Elizabeth Bowen's Selected Irish Writings

Elizabeth Bowen's Selected Irish Writings

edited by

ÉIBHEAR WALSHE

First published in 2011 by
Cork University Press
Youngline Industrial Estate
Pouladuff Road, Togher
Cork, Ireland

British Library Cataloguing in Publication Data
A CIP catalogue record for this book is available from the British Library.

ISBN-978-185918-4493

Typeset by Tower Books, Ballincollig, Co. Cork
Printed in the UK by CPI
www.corkuniversitypress.com

For Dermot Keogh

Contents

Acknowledgements

In putting this collection together I was given great assistance by the direct help and by the writings of many Bowen scholars and I want to thank Pat Coughlan, Vera Kreilkamp, Neil Corcoran, Clair Wills, Anne Fogarty, Roy Foster, Victoria Glendinning, Heather Bryant Jordan, Hermione Lee, Bill McCormack, Declan Kiberd, Margot Backus, Heather Laird, Mary Breen, Tina O'Toole, Julie Anne Stevens, Noreen Doody, Derek Hand, Sinéad Mooney, Nicholas Royle, Andrew Bennett, Maud Ellmann and others for feedback and inspiration. I owe Phyllis Lassner a great debt for her kindness in reading the introduction and her generosity in providing me with a great deal of feedback and the benefit of her ground-breaking Bowen scholarship. Donald O'Driscoll's valuable suggestions on this essay and his support throughout this project is much appreciated. Allan Hepburn was most generous in sharing his extensive research on Bowen's essays and also in answering my questions and queries and I relied on his scholarship in his two collections of Bowen essays for a definite text here, particularly *People, Places, Things* (Edinburgh: Edinburgh University Press, 2008). I would like to mention my doctoral student Mike Waldron for his innovative thinking on Bowen. My UCC friends, in particular Anne Fitzgerald, Hilary Lennon, Eamonn O'Carragain, Graham Allen, Elaine Hurley and Carol Quinn gave great help and assistance. Camilla Hornby and Sarah Lewis of Curtis Brown were very co-operative in terms of permissions. I would like to acknowledge the help of the National Archives in London in tracing Bowen's wartime reports. Thanks to the Crawford Art Gallery, Cork, in particular, Peter Murray and Anne Boddaert, for permission to use the Bowen Hennessy portrait on the cover and to Tomás Irish for supplying the author photograph used on the cover. The College of Arts, Celtic Studies and Social Science UCC Publication Fund and the National University of Ireland Publication Fund gave me much appreciated grants towards the cost of the volume. Ciaran Wallace and Sebastian Enke helped me trace some of these writings and I thank them both very much for this. My research happened thanks to grants from The UCC Arts Faculty Research Fund to visit London and from the Royal Irish Academy Mobility Grant to work on the Bowen archives in the Harry Ransom Center at the University of Texas at Austin. In Texas, Elizabeth Cullingford, Margot Backus and Molly Schwartzenburg were very hospitable and of great assistance. I would also like to thank Brendan Barrington and the *Dublin Review* for publishing my essay on Bowen and Rome; Caroline Walsh for asking me to review and write on Bowen for *The Irish Times*; the Dean of St Patrick's Cathedral, Dublin, Dr Robert McCarthy, for invitations to speak at the Bowen commemorations in Farahy; Dr Marie Bourke for an invitation to talk about Bowen at the National Gallery of Ireland, and Liam Cusack for invitations to talk at the Bowen/Trevor school in Mitchelstown. Dr Eve Patten in School of English, Trinity College, and Dr Poul Holm, Dr Jason McElligott, Dr Jennifer Edmond and Eva Mulhause at the Long Room Hub, Trinity College, were most helpful and Mike Collins, Sophie Watson and Maria O'Donovan of Cork University Press were invaluable in guiding this manuscript through each stage and I would like to thank them for their patience, professionalism and support.

I have dedicated this study to Dermot Keogh in gratitude and recognition of his support, outstanding scholarship, encouragement and invaluable friendship.

Introductory Essay

'The Indefinite Ghosts of the Past': Elizabeth Bowen and Ireland

The title of this introduction is a phrase taken from Bowen's 1940 essay 'The Big House'[1] where she writes: 'The indefinite ghosts of the past, of the dead who lived here and pursued this same routine of life in these walls add something, a sort of order, a reason for living, to every minute and hour.' But did these ghosts add to her understanding of her Irish present, her own country as it developed and changed in the years after independence? I would argue that her past did add immeasurably to the complex, multi-layered and compelling texture of her fictive writings. At the same time, the heritage of this past complicated her critical writings on the changing cultural and political complexion of her country. Bowen acknowledged the darker implication of her past heritage when she wrote in an afterword to *Bowen's Court* in 1963 that: 'My family got their position and drew their power from a situation that shows an inherent wrong' and it is clear that she understood the burdened nature of her heritage, both the brutal history and also the contentious present in Ireland. The texts assembled here cover a time span when her own class, the Anglo-Irish, was becoming increasingly marginalised in Irish political and economic life. In his study, *The Decline of the Big House in Ireland*, Terence Dooley observes that 'Over a relatively short period of time . . . the whole fabric of Irish landed society was totally transformed by economic, social and political developments. Most of these were outside the control of landlords and thus there was very little they could do to prevent revolutionary change irrevocably altering their lives.'[2]

As a result, in these critical essays and writings, Bowen tried again and again to evoke her past as something solid and continuous. Thus, as Allan Hepburn astutely observes, 'Bowen invariably conceives of the present moment as historical in its implications. By imperceptible degrees, historical events alter the climate of a place in so far as those events are lived out and lived through.'[3] This leaves her well-placed to discuss the radically altered role of the Anglo-Irish in independent Ireland from the late 1920s until the early 1970s.

Her working life was in England when the subject of Ireland and the history of Anglo-Ireland loomed large in her critical writings. In this study, I have assembled a chronological selection of her views on Ireland, starting with her review of Constantia Maxwell's book on Dublin for the *New Statesman and Nation* in 1936 and ending with her final *Spectator* review of Violet Powell's study of Somerville and Ross in 1970. In putting together this account of her engagement with Ireland, I choose representative essays, reviews, newspaper articles, and broadcasts; I also provide a bibliography of her Irish works, including reviews and essays not published here. (I have omitted extracts from her Irish short stories or her novels from this collection, as these are all in print.) Many of these critical writings have already been published in various forms and I am particularly indebted to the scholarly work of Hermione Lee and Allan Hepburn in their collected editions of Bowen's critical writings.[4] Thanks to their valuable archival research and also the Bowen archive at the Harry Ransom Center in, Austin, Texas and the National Archives in London, I was able to include a wide selection of Bowen's varied writings on Ireland. In putting together this representative collection of her views on Ireland, my purpose is to provide a context for Bowen's place in Irish literary culture and also for the place of Ireland within her own imagination.

Bowen wrote about Ireland from the late 1920s onwards, at a time when her own class was recovering from the upheavals and house burnings of the Irish War of Independence; the Civil War and where some elements of the Anglo-Irish political class still exerted influence. By the end of the 1960s, her class had become much more marginal to the political working of the Irish Republic, and so Bowen's lifelong wish to explain and mediate her class and her country was in the face of this gradual shift in power. In this introduction, I trace her lifelong writing connections with Ireland, her contacts with other Irish writers, her place in Irish literary culture and, lastly, reviews of her work by other Irish writers.

In a 1941 *Spectator* review of Jim Phelan's wartime study of Irish neutrality, titled *Ireland–Atlantic Gateway*, Bowen comments, admiringly, that 'Mr Phelan writes as an Irishman who, both for the sake of his own country and in the general interests of Western peace, desires good understanding between Eire and Britain.' In a sense, Bowen was describing herself. An important strand within her writing career was her need to promote a greater political and cultural understanding between Ireland and Britain from the late-1920s to the late-1960s. These were crucial years in the formation of the new Irish State and a time of political tension between the two countries. As this collection demonstrates, Bowen wrote essays and articles about Ireland in one form or another all through her life, but rarely in Irish journals. However, this impulse to explain and to mediate between Ireland and Britain in the aftermath of colonisation was compromised by her own hyphenated identity. Maud Ellmann suggests rightly that 'Bowen's background gave her ample cause for skepticism about national identity,'[5] and I would argue that, at the same time, Bowen had an underlying conviction that she occupied some sort of enabling ideological middle-ground between the British and the Irish. Bowen believed that her unique class position empowered her to explain and to justify the newly emerging Irish Free State to Britain, but my sense is that she was not always successful in her desire to locate continuity and relevance for her own class identity. In fact, as these writings demonstrate, there is a wishful quality in Bowen's essays concerning the role of her own class, often contradicted by her representations of Ireland and the Anglo-Irish in parallel novels and short stories. Ellmann also argues that 'when challenged, Bowen insisted on her standing as an Irish writer, yet she credited England with making her a novelist'.[6] In many ways, Bowen always saw her own Irish identity in light of her Anglo-Irish heritage and her understanding of the rapidly changing nature of Irish society in the mid-twentieth century had, at its core, a kind of disjunction. On the one hand, she argued for the political and cultural assimilation of the Anglo-Irish into the new Irish state in many of her essays and reviews. At the same time, in her novels and short stories, there is an imaginative recognition of the alienated place of the Anglo-Irish Big House in twentieth-century Ireland. In her critical writings, she often deploys metaphors of continuity and consolidation as her class was being pushed more and more towards the margins of political and economic life. Interestingly, her fiction often turns on contradictory metaphors, deploying contrasting images of disillusion, unease, fragmentation, loss.

Bowen wrote essays and reviews about Ireland all throughout her working life but her fictive writings set in her own country were sporadic. Two of her novels are set exclusively in Ireland, *The Last September* (1929) and *A World of Love* (1955), and two other novels, *The House in Paris* (1935) and *The Heat of the Day* (1948), feature lengthy interludes set in Ireland. Only ten of her stories have identifiable Irish settings,[7] and six of these were written during the Second World War at the same time as her two Irish memoirs. War and conflict often led Bowen back to Ireland as a subject and it is worth noting that Bowen's style of short-story writing on the theme of Ireland stands in marked contrast to her essay style on the same subject. As a reviewer and essayist on Ireland, Bowen is confident, impressionistic, deft, witty, always in command of her subject and assures her English or American readership of her knowledge and authority on Ireland, its class structures and political system and the nature of social and cultural life in the new state. Her fictive writings are more nuanced, even ambivalent, deploying the same style but to much different effect. In her novels, she deals with broad social and political changes, the Irish War of Independence in *The Last September,* the Second World War and Irish neutrality in *The Heat of the Day* and 1950s Ireland and emigration in *A World of Love.* In her Irish stories, Bowen's imagination is at its most illuminatingly ambivalent. In many of these stories, her Anglo-Irish characters are presented as both heroic in terms of courage and endurance, but on the other hand, willfully blind to the lurking menace in the fields and to the inexorable rise of the New Ireland. Her Irish narratives, although written at various times in her life, have in common a preoccupation with elements of the gothic or the uncanny and Bowen's two essays on Sheridan Le Fanu identify him clearly as an influence on this aspect of her imagination. In her introduction to *Uncle Silas*, she was the first critic to identify the Anglo-Irish elements in his gothic tale: '*Uncle Silas* has always struck me as being an Irish story transposed to an English setting. The hermetic solitude and the autocracy of the great country house, the demonic power of the family myth, fatalism, feudalism and the "ascendancy" outlook are accepted facts of life for the race of hybrids from which Le Fanu sprang.' She went on to write that '*Uncle Silas* is, as a novel, Irish in two other ways: it is sexless, and it shows a sublimated infantilism.' Bowen's shrewd identification of Sheridan Le Fanu as Anglo-Irish was timely and influential[8] and, not surprisingly, many of these Irish gothic elements crop up in her Irish stories. 'Her Table Spread', 'The Good Earl' and 'The Tommy Crans' all centre on young protagonists oppressed and limited by over-bearing or duplicitous guardians or parental figures, as does 'A Day in the Dark'. In stories such as 'A Love Story', 'Sunday Afternoon', 'Summer Night' and 'Unwelcome Idea', Bowen highlights moments and incidents from everyday life during the Second World War in Ireland and thus Irish neutrality is seen in a more negative and questioning way than in her secret reports. In these wartime stories, the Anglo-Irish in neutral Ireland find themselves, fatally perhaps, at a distance from the idea of war and of any real sense of engagement with Europe and the struggles against fascism. Three of her Irish stories are ghost stories, 'Hand in Glove', 'The Back Drawing-Room' and her best story, 'The Happy Autumn Fields', where the evocation of a prosperous nineteenth-century Anglo-Irish Big House stands as a dream and an escape from the dangers of Blitz London. However, in this subtle and multi-layered ghost story, the Big House, initially a place of refuge, finally becomes a haunted place of murder and loss and the uneasy legacy of the past a source of horrified fascination for the contemporary narrator.

Her style in her essays is often shrewd, perceptive and firmly grounded in her sense of place, be it Dublin, Cork or the countryside around Bowen's Court in Farahy. In her critical writings, her preoccupation with the past often led her to underestimate the emotional sensitivities around political allegiance on both sides of the Irish Sea and I would argue that, to some degree, Bowen's lifelong desire to act as translator between the two countries was often thwarted. This makes her Irish writings even more illuminating and illustrates the ambivalent position of the Anglo-Irish within the new Irish state. This ambivalence arises from the sense that the Anglo-Irish almost constituted another nation. Bennett and Royle suggest that: 'The Anglo-Irish constitute a nation at once within itself and beside itself, paranational.'[9] Bowen's desire to mediate is seen most dramatically during the Second World War when she volunteered to write reports for the Ministry of Information. It was a well-intentioned but ultimately naïve undertaking that clouded her reputation in Ireland and exposed her lack of insight into Irish antipathy towards Britain. Born and raised at a time of imperial decline, she was unable to understand the resentful attitude towards Britain then held by the Catholic majority of the Irish state and the keen antipathy towards any perceived allegiance to the British crown by the Anglo-Irish.

In the past twenty years, new critical essays on Bowen's Anglo-Irishness have located her more precisely within twentieth-century Irish literary and cultural identities,[10] and 'Bowen the Irish Writer' is now a fruitful area for studies of her work. This collection traces the trajectory of Bowen's imaginative and intellectual engagement with her own country.

It is clear from her correspondence with her agent Curtis Brown that Bowen paid great attention to the business side of her writing life, under pressure as she was to maintain Bowen's Court. Phyllis Lassner writes that, 'if she learned from her extravagant ancestors to live in great style, above all she felt the need to work'.[11] This meant producing a great deal of 'soft' journalism to make an income from her writing, but it is striking how little she published in Irish journals and newspapers, apart from work elicited by personal contacts with Irish writers such as Sean O'Faolain and Robert Gracken. Bowen inherited her family home in 1930 and lived between England and Ireland from 1930 right up to the early 1950s. In the various reviews she wrote in the 1920s and 1930s, her interest in the history of her own caste, the Anglo-Irish, is most clearly reflected, as are her personal links with Irish writers such as Constantia Maxwell and Joseph Hone, whose brother was married to her cousin.

Bowen published her first collection of short stories, *Encounters*, in 1923 and went on to produce six successful novels and two more short-story collections during the 1920s and the 1930s. However, it is worth noting that in these, her defining years as an emergent artist, her writings on Ireland were few and far between. It was as if she needed to establish her sense of herself as a novelist within the mainstream of English writing before attempting Ireland. Also, Bowen wrote best about Ireland at times of war and disorder and so her primary engagement with Ireland during this period was her novel of the Irish War of Independence, *The Last September*, published in 1929. During this period of writing, Bowen was living in England with her husband, Alan Cameron, firstly in Northamptonshire just after their marriage in 1923, then moving to Oxford in 1925 when Alan was appointed Secretary of Education. During her Oxford years, her father died and she became the owner of Bowen's Court in 1930 and thereafter spent her summers in North Cork. Bowen, by now a successful mainstream novelist, moved to London in 1935 with her husband when he was appointed to the BBC's education department. I would argue that in these years, at least, Bowen offers little sense of relevance to her generation of Anglo-Irish within the new Irish state. For example, her first Irish story 'The Back Drawing-Room', published in 1926, reflects the ghostly heritage of grief, loss and violence for the Anglo-Irish in the years after the setting-up of the new Irish state. In the words of Sinéad Mooney, this story 'embeds an Anglo-Irish story of dispossession, loss and exile within a modish framing narrative of fashionable London drawing-room hermeticism or spiritualism'.[12] Likewise 'Her Table Spread', published in the year she inherited Bowen's Court, 1930, has as central character, the demented

Anglo-Irish heiress, Valeria Cuffe, described by Bowen as being 'still detained in childhood' at the age of twenty-five and in 'The Tommy Crans', published in 1934, Bowen further explores this theme of the blighted lives of the children of the Anglo-Irish, their future bankrupted by the extravagances of the previous generation.

Her novel *The Last September* is her most sustained engagement with Ireland and it is worth remembering that Bowen was out of Ireland during the War of Independence and wrote the novel ten years later. Bowen wrote about her composition of this novel in these terms: 'When I sat in Old Headington, Oxford, writing *The Last September*, 1920 seemed a long time ago. By now (the year of the writing: 1928) peace had settled on Ireland; trees were already branching inside the shells of large burned-out houses; lawns, once flitted over by pleasures, usefully merged into grazing land. I myself was no longer a tennis girl but a writer; aimlessness was gone, like a morning mist. I *was* the child of the house from which Danielstown derives. Bowen's Court survived – nevertheless, so often in my mind's eye did I see it burning that the terrible last event in *The Last September* is more real than anything I have lived through.'[13] In 1937, having read the novel for the first time, her lover, the one-time IRA volunteer, Sean O'Faolain, wrote to her that 'It's so entirely Irish –as if that matters a damn.'[14]

Despite her own self-doubts about her critical writings, Bowen began reviewing for the *New Statesman and Nation* in the early 1930s, partly because of her friendship with the literary editor, Raymond Mortimer, and the bulk of her Irish-themed reviews from this period concentrate on her own Anglo-Irish heritage or her interest in Dublin or in the sweep of Irish history. (Bowen was not above reviewing the work of her acquaintances; Constantia Maxwell, Professor of History at Trinity College Dublin, was a friend and Stephen Gywnn a relation.) Likewise, her travel piece on Ireland, published in the short-lived journal *Night and Day*, was commissioned by the editor Graham Greene, who also employed Bowen as a drama critic.

This lack of contact with Irish writers was to change with her most important Irish literary connection from the late 1930s, Sean O'Faolain. O'Faolain and Bowen had known of each other from the early 1930s and had been reading each other's novels and stories but, in his memoir, *Vive Moi!*, O'Faolain remembers that he finally met Bowen in person in 1937, when he invited her home to meet his wife Eileen. As a result, Bowen then invited both Sean and Eileen to Bowen's Court but Sean came alone, despite his wife's wish to accompany him. Bowen and O'Faolain soon became lovers, travelling together to Salzburg in the summer of 1937 and this relationship lasted until Bowen met Charles Ritchie in early 1942. His daughter, the novelist Julia O'Faolain, remembered that 'throughout my childhood, 'La Bowen – as my mother called Elizabeth Bowen – was an offstage source of contention in that she invited you (her father) but not Eileen to house parties'.[15] In a letter dated 22nd April 1937, he wrote to Bowen about his admiration for *The Last September*, her sole Irish novel at that point and the one he was then reading for the first time:

> I adored the un-underlying atmosphere. I could smell the hay, the wet, the mountain-line. . . . I could imagine a novel called *The Island* where the Big House was an island, within the island of the Irish isolated countryside, and that the heft and weight and bloom of heat of the land weighted it down, and closed it in and it all had a kind of tropical intensity of emotion by reason of that double compression.[16]

Thus Bowen wrote regularly for his journal, *The Bell*,[17] and her close involvement in his journal is unusual, given her lack of connection with other Irish writers or Irish literary culture.[18] O'Faolain founded *The Bell* magazine to counterbalance the oppressive cultural insularity and xenophobia of Ireland in the 1930s and 1940s and he invited Bowen to speak up, as it were, for the marginalised, antagonistic Anglo-Irish of post-independence Ireland. Bowen seized this opportunity to argue for a valid place for the Anglo-Irish in contemporary Ireland. O'Faolain was a profound influence on her in many other ways. They came from vastly different Irish worlds, although both connected with Cork city and county; Bowen, the Ascendancy owner of Bowen's Court and O'Faolain, originally working-class and urban, a lapsed Catholic, a former Irish revolutionary and now at odds with the new Irish state he had helped to establish. Their professional lives intersected on a number of levels – she reviewed his biography of Hugh O'Neill in the *New Statesman and Nation* in 1943 and found that:

> Mr. O'Faolain's study must stand or fall by the importance he succeeds in giving its subject – and to my mind it stands triumphantly: shrewdness and a perception on the poetic level are equally present in the interpretation.[19]

This study of O'Neill would later influence her reading of Irish history, particularly as seen in her 1966 'Kinsale, Son et Lumiere',

Indeed Bowen took on his views of Irish state and Irish language, as evidenced by many of her other writings on Ireland. O'Faolain reviewed *The Demon Lover* in *The Bell*.[20] On his side O'Faolain proposed her as a member of the Irish Academy of Irish Letters in 1937 and also tried, unsuccessfully, to have *The House in Paris* awarded the Harmsworth Award, a move that was opposed by Yeats. Bowen introduced him to Virginia Woolf while he introduced her to Yeats.

O'Faolain interviewed her in an article for *The Bell* called 'Meet Elizabeth Bowen' in September 1942, appropriately enough in the Shelbourne Hotel in Dublin. It is worth considering the terms he used to describe her in this interview where Bowen was at pains to identify herself as an Irish writer, already aware that such a classification was under question. O'Faolain calls her 'primarily an aristocrat'[21] and referred to her as having 'that curious period quality',[22] conveying the sense that Bowen is not of her age, or of contemporary Ireland. Bowen, who tells him that she is working on a history of her family home, declares emphatically that 'I regard myself as an Irish novelist.' As long as I can remember I've been extremely conscious of being Irish – even when I was writing about such un-Irish things as suburban life in Paris or the English seaside . . . I must say it is a highly disturbing emotion. It is not, I must emphasise – sentimentality.'[23] Bowen goes on to make the prediction that 'When the Really Great Irish Novel comes to be written, I fancy you'll find that it has been written by a Protestant who understands Catholicism and who, very probably has made a mixed marriage.'[24]

They remained close friends for the rest of their lives, even after she refused O'Faolain's request to include her story 'Her Table Spread' in his 1947 edited collection of Irish stories because he didn't offer the usual eight guinea fee. She did review his *Come Back to Erin* for *The Bell* in December 1950. After her death, he wrote:

> If there ever was a writer of genius, or near genius – time will decide – who was heart-cloven and split-minded it is Elizabeth Bowen. Romantic-realist, yearning-sceptic, emotional-intellectual, poetic-pragmatist, objective-subjective, gregarious-detached (though everybody who resides in a typewriter has to be a bit of that), tragi-humorous, consistently declaring herself born and reared Irish, residing mostly in England, writing in the full European tradition: no wonder all her serious work steams with the clash of battle between aspects of life more easy for us to feel than to define. It is evident from the complex weave of her novels that it can have been

> no more easy for her to intuit the central implication of any one of those conflicts – she never trod an obvious line; nor easy for her to express those intuitions in that felicitous language which, more than any other writer of her generation, she seemed to command as if verbally inspired. But that suggestion of inspiration lifts a warning finger of memory.[25]

The connection between the two was a very important one for Bowen but I would make the point that the difference between them on the subject of Ireland was profound. Bowen attempted to write herself and her class into the new largely Catholic state by invoking the certainties of a vanished Anglo-Irish cultural heritage while O'Faolain was in active dissent from the Ireland he had once fought to create. O'Faolain understood and disapproved of the New Ireland whereas Bowen constantly attempted to re-invent it to her own satisfaction.

One consequence of Bowen's bond with O'Faolain was that she chose to write about Joyce in *The Bell* and this is worth noting, as she rarely engaged with any other Irish novelists outside her own tradition, mainly reviewing and writing about Somerville and Ross, Le Fanu and other Ascendancy writers. It seems to me that what interested Bowen most was his crucial importance as a modernist novelist but, interestingly, in her essays, she often connects herself with Joyce in terms of his Irishness. On Joyce's death, she wrote one of her finest pieces of critical work with a long essay for *The Bell* in 1941. She also reviewed Herbert Gorman's book on Joyce in 1941, as well as writing a preface to a 1945 edition of *Dubliners; Finnegan's Wake*; and reviewing a book by Patricia Hutchins on Joyce in 1957. In her essay for *The Bell* in 1941 she states that 'Joyce had that kind of *hauteur*, independent of circumstance, that Stendhal calls *espagnolisme'* and this interpretation also surfaces in her review of Gorman, where Joyce becomes almost Anglo-Irish, in her re-reading of his life: 'He had the Irish qualities shaped and steeled, and Joyce was heroic to withstand poverty. In her essay for *The Bell*, she lets slip that she once met Joyce in Paris, not specifying when and where, and that she thought that Ireland didn't know him but 'It was the grit in his oyster shell'. As always, when speaking or writing for an Irish periodical, Bowen sees herself as undoubtedly Irish, claiming that 'The English can never know us' and linking herself to Joyce as 'A writer out of the Irish people'. This contrasts with her persona in some English journals where she presents herself as English.

Apart from her writings on Joyce, there is biographical evidence that by the end of the 1930s, Bowen was engaging more with Irish literary culture, perhaps because of O'Faolain. She reviewed Lady Carbery's *The Farm by Lough Gur* for *The New Statesman and Nation* in October 1937 and later, in June 1939, on her birthday, Bowen was guest of honour at the fifth annual banquet of the Women Writers' Club in the Gresham Hotel in Dublin where she made her identification as an Irish writer clear. 'I think that we Irish people are in the happy position of being able to use the English language as few English people have been able to use it.'[26]

Bowen was in London when war broke out and she and Alan Cameron stayed on in their Regent's Park flat for most of the Blitz until they were finally bombed out and were forced to leave in 1944. She later wrote that 'I would not have missed being in London throughout the war for anything: it was the most interesting period of my life.'[27] Her creative output was intensified during this period, as life in wartime London stimulated her imagination, possessing her with what she herself termed in her preface to her wartime stories, *The Demon Lover and Other Stories*, a 'kind of lucid abnormality'.[28] As she put it: 'During the war I lived, both as a civilian and as a writer, with every pore open . . . arguably, writers are always slightly abnormal people: certainly in so-called "normal" times, my sense of the abnormal has been very acute. In war, this feeling of slight differentiation was suspended: I felt one with and just like, everyone else . . . We all lived in a state of lucid abnormality.' Out of this lucid abnormality came a flood of writing about Ireland: *Bowen's Court* in 1942, *Seven Winters* in 1943 and stories like 'The Happy Autumn Fields' and 'Summer Night' in 1945. In all of these Irish writings, Bowen looked homewards to North Cork as a place of stability and loyalty in an endangered and treacherous world and her vision of Anglo-Ireland becomes her talisman, her source for imaginative power in war-disordered London. However, unease continues to lurk out in the North Cork terrain. The tensions of being Anglo-Irish at a time when Britain was at war while Ireland remained neutral accentuated Bowen's ambivalent attitude towards Ireland. These skirmishes meant that, even in her most celebratory work, her childhood memoir, *Seven Winters*, she still writes of her birth in the following terms: 'So by having been born where I had been born in a month in which that house did not exist, I felt that I had intruded on some no-place.'[29]

Bowen's writing on Ireland also benefited from this heightened sense of awareness and lucidity and in this section I have included her controversial reports to the Ministry of Information. War brought out a new aspect in Bowen's relationship with Ireland, one which was to damage her reputation: her fact-finding activities to provide secret reports on Ireland and Irish neutrality for the British Ministry of Information. Bowen was paid for this work but kept it secret from her Irish connections and friends and this was, retrospectively, seen in some quarters in Ireland as spying. Eunan O'Halpin writes that 'She submitted a number of critical but perceptive reports on the emotions and calculations underpinning Irish policy. One, which concluded that in existing circumstances neutrality was the only feasible policy for de Valera, was commended to Churchill by the Dominions Secretary Cranbourne in November 1940, a chance which later contributed to the accusation that she had been a British intelligence agent as distinct from a well-informed observer.'[30] These reports have sparked off much critical debate. Clair Wills argues that 'While espionage is too strong as well as too narrow a term for what Bowen called her 'activities' in Ireland, they did involve sending secret reports to the Ministry of Information and meetings at the Dominions and the War Office, conveying her sense of the climate of opinion: taking the temperature amongst writers and intellectuals in Dublin, and amongst country people near her home in County Cork. But it was principally a response to the catastrophic situation for Britain following the fall of France. The stakes could not have seemed higher and the sympathies and loyalties of Allied supporters in Ireland became unbearably stretched.'[31]

In these reports, Bowen attempted to defend the Irish decision to remain neutral, but in terms that highlighted her own class allegiances. There was a real sense of engagement in the war effort in Bowen's writings, as Robert Fisk has commented: 'Elizabeth Bowen and the other writers in Dublin in the winter of 1940 were all struck by the Irish predilection for ignoring the ideology of the war.'[32] But Bowen's reports do have their flaws, as when she completely misinterprets the political opinions of the main opposition leader, James Dillon, the Fine Gael politician, by declaring him a Fascist sympathiser when he was precisely the opposite. Her attitude towards Ireland's neutrality changed as the war progressed, as R.F. Foster explains: 'After two years war experience in London, Irish neutrality seemed less defensible.'[33] After her death, the revelation that she had written these confidential reports did much damage to her name and reputation in Ireland, particularly in North Cork. Robert Fisk comments, for example, that 'Dillon had no idea that Bowen reported to the British government on their conversation until the author of this book (Robert Fisk) showed him a copy of her secret memorandum in 1979. Now aged 79, Dillon read it carefully. It was typical of him that he expressed no anger at Bowen's unflattering references to him, only at the way in which she had abused his hospitality in 1940 by breaking the confidentiality of their meeting. Of Bowen's remarks about his 'religious fanaticism', he commented: 'Poor woman, you can see her unhappy agnosticism.'[34] Her English friends knew of her war reports, but her Irish friends, including O'Faolain, did not. Her reports show Bowen at her critical best in that she adapts and shapes her view of Ireland to accommodate this new Irish crisis of identity. War drew out her understanding of the divisions in Ireland and also within herself and her heritage.

This ambivalence was also at the heart of her wartime fictions. In times of violence, Bowen used her learning and her sharp critical intelligence to locate some kind of solid ground, but her literary imagination was moved by a contradictory impulse to explode permanence. Bowen's underlying desire was to present a sinister threat of extinction lurking somewhere out there in the North Cork landscape. Her fiction reveals a darker version of her anxiously utopian vision of the fields around Farahy presented in her memoirs and essays. Memoir and personal history were a refuge for Bowen in wartime but a refuge that came at a cost. To compensate, Bowen's critical writings of the early 1940s show her at her most determinedly optimistic about the role of the Anglo-Irish. The most revealing example of this kind of writing comes with her 1940 essay 'The Big House' mentioned earlier. This essay is a plea for assimilation, a utopian vision of a harmonious relationship between house and landscape. Her tone throughout the piece is jaunty: 'The loneliness of my house, as of many others, is more an effect than a reality . . .' Yet, despite her need to create a place for the Big House in twentieth-century Ireland, her particular sense of the unease for the Big House within the countryside inevitably breaks through: 'The Big House people were handicapped, shadowed and to an extent queered by their pride, by their indignation at their decline and by their divorce from the countryside in whose heart their struggle was carried out.' She concludes her essay with a call for political and cultural accommodation between the Big House and surrounding towns and villages: 'The Big House has much to learn – and it must learn if it is to survive at all. But it also has much to give . . . From inside many Big Houses (and these will be the survivors) barriers are being impatiently attacked. But it must be seen that a barrier has two sides.' Thus her essay is a plea for assimilation, a utopian vision of a harmonious relationship between house and landscape.

In all of these Irish writings, Bowen looked homewards to North Cork as a place of stability and loyalty in an endangered and uncertain world and her vision of Anglo-Ireland becomes her talisman, her source for imaginative power and stability in war-disordered London. However, this was never a simple process for Bowen. The tensions of being Anglo-Irish at a time when Britain was at war while Ireland remained neutral accentuated Bowen's ambivalent attitude towards her own country. In the words of Heather Bryant Jordan, 'Unable to abandon her colonial training, Bowen found herself in the midst of a battle with institutions that echoed her own skirmishes with herself.'[35]

She took a flat in Dublin during the war despite the travel restrictions and did seem to be part of general literary culture in Dublin, as a letter in 1942 to *The Irish Times* from a Mary M. Macken[36] attests. Macken was writing to correct a newspaper report of her lecture on North Cork. It claimed that she had said that Bowen had been hidden in a clock in Doneraile House, near Bowen's Court in North Cork, accidentally overhearing the Masonic rituals during a Freemason's Lodge meeting there and, as a result, Bowen had been inducted into the Freemasons, thus becoming one of the few women ever to have been made a Lady Mason. Of course, Macken had been referring to a Miss St Leger Aldworthy in the eighteenth century and she protested that 'I am as much an innocent victim as the distinguished author of *Bowen's Court* herself.'[37] Other contacts from the war years in Ireland included Bowen's review of Sean O'Casey's *Pictures in the Hallway* in *The Spectator* in May 1942 and the contribution of the story 'A Love Story' to Robert Greacan's collection *Irish Harvest*, published by Maurice Friberg in September 1946. She would review the book by Patricia Hutchins, Greacan's wife, on Joyce for the *Tatler* in 1957.) Bowen also wrote an essay to accompany Jonathan Cape's illustrated edition of *Dubliners* published in 1945.

Bowen's most ambitious wartime writing on Ireland was a history of her family home, *Bowen's Court* (1942). Jonathan Cape, her usual publisher, turned it down because, in his opinion, it contained controversial Irish materials but Longman published it instead. In this family chronicle, she proudly presents successive Bowen patriarchs and landowners as members of a powerful dynasty and addresses the difficult question of attempted harmonisation between the Big Houses and the surrounding lands. However, blankness and non-being threaten to descend on the Big House and the possibility of violence is never quite exorcised. Overall, as Clair Wills writes, 'In *Bowen's Court*, the family history that she had begun in 1939 (presumably while still feeling 'wedded' to the country through her "marriage" to Sean O'Faolain), and which she completed during her intelligence-gathering trips in 1940 and 1941, Bowen recorded the "centripetal and cut-off life" of the Protestant ascendancy in Ireland.'[38] *Bowen's Court* was extensively reviewed in Ireland and the most significant review was that by her fellow Irish novelist, Kate O'Brien, published in *The Spectator* on 3 July 1942.

Kate O'Brien, Catholic, middle-class and university-educated, spent most of her working life in England, living in London from the mid-1920s onwards and she knew Bowen slightly. All through the 1930s and 1940s O'Brien lived in flats around Bloomsbury, Gordon Square, Great James Street, near to Bowen's Clarence Terrace flat in Regent's Park. Once or twice, their professional lives interconnected. They worked together on a volume of patriotic essays, *The Romance of English Literature*, edited by O'Brien and published in 1944. However, they were never close friends and there is little or no sense of connection between them as Irish women writers. O'Brien reviewed two of Bowen's short-story collections for *The Irish Times*. In March 1941 she reviewed *Look at All Those Roses* in these terms: 'In spite of the fact that one is inclined to compare all short stories with those of Maupassant, *Look at All Those Roses* is a book that will be read time and time again, even by the most ardent Maupassant "fan".' O'Brien also reviewed *The Demon Lover and Other Stories* for *The Irish Times* in January 1946 and wrote, 'It is a very fine and sorrowful collection. These stories, deeply matured in sadness, elegiac and even desperate, show a very great advance in their author's power over their medium. There is little to be found here of that somewhat arid elegance which in the past seemed at times to threaten the movement, and even the very life, of her ideas. The last in the book, 'Mysterious Kor', the most beautiful and pitiful, sums up the lonely passion of the whole. They are passionate, powerful stories, and they compel us to read on with an arrogance, almost rough, almost insolent sometimes, which Miss Bowen has not troubled to use heretofore.'[39]

O'Brien's most significant review came in 1942. Titled 'Amende Honorable–Bowen's Court by Elizabeth Bowen', Kate O'Brien's review is worth quoting at some length, given the very different class perspectives of these two Irish women and accounts for the lack of any real closeness or friendship between the two London-based writers:

'... My family got their position and drew their power from a situation that shows an inherent wrong. In the grip of that situation England and Ireland each turned on the other a close, harsh, distorted face.' From the sobriety and care which inform these quoted lines the dominant tone of Miss Bowen's history of her family may be justly apprehended; and from among many excellences and pleasures which await its readers I choose first to praise in it this sustained duality of *tone* – a pervasive spiritual idiom, blended of delicacy, patience, detachment, and poetic feeling, all bound together and made purposeful by the courage which can grasp the nettle . . . There are nettles to be grasped, all along the author's road of three hundred years. The lands distributed by Cromwell to his 'Adventurers' and troops at the expense of the dispossessed Irish are still most passionately resented, for there was the first real methodical beginning of our national misery; here was the first truly businesslike establishment of prosperity upon visible woe. 'To hell or to Connaught' was *par excellence* a go-getter's slogan, and its echoes are a long time dying – naturally enough, as is recognised by this daughter of a line that rose to power and wealth when the savage cry was first flung out . . . By chance, from a different angle, I am familiar with much of the atmosphere, history and hearsay which support Miss Bowen's record. Eighteen months earlier than she, I was born about fifty miles north-west of the Bowen lands, in the city of Limerick, in a family of the Catholic and Nationalist middle-class. My father adhered to John Redmond and grieved always for the tragedy of Parnell. I was schooled in Ireland, and by an accident of unusual intellectualism in one of my schoolmistresses, was early set to work in the reviving Irish language. My mother's people came from the Limerick side of those Ballyhouras hills that shelter Bowen's Court on the north, and next best after my own county and West Clare, I knew in childhood the country of the Blackwater. So I respond with a doubled ease to many of these pages – not solely because of their intrinsic, rich evocativeness of scene and custom, but because for me they do so particularly wash and brighten memory. Also, of course, I do admittedly read Miss Bowen's various *précis* of periods of Irish history in some measure by the uncertain candle of inherited prejudices and emotions. Yet, if I hold my scepticism in check while she makes a plea for Lord Salisbury's Conservative Experiment, I am rewarded, and perhaps admonished, by the accuracy and justice of her appraisal of the Gaelic Revival, and her later summary of 'the troubles' . . . It has not won me from my dislike of that shadowland where biography embraces fiction . . . The time

> for that must come – and a book such as *Bowen's Court* seems to bring it perceptibly nearer. Moreover, it is itself one more of those very gifts and embellishments – an *amende honorable* of singular beauty and distinction.[40]

This review by O'Brien is significant in that it reveals the very strong divergence between the two as to the interpretation of recent Irish history. O'Brien, like O'Faolain, was no apologist for the new Irish state, rather the reverse, as her novels had been banned there in 1935 and again in 1942 and she became disenchanted and estranged from de Valera's increasingly paternalistic Catholic state. Nevertheless, O'Brien still found herself, as she said, respectfully sceptical about Bowen's view of the course of nineteenth-century Irish political history, written as it was from the perspective of the Big House. For O'Brien, as for many dissenting Irish Catholic intellectuals of this time, Bowen's valorisation of her own social position would still have been difficult for them to accept. Class difference accounts for this divergence. Bowen and O'Brien had parallel fictive attitudes towards the representation of Irishness in their fictions. Both women valorised their own class identity, Bowen seeing the Anglo-Irish as heroic and courageous and O'Brien seeing her own Catholic bourgeois as civilised, cultivated and intellectually gifted. In contrast Bowen's friend and fellow Anglo-Irish novelist Molly Keane wrote to subvert and query the ethos of civilised behaviour in the Anglo-Irish Big House. Bowen was close only to women of her own caste and had little or no empathy with Irish women writers from other classes or traditions.

Other reviews in Ireland were equally positive. In the *Sunday Independent* on 5 July 1942,[41] the reviewer saw the book as 'The result of an earnest and sustained effort on her part to stick to the known historical truth' and the *Irish Independent* of 13 July 1942 talked of Bowen's 'scrupulous fairness' and her 'graceful literary achievement'.[42] In *The Irish Times* on 4 July 1942, Bowen's friend Constantia Maxwell wrote, 'Very few of them, unfortunately, have found biographers, for the Anglo-Irish, to whom they chiefly belong, are not very articulate. When such a brilliant novelist as Elizabeth Bowen, therefore, sets herself to the task, we expect, as, indeed, we find, a distinguished performance.'[43]

After the war, Bowen maintained her interest in Irish literary and political culture, publishing an essay on Ireland in *Vogue* in 1946, stressing the Irish setting for many of *The Demon Lover* stories (in particular, 'The Happy Autumn Fields'). She used her contacts with the

Cork Examiner to be accredited as their correspondent for the Peace Conference in 1946, presenting her views of European politics written for an Irish audience. She opened an exhibition of Cork landscape paintings by her North Cork neighbour and friend, Silvia Cooke-Collis, at the Grafton Gallery in Dublin in May 1947 and on 20 October 1947, she spoke at Trinity College Dublin on 'Arrangement of Good Taste', a night organised by the Modern Languages Society. Even in London, she was involved with other Irish-themed projects. In February 1948, *Castle Anna* opened, a Big House three-act play written by Bowen and John Perry, the Anglo-Irish novelist Molly Keane's friend and dramatic collaborator. In 1949, Trinity College Dublin awarded Bowen an honorary doctorate.

Her war novel, *The Heat of the Day*, was published in 1948 and sold 45,000 copies almost immediately. Neil Corcoran calls it 'a story about entangled loyalties and treacheries – in war, in love and in relationships across the generations – itself generated out of a radical sense of the destablisations or erosions of identity consequent on wartime displacements and disorientations'.[44] In Bowen's novel, cultural lines and debates around treason are uncompromising and it is interesting to note that the idea of Ireland operates in this wartime novel as a metaphorical locus for loyalty and stability. Ireland is the place where Stella visits her son's Anglo-Irish Big House Mount Morris and experiences a sense of uncomplicated, liberating allegiance to the allied cause. It is also the place where she finds proof that her lover Robert Kelway is a traitor and she returns to London to confront him with his disloyalty. Thus, in this fictionalised version of the Irish Big House, Bowen allows a sense of untroubled patriotic love between house and land to predominate. This is of a piece with much of Bowen's wartime sense of Anglo-Ireland as a loyal, stable place and the Anglo-Irish home becomes symbolically implicated with eventual Allied victory. During her stay in Ireland, Stella comes to see this Irish Big House as an oasis of feudal certainty and this certainty is contrasted unfavourably with the suffocating, traitorous suburban villas of the English Home Counties. Yet, at the same time, the interior world of the Anglo-Irish Big House is also a place of lurking madness and unhappiness for Anglo-Irish women and Bowen does allow this contradictory note to intrude, the one drawback to this house of peace, loyalty and safety in a time of war and of suspicion. 'After all, was it not chiefly here in this room . . . that Cousin Nettie Morris – and who now knew how many more before her? – had been pressed back, hour by hour, by the hours themselves, into cloudland? Ladies had gone not quite mad, not quite even that, from in vain listening for meaning in the loudening ticking of the Clock.'[45] However idealised the Irish Big House seen by Bowen from the fraught atmosphere of London, may be she is careful to show the double-sided nature of the Anglo-Irish heritage: the keeping up of a civilisation and a tradition at the cost of the sanity of the women of that class.

The Irish landscape around Mount Morris is viewed by Stella in terms of loyalty and stability in contrast to Lois's troubled vision of the rebellious terrain around Danielstown in *The Last September*. Mount Morris is the place where Stella first hears of the Allied victories in North Africa, the turning point of the war. So, it seems as if Anglo-Ireland, and the figure of the Irish servant girl Hannah Donovan, is transmuted into a uniquely loyal, safe and trustworthy terrain by the experience of the Second World War. Ireland arms Stella for confrontation and right at the end of the novel, the two protagonists, the wartime lovers Stella and Robert, debate as to the nature of patriotism and its dark opposite, treason. *The Heat of the Day* was positively reviewed in the *Irish Times* on 26 February 1949.

After the Second World War, Bowen's relationship with Ireland began to change. When she published her history of that icon of Ascendancy tradition, *The Shelbourne*, in 1951, her friend Joseph Hone reviewed it in *The Irish Times* and criticised her for her over-reliance on *A History of Ireland, 1798–1924* by James O'Connor, but concluded that, 'The Shelbourne is indeed fortunate in finding a biographer with so fine a sense of literary form.'[46] The reviewer in the *Irish Independent* called NN was not so kind, objecting to her account of the Irish War of Independence – 'What Miss Bowen is pleased to call "The dreadful story" of the years of guerrilla war against the British. One might as readily have hung the story from Kingsbridge Station or from Trinity College or for that matter from the top room of any tenement house in Dominick Street. Still it makes pleasant if not very profound reading; at any rate she surveys the changes and revolutions with more understanding than, say, the English politicians and the English journalists who so often studied, or thought they studied, the Irish nation from the steps of the Shelbourne.'[47]

Profound change came to Bowen's personal life in the early 1950s. As he grew older, her husband Alan's health began to fail and he retired from his work. In early 1952, they gave up their London flat to retire permanently to Bowen's Court but, unexpectedly, he died in August of that year. She buried him in the small churchyard in Farahy, near to her father's grave and next to the Church of Ireland chapel where generations of Bowens had worshipped and where tablets to their memory lined the walls. Bereft of his help and great administrative ability, Bowen struggled unsuccessfully during the 1950s to maintain Bowen's Court. She disliked her new status as single woman intensely. As she wrote to Charles Ritchie from Rome in 1959: 'I sometimes wonder whether even you, knowing me as well as you do, really realise my horror of my state as a *femme seule* (legal definition). It seems to me abnormal, it fills me with a sense of ghastly injury, that I should have to organize my own life. It seems abnormal that any woman should have to do so . . . look at my life since Alan died.'[48] Bowen had been married from her early twenties, and now her status as a widow within quite a conservative society meant a great deal of social isolation and some mistrust. Unfortunately for her, the other men in her life were also leaving or becoming less available. Most upsetting of all was the fact that her long-term lover Charles Ritchie had married his cousin only a year before Alan's death.

Her return to Ireland resulted in more critical and reviewing writings on Ireland but, as the papers in the Harry Ransom Center show, very little of these works actually ended up in Irish journals and newspapers. She turned down writing work from the editor of the *Cork Examiner* despite promising to review a book for him and also despite the fact that he had procured her a press card to attend the Peace Conference in Paris just after the end of the war. She also turned down the Trinity College Dublin Elizabethan Society when they requested a lecture, and the editor of the *Irish Housewife*, Hilda Tweedy, who asked for a contribution. However, she did write a nativity play for the Church of Ireland in Kilmallock[49], directed by her friend Major Stephen Vernon, in 1953. Unusually, she also contributed a story, 'Tears, Idle Tears' to *The Blarney Magazine* in February 1954, corresponding with the editor, Joseph Reilly, Professor of Chemistry at University College, Cork. In June of 1954, the editor of *Irish Writing*, David Marcus, asked her to contribute to a special edition on Irish women writers, offering five guineas and telling her that Kate O'Brien, Mary Beckett and Mary Lavin had already agreed to write – Bowen gave him an extract from the forthcoming *A World of Love*.[50] In the *Tatler and Bystander* in 1954, she reviewed *The Stranger in Ireland* by Constantia Maxwell and Honor Tracey's novel *The Deserters*. Most of the review concerns her friend Maxwell and Bowen laid great stress on the hospitality of Irish houses but showed less interest in Honor Tracy's writing: 'The language, used as required, may cause readers to blink. But it would not, I think, be too much to say that there is not a dull moment in *The Deserters*.'[51] A later review for the *Tatler* of fellow Irish woman writer Mary Lavin's short-story collection *The Patriot Son* in April 1956 is an unusual connection with another Irish women writer who was not of her own class: whereas her review of her Anglo-Irish relative, the poet Sheila Wingfield, for the *Tatler* in January 1955 was more characteristic. Bowen had also begun to review for the *Observer* at this time and mainly chose books about Ireland or the Anglo-Irish for her subjects. In May 1952, she reviewed *Wait Now!*, a novel about Anglo-Ireland by an English woman, Rachel Knappett, and remarked that 'Miss Knappett, to her own knowledge, never exaggerates: whether she was not sometimes imposed upon by our Irish tendency to play "stage Irish" for newcomers, one feels less certain'.[52] In a later piece that year about a study called *The Anglo-Irish* by Brian Fitzgerald, she struck a familiar, even unchanging note about her own class: 'The contribution the Anglo-Irish have made to Ireland is now recognized: it is one sign of a happier epoch that the extent, nature and worth of the contribution should be, by general consent, examined.'[53]

However, Bowen's own place in Irish literary culture was ambiguous. In *The Irish Times* in 1954, a series of articles by a columnist 'Thersites' (the pen name of a member of the Department of External Affairs called Thomas Woods) seemed intent on seeing Bowen's writing as unreadable In the *Irish Times* of 6 February 1952, he commented on an essay written by the Irish academic Lorna Reynolds on 'Thirty Years of Irish Letters', published in the Irish literary journal *Studies*: 'Women mostly write badly . . . Miss Bowen is a fair example of this. Of her decided abilities, her sensitivity, her acute perception and so on, I have no doubt. It still remains that three pages of any of her novels can be guaranteed to leave me whirling in an intellectual StVitus dance. Reading Miss Bowen is rather like attempting to walk a tight-rope which is being vigorously shaken at one end. Not even the most neurotic of male writers – Proust, for instance – produces this effect on one's heart missing a beat during sleep.' This was not an isolated moment. In July 1954, commenting on the special edition of *Irish Writing* on women writers, edited by David Marcus and Terence Smith, 'Thersites' reminds readers that 'only a few pages of Miss Bowen's prose are enough to make me feel that I have forgotten to fasten my safety belt'.[54]

A new departure came for Bowen when she was asked to script the narration for a television documentary on Ireland for an American audience, called 'The Tear and the Smile'. Directed by Willard Van Dyke, this documentary was part of a popular American television series called 'The Twentieth Century', made by CBS and narrated by Walter Cronkite. The film had the initial approval of the Irish government after the executive producer, Isaac Kleinerman, visited the Secretary for the Department of the Taoiseach, Padraig O'Hanrahan, in August 1960 for permission to interview Seán Lemass, and Éamon de Valera. The programme was to address social, political and economic developments in the country and the Irish Government was happy to help, and asked to see the shooting schedule. (The government did not know at this point that Bowen was the writer, perhaps if they had, they might have had some reservations, given her Anglo-Irish allegiances.) As it happened, Lemass read the schedule and saw it as flawed, disliking the proposed opening moments set in a Dublin pub. (Walter Cronkite had said he wanted to see the Irish at their favourite occupation, talking and drinking.) The programme makers proposed interviewing an IRA volunteer and shooting footage of men dancing together because of the scarcity of young women in small country towns and also wanted to see two men arrange a marriage. O'Hanrahan wrote to Kleinerman to protest: 'Ireland unfortunately only too often has been represented as a country where the amenities of modern life are practically unknown [and] whose people live under conditions bordering on the primitive.'[55] Kleinerman replied: 'We have no desire to alter, distort, or in any other way create a false or misleading impression.'[56] In the end, both Lemass and de Valera finally agreed to be interviewed.[57]

On 19 September 1960, Bowen was approached by Spencer Curtis Brown, her agent, with a proposition to write scripts for these two half-hour CBS documentaries. Curtis Brown wrote to tell her that 'Apparently a man with the characteristic name of Isaac Kleinerman wrote to you from CBS in America asking if you could do a commentary to go with two half-hour films on 'Ireland Today' which CBS have made. I gather that the commentary would run for about fifteen minutes on each film and they offer $1,200 for each. I imagine that they can arrange a showing of the films in London. They say they have never had any reply from you and quite possibly you have never got the letter. Are you remotely interested in earning £800 in this way? They seem, as always, to be in a great hurry so perhaps you could wire or phone me about it.[58]

Bowen accepted the proposal from CBS and sent the script to New York in late December or very early January. It is not clear where exactly this script ended up. Among her papers in the Harry Ransom Center is a typescript called 'Ireland Today,' reproduced here in Chapter 4. The date of composition of this essay is uncertain and, if it is the script Bowen, submitted for the television documentary in 1960 then it was never used, despite the fact she was paid for the writing and is credited as the author at the end of each programme. The narration lacks any sense of Bowen's voice – her script may have been completely abandoned. Bowen herself certainly believed so.

When the programmes were broadcast in the US on 29 January and 3 February 1961, there was a negative response from the Irish viewers. The Irish ambassador to Washington wrote a report to Lemass on 6 February 1961[59] complaining that the programmes depicted 'A poverty-stricken country riddled with backwardness, unemployment and emigration . . . a general air of fatalism'. Lemass held an internal review to decide if the programme was in breach of the agreement, and, in the end, a letter of protest was sent, but no more was done in official quarters.[60] Charles Ritchie wrote up the unhappy occasion in his diary the next day: 'Last night we had a gloomy little gathering to hear E's script on the TV. It was Ireland "The Smile and the Tear," and the Irish Ambassador was here. They didn't use her script at all. She sat on the sofa drinking martinis and saying at frequent intervals in a sepulchral-furious voice, "I didn't write that, I didn't write that," and finally announced that she was going to use the money she had earned for the script to sue the CBS.'[61]

In the later 1950s, Bowen spent time in Rome gathering materials for a travel book. This trip took place at time of personal crisis for Bowen, as is clear from her letter on 16 June 1958 to her lover, Charles Ritchie. Written, as she tells him, standing up in the General Post Office in Cork City, Bowen gave Ritchie the gloomy news that 'I've come in for the rather depressing purpose of selling a good deal of silver and some pieces of good jewellery I unearthed. I am having the most unspeakable dreary financial crisis. Can you possibly send me a hundred dollars? No use beating about the bush and saying I hate asking you: obviously I do; but would be a help. Will you send the cheque to the Rome address and I'll post it to my Dublin bank. Everything will be all right when I've got the Rome book done . . .'[62] When she had finished her time in Rome, she went back to Ireland in 1959, and began to unload the responsibility of her house. In the words of Heather Bryant Jordan, 'The clearer it became that she would have to part with the house, the more impassioned her writings about it became'[63] The connection between Bowen and the North Cork landscape around her home had become almost elemental, so much so that, as she wrote in the 1963 afterword to *Bowen's Court*, 'the land outside Bowen's Court's windows left prints on my ancestors eyes that looked out: Perhaps their eyes left, also, prints on the scene? If so, those prints were part of the scene to me.' The house that had survived burning during the War of Independence was now about to be voluntarily abandoned. As the loss of the house became more and more inevitable, Bowen began to withdraw emotionally from it. She wrote to Ritchie from Bowen's Court saying, 'You've strengthened me, cheered me and cleared my mind about the decision I've had to take . . . Oh Charles, I am getting bored here, and that's a fact. I supposed it is the effect of hardening my heart: when one can no longer afford to support an illusion, one rather welcomes seeing it break down – or perhaps, rather, in this case, run down.'[64] Charles Ritchie noted the decision with sadness in his diary. 'I feel as if my home was going' and went on to make the odd, significant observation: 'What is driving her away? Some complication she has got into? Is it the pull of Rome – I mean the city, not – at any rate yet – the religion? Does she know how much this will hurt when the time comes?'[65]

First she offered the house to a male Bowen cousin who could not afford to take it and so had to refuse. Then, without telling family or friends, she put the house up for sale through her local Cork solicitor and accepted the first offer she received. Throughout, her financial sense was poor. Bowen would have welcomed Alan Cameron's good business head at this time. The contents of the house, the books, furniture and paintings went for sale to a local auctioneer in Cork, rather than the large London auctioneers where they would have gained much greater prices. Bowen's haste and secrecy suggest that she was embarrassed by what she must have seen as a failure in duty and inherited responsibility. As she wrote in her 1940 essay 'The Big House', 'It is something to subscribe to an idea, even if one cannot live up to it.' Now she was failing to live up to this idea of duty.

Bowen had hoped that the new owner would live in Bowen's Court with his family, but within a year the house was demolished and the valuable trees cut down. Her friend Eddy Sackville West said that when she came back for one last look at her home, after the sale, she looked like someone who had attended her own execution. In a re-issue of her family history, *Bowen's Court*, in 1963 she laments in an afterword that 'the house, having played its part, has come to an end. It will not, after all, celebrate its two hundredth birthday – of that it has fallen short by some thirteen years. The shallow hollow of land under the mountains, on which Bowen's Court stood, is again empty. Not one hewn stone left on another on the fresh growing grass. Green covers all traces of the foundations, today so far as the eye can see; there might never have been a house. One cannot say that the space is empty . . . It was a clean end. Bowen's Court never lived to be a ruin.'[66] The *Irish Independent* reviewed the re-issue of *Bowen's Court* warmly. The reviewer, F.J. Keane, wrote that 'Miss Bowen sheds no tears and ascribes no blame for anything . . . The result is a book that is not alone admirable in itself but which could serve as a shining example for all too many querulous Irish writers who spend so much time snarling at everything around them.'[67]

Clean end or no the loss of Bowen's Court was a difficult one for Bowen. To some degree, the loss of her house liberated her from what she called, in Rome, the thicket of the self, and her final novel, *Eva Trout*, published in 1969, four years before her death, is arguably her most radical, a devastating account of a wealthy heiress a 'lunatic giant'. Her sense of profound displacement was now released and given full fictive life. She did continue to write and broadcast on Irish subjects. For example, one unique departure came for Bowen when she was asked to write the narration for the light and sound performance 'Kinsale, Son et Lumiere', performed at Charles Fort in Kinsale on 22 May 1966 as part of a local arts festival. Her narration is an account of the various wars and battles fought in Kinsale and in her epic sweep through Irish history, she moves deftly from Vikings to the Battle of Kinsale, from Raleigh and Spenser to the Williamite wars and onwards. In her interpretation of the course of Irish history, Bowen draws heavily on O'Faolain's book on the Great O'Neill, which she had reviewed. Throughout, Bowen is, as always, even-handed, valorising the English administrator and general Mountjoy on the one hand, while praising the Irish hero Hugh O'Neill, thus trying to reconcile two traditions in Irish history, Wild Geese and planter. In terms of historical allegiance, Bowen is sympathetic to the plight of Catholic Ireland in the seventeenth century but she does make a sympathetic link with John Churchill and his descendent, Winston Churchill. There is a (very) brief mention of Cromwell, but Bowen's method throughout is to take the broad sweep of Irish republican history and balance it with a subtle validation of her own tradition here and there.

In June 1965, she broadcast a review of Elizabeth Coxhead's book *Daughters of Erin*, a study of Maud Gonne, Sarah Purser, Constance Gore-

Booth, and Sarah and Molly Allgood. Bowen wrote: 'as Irishwomen they drew on primitive strength – for Ireland is, fundamentally, a primitive society; in which there is – I would argue – still more than a trace of the matriarchal . . . The *Irish RM* stories are less cut-to-pattern in comicality, turn less undeviatingly on blood sports, than anti-blood-sport generations have preferred to suppose. In these tales are no meaningless antic caperings: on the contrary, outsize characters, clashes, crises, realistic in their very delirium. These not only *were* Ireland – they still are Ireland, under the skin.'[68] Yet, a few years later, as R.F. Foster reports, 'Shortly before her death in 1972, she astounded her friend the writer Hubert Butler and his wife Peggy by the vehemence with which she said, "I *hate* Ireland." It had grown away from her – or away from the collusive, stylish, never-never land which she had chosen to inhabit.'[69]

She relocated to Hythe in Kent where she had spent much of her vagrant childhood and where her mother had died. There she went on to write two more novels before her death in 1973, although she did request to be buried in Ireland, in the churchyard in Farahy. (*The Irish Times* paid lavish tribute to Bowen at the time of her death, under the headline 'Elizabeth Bowen dies at 83', thus adding ten years to her age!)

Overall, my sense of Bowen's relationship with Ireland accords with that of Heather Bryant Jordan, where she writes, 'Although she sought to find the everlasting resolution of these personal struggles in Ireland, in fact there she learned of the existence of more uncertainties'.[70] It is, I think, to Bowen's credit that she applied herself with so much rigour and self-scrutiny to understand these uncertainties in her critical writings and furthermore I would argue that she benefited immeasurably as a fictive writer from her lifelong career as a reviewer and an essayist on Irish themes, subjects and history. For Bowen, Ireland drew out essential contradictions within her imagination, and the critical works in this collection will, I hope, illuminate this most important source for her imagination, her own hyphenated identity.

WORKS CITED

Bennett Andrew, and Royle Nicholas. *Elizabeth Bowen and the Dissolution of the Novel* (Hampshire: Macmillan, 1995).

Corcoran, Neil. *Elizabeth Bowen: The Enforced Return* (Oxford: Oxford University Press, 2004).

Dooley, Terence. *The Decline of the Big House in Ireland* (Dublin: Wolfhound, 2001).

Ellmann, Maud. *Elizabeth Bowen: The Shadow Across the Page* (Edinburgh: Edinburgh University Press, 2003).

Fisk, Robert. *In Time of War* (Dublin: Gill and MacMillan, 1996).
Foster, R.F. *Paddy and Mr Punch: Connections in Irish and English History* (London: Penguin, 1993).
Foster, R.F. *The Irish Story* (London: Penguin, 2001).
Glendinning, Victoria. *Elizabeth Bowen: Portrait of a Writer* (London: Weidenfeld and Nicolson, 1977).
— and Judith Robertson. Editors. *Love's Civil War* (London: Simon and Schuster, 2009).
Hepburn, Allan. Editor. *People, Places, Things: Essays by Elizabeth Bowen* (Edinburgh: Edinburgh University Press, 2008).
Jordan, Heather Bryant. *How Will the Heart Endure? Elizabeth Bowen and the Landscape of War* (Ann Arbor: University of Michigan Press, 1992).
Lassner, Phyllis. *Elizabeth Bowen* (Basingstoke: MacMillan, 1990).
Lee, Hermione. *Elizabeth Bowen: An Estimation* (Totowa, NJ: Barnes and Noble, 1981).
—. *The Mulberry Tree* (London: Virago Press 1986).
O'Faolain, Sean. 'A Reading and Remembrance of Elizabeth Bowen', *London Review of Books* (4--17 March, 1982).
—. *Vive Moi* (London: Sinclair Stevenson, 1993).
O'Halpin, Eunan. *Spying on Ireland* (Oxford: Oxford University Press, 2008).
Osborn, Susan. Editor. *Elizabeth Bowen: New Critical Perspectives* (Cork: Cork University Press, 2009).
Wills, Clair. *That Neutral Island: A Cultural History of Ireland During the Second World War* (London: Faber and Faber, 2007).
Walshe, Éibhear, Editor. *Elizabeth Bowen: Visions and Revisions* (Dublin: Irish Academic Press, 2009).
—. Editor. *Elizabeth Bowen Remembered* (Dublin Four Courts, 1999)

Chapter 1

Oblique, Frayed Island
1929–1940

Dublin Under the Georges, by Constantia Maxwell, 25 July 1936, *New Statesman and Nation*, Review

Dublin and New York are two standard examples of the grand manner – the eighteenth century's and the twentieth's. Dublin exhales melancholy, the past and the sense of an obliterated purpose that no New World activity can exactly renew: an anticlimactic, possibly endless pause hangs over her large squares, long light streets and darkening Georgian façades. Meanwhile New York, congested on her narrow island, as beautifully brittle-looking as candy in the air, shoots higher yearly, throws out bridges across the Hudson and speedways across the State, tears herself down, re-piles herself in toppling masses and infuses the century with her nervous life. New York grew on a series of impulses; Dublin is rooted in political stubbornness: her great phase had the unity of a social idea.

Miss Maxwell has chronicled what remains – with every salutation of the new Ireland – Dublin's most fully vital, if not her most happy, phase. Under the Georges she was a European capital: as that she has still to find herself again. Strife and complexity, danger and bitter feeling have never released their grip on this unhappy town, but in the eighteenth century, under Grattan's[1] Parliament, the Irish of the Ascendancy turned to them their most nearly unknowing face. Hemmed in by country trouble and shaken by city strife, the aristocratic dwellers on each side of the Liffey maintained an almost Venetian level of gaiety. Entertainments were princely. Whatever else happened, they had a good time. Security may have bred, elsewhere, a sounder magnificence, but never magnificence at such fever pitch. Here the great were often shady, but few were shoddy. Trinity College threw out crabbed and mordant wits. The deaneries were headquarters of good company. The Archbishop's wife drove round Dublin in one of the most dashing turnouts on record. The theatre, in spite of the difficulty of keeping the audience off the stage (on one occasion Sheridan[2] had to clear the Smock Alley theatre with firearms), kept, at least to the time of the Union, a notably high form; concert rooms were packed with exacting audiences, and enthusiastic peers composed a private orchestra. The ladies' conversation was full-blooded and snappy, if not always informed. In clubs and drawing-rooms the rate of play was high; the consumption of drink and victuals at dinners was astounding. Elegance in the exact sense may have been rare: spleen and a tough, drink-pickled melancholy underlay much of the glitter: the glitter itself had a tarnish. The scandalous and infinitely regrettable Union struck all this fun in Dublin a fatal blow.

The conditions in which the poor lived were nauseating, even for the period. A certain amount of relief led to some grand building, though even the new Lying-in Hospital seems to have been open to criticism. The other hospitals, the prisons and orphanages were charnel-houses, with an immense mortality. Liffey floods increased the horrors of a very negative sanitation. English policy and foreign wars struck repeated blows at the Dublin industries: the city's distress-pressure was heightened by influxes of futureless, disaffected country workers. Protection supported by bloodshed, sacked foreign-goods warehouses, burnt effigies and nocturnal howlings – did what it could. The fortunate classes, in so far as fashion and expediency allowed them, stood by what Irish industries there were. The charming and ill-fated Lord Edward Fitzgerald[3] was not alone, though he was the most militant, in espousing a romantic nationalism. A curious and unspoken complicity of spirit between all classes must account for the fact of there not being, in a city of such extremes and such constant feverish pressure, more, or in fact any, sustained, class-hatred.

Miss Maxwell's book, which deals with many more, and more complex, aspects of eighteenth-century Dublin than I have given here, is the fruit of wide, thorough, unbiased and enterprising research. She is admirably documented as to the city's political, social, industrial, academic and artistic life during the period she covers, and she has set out her material most ably. Her style is unaffected, unemotional (though a curious, wry emotion exhales from its matter), concrete, and therefore, I think, excellent.

A Biography of Dublin, by Christine Longford, 7 November 1936, *New Statesman and Nation*, Review

Lady Longford's story of Dublin is tactful and spirited; it cannot displease the native, it will amuse the visitor. Her book – the first of a series of city biographies – had to be very short: she has done very well with it. She rushes through history with rapid discrimination, making pauses only for anecdote: rightly, for Irish history is a constellation of anecdotes glittering on a profound and untracked gloom. Briskness is essential to Lady Longford's manner and to the form of her book; only two subjects tempt her to potter – the Anglo-Irish (who first began to make trouble centuries back, while still called the Old English) and the Dublin theatre. It will be interesting to see whether other towns in the series – Jerusalem, Moscow, Los Angeles – offer as much as Dublin to common sense and fun. The Irish discussing themselves are often boring, long-winded and full of vanity: they have been given style recently by a new *désabusé*[4] kind of English wit. It took an Englishwoman – and one with flair – to write this agreeable, vivid, smooth, un-bitter book. Her style and tone have their dangers: she comes in places a little too near smartness, but she gives tragedy place by respectful understatement; honours the fantastic and the heroic, and shows throughout a sober regard for fact. Dublin has loomed in art through a haze of native sentiment, often a tortured sentiment. But taste – of which so great a part is intelligent and voluntary – better qualifies the biographer. Lady Longford ably paints the city's portrait and summarizes its past.

Dublin, on the east, the Europe-regarding coast of Ireland, owes her vitality and complexity as a city to a continuous influx of foreign life. The invader, the trader, the opportunist, the social visitor have all added strife or colour. The Norsemen found her a village – called Baile Atha Cliath, or Fort of the Hurdles – on the lowest ford of the Liffey. The river's mouth made a fine harbour, her position was strategic; since their day until lately she was garrisoned by invaders, whose ostentation has always been uneasy. Once her walls went up she became a capital, full of heady passions. The Normans, invited over, gave a bad deal, but got a worse deal than they had time to see. Prince John's[5] lordship of Ireland was not happy; he was frivolous, tactless and overbearing, offended the older Normans, who had been settling down, and gave early support to an Irish theory that when the English come over they go to bits. Richard II found enlightenment did not work. The Fitzgeralds, of Norman origin, made perpetual trouble; Lord Edward, finally, led a forlorn hope. Dublin, connected with Ireland by a system of nerves, registered and reacted to trouble throughout the country: the relation of Paris to France provides no analogy. She became the headquarters of Protestant domination, of aristocratic pretension, of bourgeois power. A minority supported by theoretic authority fled to her at any crisis, to be fortified. Under Henry VIII, the Protestant aggression had its way in Dublin: George Browne, the Archbishop, found the greater part of Ireland unsatisfactory; he complained to Thomas Cromwell[6]: 'The common people of this isle are more zealous in their blindness than the saints and martyrs were in the truth.' Puritanism, later, found the city slippery in its grip. Dublin has always been foreignly irresponsible; an uninformed enthusiasm commands it, and the Stuarts, attractive and kingly, were warmly supported there. The Restoration was signalized by a great burst of fun: the theatre (precious to Lady Longford) first came into evidence, and Roman Catholics were tolerated. In spite of defeat James II, owing to personal characteristics, became unpopular. Under William and Mary some hanky-panky over the linen industry brought capitalism into the open as a declared force. Longer lapses between violence made constitutional difficulties more apparent. 'The work of the Irish Parliament was very much obstructed by the fact that certain officials were English, and only came to Ireland in their spare time.'

Lady Longford makes place for portraits of Swift, Molyneux[7], Wolfe Tone[8], Grattan, Lord Edward Fitzgerald, Emmet[9], O'Connell[10] and Parnell[11]. Her desire, which is honourable, to place Swift in the gallery of enthusiast patriots makes her overlook, or ignore, the in-turning edge of his wit. To burn for Ireland is not to burn for truth: Swift never buried for Ireland the quality that he had. Lady Longford, referring to Swift's last charity – the leaving of his money to found a hospital for lunatics in Dublin – suppresses in her quotation his next couplet:

> He left the little Wealth he had
> To build a House for Fools and Mad;
> *And shew'd by one satiric Touch,*
> *No Nation wanted it so much.*

The anecdotes are well chosen, pleasant and pithy. There are pictures of pre-Union Dublin in redundant and crazy flower. The nineteenth century is summarized; there is a sympathetic family picture of the Wildes; a broad daylight photograph of the Celtic Twilight and a respectful resume of 1916. Lady Longford does justice to Dublin's present urbanity: the startled and somehow not yet quite authentic glitter of cinemas and all-night cafés, the inexhaustible talk with its malice and unfocused uplift, the Grafton Street animation, the morning coffee, the theatre. Prolonged European disturbance offers Ireland an opening; she bids fair to become for the English a more accessible Switzerland, an amiable, rural country, now that the rifles have cooled there, poetry with the sting drawn, a country with a decay-glamour, a touch of the Old South. Dublin may make a bid to be Basle and Berne, the clearing-house for the sensitive tripper, the intelligent pause on the way to country house visits, the gateway to bay and bog. For this her biography, informed and sophisticated, is exceedingly well-timed. But the city is not in tune yet; she is overcast like a yesterday one remembers with no pleasure; her trams give her away, they have no Continental brightness; they crawl through the Georgian quarters with a rasping vibration and the red plush inside gives out a dusty and charnel smell.

Letter from Ireland, 28 October 1937, *Night and Day*, Essay

Cork city has been very gay of late. Summer weather persisted, just lightly chilled, and on long gay glassy evenings the Lee estuary looked like the scene set for a regatta. Galway oysters reappeared at the Oyster Tavern, off Patrick Street: this is a long cavern of dusky mirrors with a grill fire (which grills really superbly) glittering at the end. The Opera House on the quayside reopened, and Jimmy O'Dea[12] packed it for two weeks. Ireland's great little comedian is a tragi-comedian. He is a pool of temperament. There is a touch of Stan Laurel, a touch of Chaplin: any affinities he has belong to the screen, not the stage, because he has such a very *exposed* nature. He is ultimately and first of all himself. He is a Dublin man, but Cork thinks the world of him.

Cork left Cork for Killarney when the All Ireland Hurley Finals were played there. Tipperary won. This was a great day for the whole of the South of Ireland; special trains were run and the roads for a hundred miles round streamed with cars and bicycles, most of them flying flags. The Tipperary contingent passed my way. Those who unluckily could not get to Killarney stood on banks for hours to watch the traffic. This is, in the literal sense, a very quiet country: the Troubles and the Civil War were fought out in an almost unbroken hush, punctuated by a few explosions or shots. Voices are seldom raised, and you can (so to speak) hear a dog bark or a milk-cart rattle or a funeral bell toll two counties away. But these great Sundays of sport galvanise everything; from the moment you wake you know that something is going on. This last year or two, the town of Killarney has begun to cash in on sport. Last year they had a Big Fight there. Hurley is the fastest game, short of ice hockey, that I have ever watched. It is a sort of high-speed overhead hockey, played with sticks with flat wooden blades, and it looks even more dangerous than it apparently is. Though a game that would melt you in the Antarctic, it is, for some reason, played only in summer. I do not think nearly so much of Gaelic football. But I have only seen this game played in a sea mist, which, milkily shrouding goals and players, added to an effect of aimless mystery: there seemed to be effort but no fun, and sea birds – this was in the flats behind Waterville, County Kerry – circled rather drearily overhead.

Yes, certainly in early autumn the Cork social season is at its height. And English visitors constantly overlook this. English people apparently come to Ireland for reasons – such as scenery pure and simple – that would get me nowhere. (I except, of course, fishermen.) They disembark their cars from SS *Innisfallen* on to the Cork quay, and rattle at high speed, with minds set on the sublime, out of one of Europe's strangest and most beautiful cities. They go in droves to stay at boring hotels on lakes or bays. These hotels seem to me boring because they have no local life; they are built for strangers who want to look at scenery. Their lounges, though often lofty, are claustrophobic, and often smell of milk pudding. Their social atmosphere seems to be subnormal. I should add that these are very good hotels for those who like to stay in hotels of this kind. The surrounding scenery is handsome and undisappointing – if this were not so, the hotels would not be there.

But so much fun is to be had in the small towns. The small town hotels in Ireland are brightening up, and are now perfectly possible to stay in. They have a great *va et vient*,[13] and their saloons in the evening are full of excellent talk. In the town, there is nearly always something going on – a fair, a funeral or a politician's visit. Or if something is not going on while you are there, something has gone on just before you arrived, and everybody is willing to tell you all about it. All summer and autumn, circuses or strolling players are on the roads: these pitch their tents nightly and give their shows at the edge of one or another town. The remoter cinemas show where good films go when they die. South Irish small towns are beautiful in an abstract manner, with painted houses, wide streets, big dusty squares, knolls of bronze beeches and dark, quick rivers. They are full of shoe-shops, china shops and 'medical halls.' Dogs lie asleep in mid-street in the hub of the town, only dislodged now and then by big red Great Southern buses. When a bus pulls up in a town a surprising number of people come out of shops and pubs and stand round the bus in a ring, as though a whale had been landed. Anybody who gets into the bus or gets out does so in a glare of gratifying publicity. When the bus has been looked at for about twenty minutes it gets up, as it were, and dashes out of the town. To those who are set on scenery, and must have it, I would explain that most small towns in the coast-counties of Ireland are set in as much beauty as anybody could wish, that most streets have a backdrop of dark blue mountain, whether close or distant, and that on fine days they are drenched in dazzling light. The official grandeurs of Ireland are generally, too, within quite possible reach.

For two or three weeks after Horse Show, Dublin sits back and looks rather desultory. That gala week in August involves the whole south of the city, which becomes a sort of annexe of Ballsbridge. Dublin goes all out, and becomes very European. It seems such a pity that Horse Show should coincide with the height of the Salzburg Festival. When we become the United States of Europe, one may hope that something may be better arranged – though it will have to be made perfectly clear, from the outset, that nothing can alter the date of Horse Show. In September, Dublin stops being anti-climatic. Early autumn brightness polishes the façades of Georgian streets and squares; russet edges the trees in the park and along the canal. This autumn the city looks very brisk. One set of traffic-lights has been installed at a lower corner of Merrion Square: the tempo of progress is setting in. Car-parking regulations are being tightened: another sign of how prosperous we all are. There is a boom in civic pride – a fine exhibition of prints and maps, depicting the past of the city, has been opened and ought not to be missed. The Irish Academy of Letters has just elected three new members. The Abbey Theatre has started its winter season. The Grafton Street shops are full of the autumn modes. Trouble was caused at the trials before the motor races in Phoenix Park by a party of peacocks that escaped from the Zoo and, in the gloom of a very early morning, filed slowly across the racing track. This is said to have happened twice. But by the crucial Saturday, the surviving peacocks were under lock and key. Ireland becomes safer, though never obvious.

My Ireland, by Lord Dunsany, 26 June 1937, *New Statesman and Nation*, Review

Lord Dunsany, perhaps a little disorientated by the largeness of his publisher's invitation, halts and hovers rather over his opening chapters, then drops into his swing and writes an engaging book. High-handed, whimsical, bland, touchy, reactionary, and impossible to pin down to any point, here he has it all his own way – and what a way it is. *My Ireland* has, throughout, a sort of contrary soundness. It is written to please himself and, please God, infuriate others. The merit of the completely personal book is that it often captures, or rather blunders upon, that general quality that makes literature. This title (not his own choice) with its possessive smugness is certainly putting-off; one is led to expect some more of those whimsical retrospections to which the country have been too prone lately. 'I shall never forget how the mountains looked as I hacked home, etc.' But here the relation felt between the man and his land is profound, subtle and reticent. The retrospections are pungent, and are so defiantly mustered that they escape sentiment. Here is, for Ireland, more than sheltered affection: this goes back further than Eton, a turn for the twilight of history, or the Kildare Street Club. And here is, for this author, a refreshing absence of mystic experience. What dominates the book is satisfied love of a country, body and spirit – love which the too apt pen, by making articulate, has too often denatured or falsified: here it is not falsified.

In these pages, Lord Dunsany may be tendentious – in fact, he is clearly out to be tendentious, with his *Sackville* Street, his pouncing inverted commas, his little digs at the new Ireland that are about as playful as would be the nudges of a surviving bog moose – but he is not phoney. His feelings are too furious to exploit. The finest part of his book, written in Ireland last winter, is more or less of a journal and is about shooting. Turgenev, Tolstoi, stake no claim on this as a subject; Lord Dunsany's experiences and reflections are his own. Art these days shows signs of decamping from enlightened Metroland, where it has lodged so uneasily; Horseback Hall is coming into its own again; we have had quite enough, for a bit, about the country from the kind hiker's angle; kindness to huntable animals is once more at a discount: art shows a re-mellowed attitude to sport.

In fact, there is now in sight rather too much extraversion and blood. But at this still apposite moment comes Lord Dunsany, squelching about Irish midland bogs with his gun, full of bloodthirsty tenderness and of rude poetry either unselfconscious or raised to the hyperconsciousness of art. He is authentic, full of tips (care of shooting boots) and of plain facts:

> The outwitting of golden plover depends, in one of its branches, on going to the right spot in a hedge, while another man goes round to

> the far side of a field and drives them over. But I did not go to the right spot in the hedge, and only got one. Then I drew a small snipe-bog blank because it had been drained. But my gamekeeper pointed out that there was no harm in that, for it would be just the same again in two or three years. And this is undoubtedly true, for soil and air in Ireland seem to be at one in bringing back the bog to its own, wherever man has lifted the spade against it. The soil seems to work for the bog, while the damp air fights against man. And so the spade is laid by, and the bog steals softly back; and in a few years there it is again, as though man had never troubled its ancient stillness . . . Memorials to this struggle may be found all over Ireland, and they mostly seem memorials to the victors, the wind and the weather.

All through: the romantic, endemic feeling for ruin:

> One does not fully understand Ireland if one overlooks the pace at which ruin floats on the gentle wind, and the grudge that the Irish soil seems to bear to civilization. Earth seems to triumph in the end over civilization everywhere, but a few decades in Ireland seem to have powers to bring down to oblivion, such as only comes with a thousand years to Egypt.

There is more, of course, to a book like this than shooting; there are personalities, hunts, legends, gossip, landscape and extinct cricket fields, now in pasture. Nostalgic and measured prose, which is at the same time vigorous, hangs over all this an iridescent veil. The book is not very happily illustrated by photographs of a Come-to-Ireland nature: these have little relation to Lord Dunsany's prose.

Lord Dunsany's turn of mind is his own, but his nature, his habit of living, are generic, inherited. The old regime throws out from time to time its artists, sports like this, minds that show degrees of creative, sometimes poetic, power – overbearing fantasists. Oddly enough – or is it odd? – lordly art has almost always a rude, sometimes not far from vulgar, and somehow saving quality: it may be orchidaceous, but it is rooted. Too cerebral bourgeois art, with its lack of attachments, is on the whole more often brittle, and so, ephemeral. There exists in one kind of art a touch of the peasant toughness that Proust saw in the Guermantes. For pages together in *My Ireland,* Lord Dunsany chooses to show himself as a quite impossible person – complacently dream-bound, 'overbearingly blind'. Many might wish to displace him. But he has gone to the making of his Ireland, and his Ireland is valid – rich as peat with its memories, ignorant, but impossible to ignore.

Bouquet, *Dublin Old and New*, by Stephen Gwynn, 7 May 1938, *New Statesman and Nation*, Review

At the first glance, Dublin nearly always delights the visitor by its grand perspectives and large light squares; its at once airy and mysterious look. Then there is a less happy phase in getting to know the city – when it appears shut-up, faded and meaningless; full of false starts and dead ends, the store plan of something that never realized itself. The implacable flatness of the houses begins to communicate a sort of apathy to the visitor: after her first smile and her first grand effect, Dublin threatens to offer disappointingly little. This stale phase in the stranger's relations with the city can only be cut short by imagination and vigorous curiosity. Dublin is so much more than purely spectacular; she is impregnated with a past that never evaporates. Even the recent past, the nineteenth century, leaves on some outlying quarters of the city a peculiar time – colour. Every quarter – from where the two cathedrals stand in the maze of side-streets, to the latest ring of growth, where red villas straggle into the fields – has, in fact, got a character you could cut with a knife. The more you know, the more you can savour this.

Unlike London, Paris, Edinburgh, the city, at each side of the river, covers flat land. The earth under it forms no romantic contours, and does not thrust the buildings up into different levels: from no point does one get a momentous view of the city. Her position, between the sea and the mountains, is beautiful, but can only be guessed at from her heart. Dublin's grandness, as a capital city, is anti-romantic; it lies in her plan, and her fine buildings, alone. Her interest lies in her contrasts, in the expression she gives to successive different ideas of living. Dublin does not represent Ireland; she is one aspect of it: she stands, or had stood, for wealth, for the imposition of power, for the generally European element that has made itself felt but never been quite absorbed. Not for nothing is she the capital of a country in which blood runs to the head: life here has been always lived at high pressure; everybody is highly articulate; this has always been a city of 'characters,' in which nothing gets done impersonally. Emotional memory, here, has so much power that the past and the present seem to be lived simultaneously. In Dublin, as in the rest of Ireland, if you do not know the past you only know the half of anyone's mind.

Mr Stephen Gwynn's *Dublin Old and New* supplies that background which the stranger will need. This is not a guide book, and not a history – though it resumes those parts of the past always most present in the

Dubliner's mind. There is information, but no bare information: what we learn is made palatable and given colour by Mr Gwynn's smiling, unhurried style. To the Dublin-born person, this book rings true and is evocative; at the same time, Mr Gwynn has known how to detach, from the web of Dublin's character, facts which will strike the stranger's imagination. He has, chiefly, traced the social growth of the city; he relates its human history in the course of a tour through the streets themselves, picking out here a statue, here a tablet, here a building or corner dark with associations. He also gives, in words, such a vivid plan that the appended map is almost unnecessary.

He is at his best with portraits, and has great command of anecdote. His eighteenth-century Dublin has been knowingly touched in, but, wisely, he has given most of his space to the nineteenth century, assembling a good deal of unwritten history, filling in a tract between fact and gossip. He has taken aspects of Dublin of which he is most fully qualified to write. *Dublin Old and New* should endow the stranger with a sense of the city's continuous, vivid and far from placid life: the residential quarters, the university buildings will no longer present an obdurate mystery. The best of Mr Gwynn's chapters have the spontaneity of talk, and follow the same compelling, zigzag line. A good deal of the traditional gloom of Dublin (which literature, lately, has reinforced) is relieved by his stories of witty lives. After the Union, Dublin declined from her aristocratic showiness: a good many families left and found their focus in London. But judges, divines, the great doctors, the Trinity College figures continued to enjoy, and to add to, the city's urbanity: there was less wildness, but there was wit, good living and dignity. In Ireland, the nineteenth century showed the best of its mellowness, without the industrial element. It had more grace here, though life was often tragic, never fully secure. His chapter on the museums and galleries, touches the unhappy subject of the Lane bequest.[14] Here, and elsewhere, something more natural than tact guides him through the complex history of a city in which almost every subject is controversial. The great quality of *Dublin Old and New* is its companionableness: it should be carried round with the guide book but not read in the street, its style is too retrospective and leisurely – read, rather, in the intervals of sight-seeing, or, best of all, in bed in the hotel. It should feed a taste for Dublin – and, also, bring to the notice those quiet and atmospheric quarters (along the canal, for instance) that the tourist often overlooks.

Irish Life in the Seventeenth Century: After Cromwell, by Edward MacLysaght, 6 May 1939, *New Statesman and Nation*, Review

The past of Ireland is an uneasy subject: controversial, bloody and bitter, with no trappings; few uninterruptedly pleasant prospects down which the eye can run. To the English mind, that past is not even stirring – it is too full of defeats. The tragedy is too plain to permit analysis – and it is for analysis, inference or the picturesque that history is read now, as an exercise or another kind of escape. Peace-lovers seek the past because it is safely over – and nothing in Ireland is ever over. England's past is at present one of her chief assets; it must have only one adjective – 'glorious.' And England's past in Ireland has not been glorious: its residue is a sort of embarrassment. When the Englishman looks at Ireland, something happens which is quite unbearable – the bottom drops out of his sense of right and wrong. That *méfiance*[15] holds good in a generation: few Englishmen who served in His Majesty's Army in Ireland in those years that just preceded the Treaty care to be reminded of that country again.

So, ignorance of Irish history, in the English and most of the Anglo-Irish, has not been seen as a blot on culture – till now. The traveller finds few monuments. Till lately, a mist covered the centuries: sieges, risings, massacres, famines, forlorn hopes had been heard of; inevitably, Ireland appeared only in English popular history where the fates of the two countries most momentously touched. Her entity as a country, her continuous, underlying existence, her conditions were very little known of – except when conditions, through some access of misery, forced themselves on the English popular eye. Her native – as opposed to the Anglo-Irish – culture was, before the height of the Gaelic movement, ignored. In fact, Ireland was not objectified.

Lately, however, this ignorance – one might say this wish for ignorance – has begun to dissipate. What was at the most a sporadic sentimental interest in Ireland has given place to a demand for exact knowledge. This is to hand: Irish scholarship has never needed an outside impetus; for years it has been thorough and self-rewarding; today, simply, it meets with a wider recognition. Also, the output of semi-popular, but informed and temperate books on Irish subjects is on the increase. Ireland appears on the European map.

Here are two books which, in different manners, uncover tracts of the past, or the Irish scene. On *Irish Life in the Seventeenth Century*, Mr MacLysaght has done useful, thorough and extended research. This particular period in Ireland has been little touched by the social historian. Ireland just after Cromwell, with that influx of violently imposed settlers – the effects on her civilization, the confluence of temperaments, the unwilling adjustments, the repercussions of constitutional and temperamental changes in England – is a fruitful subject for study. Mr MacLysaght has not aimed at a facile 'picture'; he has given no emotional colour. He has, more usefully, weighed and collated facts, then left the reader's judgment and imagination to work. He has drawn largely on letters and manuscripts – accounts by settlers, travellers and officials. One of his merits is, he examines every authority, allows, in any account he quotes from, for the writer's predispositions or temperament, and is as careful to warn against the hasty deduction as he is to avoid the hasty deduction himself. Especially where the matter is controversial (as in the chapter on the subject of 'Morals'), he does not neglect to balance opposing views. At times this impartiality is carried almost too far: it becomes hard for the reader to draw any final inference – even so, one must commend his fullness and honesty.

As a result of this serious, dogged work a clear picture of seventeenth-century Ireland does come to form in the mind. The opening chapter on 'Characteristics and Traits' is general, but not blurred by generalizations. In 'The Gentry and their Dependants' appears the inevitable contrast between the unwelcome, enforced new upper class and their predecessors. There is an interesting note on the strong ties formed by the foster system. The absorption – in some happier cases – of the newcomers into the native background, the weathering-down of their foreign traits, is well shown; the idea that Ireland is predisposed to feudality is examined. Sports and recreations, within the period; life in Dublin and city life in general; 'The Clergy and the People,' amenities, culture and communications make the stuff of succeeding chapters. The writing, admirably concrete, is enlivened, though not overloaded, with anecdotes and quotations. Both for the initial interest of its method and subject, and for its promising value as a book of reference, this solid, sufficiently graphic study of seventeenth-century Ireland should be recommended very highly indeed.

The Sword of Light, by Desmond Ryan, 6 May 1939, *New Statesman and Nation*, Review

Mr Desmond Ryan's *The Sword of Light* treats a heroic subject – the survival of Gaelic in Ireland – in a heroic manner. Mr Ryan's rather too highly dramatized style should not be allowed to detract from the seriousness of his argument. Sub-titled *From the Four Masters to Douglas Hyde,* the book begins with the early seventeenth century, with the four Annalists of Donegal Bay and their contemporary, the less exact Dr Keating. Then there is blind O'Carolan, the last of the Irish bards, who sang from house to house in the eighteenth century, a chapter on the Ossian controversy, and a picture of Miss Charlotte Brooke[16] in Co. Cavan, her ardour, her limitations, the impetus that she gave. The Gaelic Society of 1808, the discouragement (stressed by Mr Ryan) that the Gaelic enthusiasts received from O'Connell, and the attempted use of Gaelic for Protestant propaganda in the early nineteenth century are the subjects of the middle part of the book. Philip Barron's[17] magnificent and abortive effort for Gaelic, sixty years too soon, the brief life of his college on the Waterford coast, makes one of the finest chapters. Mangan[18] the poet, John O'Donovan[19] 'the Fifth Master' are drawn with feeling – both as persons and forces – and the Gaelic League, Dr Hyde[20] and the present-day 'victory' for the Irish language bring the book to its close as the history of a culture (and something deeper than a culture) that was threatened, ignored, persecuted, belittled but not lost. Sources of the antagonism to Gaelic have been by turns political, snobbish, religious. Mr Ryan, with good will and a degree of fairness, examines them all. His work is creditable; it may also be popular.

The Moores of Moore Hall, by Joseph Hone, 25 November 1939, *New Statesman and Nation*, Review

George Moore, the merchant of Alicante, built Moore Hall when he returned from Spain. The site, on the top of a wooded hill overlooking an inlet of Carra Lake, caught his eye – no doubt it embodied his Irish dreams. He had meant to improve, and to settle at, Ashbrook House, the more modest home of his family; but, like other Irishmen of his period, he could not but deviate into the grand idea. He had the means: he had more than made good during his term abroad – perhaps his ability came from his mother's side; she had been an Athy of Renville, and the Athys head the roll of the great Galway burgher families. Now, backed by a solid fortune, this first George Moore set out to buy up land at a time when land in Ireland cost more than it does now. He had a right, also, to his wish for the grand, for he had soared out of the Anglo-Irish ambiguity by taking out a patent of nobility in order to attend the court of Spain. He had established, as far as one knows rightly, descent from the Yorkshire family of the Blessed Thomas More. He and his wife (*née* Miss de Kilikelly, or Kelly, reared in Spain and married by him at Bilbao) had thus made part of the aristocratic society of Catholic *émigré* Irish that gathered at Catholic courts. The Catholicism of the Moores – as the fourth and last George Moore was not slow to point out – was recent, and on the whole unimpassioned: that Miss Athy, the merchant's mother, had been a Catholic and brought the religion in. Miss de Kilikelly confirmed the matter, of course. In the clement, propitious Spanish air, the George Moores got from their religious background advancement, poise. But back in Ireland, in Mayo, the position of Catholic gentry was not too good.

However, a chapel was built at the top of the new house, and the family practised its own religion in an easy, unbigoted way. Later, they were to attract Miss Edgeworth[21] and her friend the Dean[22] by their liberalism, their readiness to discuss. With the Moores, there were no mines in this area; their fanaticisms worked out in other ways. The last George Moore's abnegation of Rome and rather wordy embracement of the Protestant faith was the first Moore act of religious fanaticism.

The woods at the top of Muckloon Hill were cleared, and Moore Hall went up. Begun in 1792, the bland Georgian house in its watchful position over the lake and islands was not to live much more than a hundred and thirty years. In 1923 it was burned down – victim, like other Senators' houses, of party violence. Mr Hone shows a dreadful photograph of the shell – not the least indignity is the ivy. While it stood, classic and bare and strong, the house embodied that perfect idea of living that, in actual living, cannot realize itself. The inside, in proportion and decoration, was of Renaissance simplicity. It was (someone said) a house built for hot days; the ceilings must have reflected the lake light. On the first floor, 'the summer room' gave, through a Venetian window, on to balcony over the portico. Had George Moore the First forgotten the rains of the West, the isolation in acres of wet woods? His son, George Moore the Second, the historian, when recalled to rule here from London, from the pleasures of Holland House, added a notable library. But it was he who said: 'Beautiful as it is, much as I love it, I have not always been able to exclude ennui from its precincts.'

As the returned merchant found, and as his son the thinker found later, to dream of Ireland is one thing, to live there another. Ireland broke each of the Moores, in her oblique way. But being spirited people, they broke well.

George Moore the First created more than a house. By building Moore Hall, and by buying much land round it, he saddled his descendants with that something between a *raison d'être* and a predicament – an Irish estate. The hold is ghostly as well as material; there is a touch of 'I have, therefore I am.' And, from the outset, nothing went very well. The former Miss de Kilikelly moped for Spain and never quite settled down. The eldest son, John, gave trouble: reared abroad, he took his transplantation to Ireland in only too good faith. He detached himself from some squalid troubles in London to plunge into revolutionary politics. The Moores, already appalled, next learned that Citizen John Moore had been, immediately after the French landing, proclaimed President of the Republic of Connaught by General Humbert.[23] John was arrested; tortuous and expensive litigation ended only with his obscure death. The unimpeachable Moores had the neighbourhood's sympathy, but nothing was bad enough for poor John.

Thus, George Moore the Second became the heir; his father's death recalled him from London to Moore Hall. He married a Mayo lady, Louisa Browne. This Louisa Moore, with her hard, brilliant dark eyes and curled upper lip, was a *maîtresse femme*. Women like this, in every few generations, dominate, in all classes, Irish family life. Her husband's frail health and his preoccupations made her master as well as mistress of Moore Hall. In her passionate dealings with people – most of all with her eldest son – Mrs Moore stopped at nothing. Anything might be used to implement a quarrel. The letters she wrote to George Henry were those of a thwarted mistress rather than of a mother. She took up an impossible position when, her second son John having been killed in a riding accident, she set herself against all horses, point blank. With George Henry, love for a faithless mistress cured itself (no thanks to the intervention of his aunt, Miss Browne) but horses continued to impassion and dominate him – as they dominated Mayo and most of Irish society. Augustus, the third son, precocious and disappointing mathematician, soon cared for nothing but horses, either. First with the Mayo squireens, then in England and with the Waterford set (who, jumped their horses in halls), the two brothers showed indomitable courage and silliness – and George Henry ran up horsey debts. Mrs Louisa Moore lived in that sort of dread that does seem able to magnetize tragedy – Augustus *was* killed, riding at Liverpool. Life for George Henry took a serious turn – he turned to the heartbreak of politics.

It was Mrs Louisa Moore who maintained, on behalf first of her husband, then of her sons, the friendship with Miss Edgeworth.

Interchanges of visits and letters between the two households were lively, affectionate, fruitful. In Miss Edgeworth's conversation, in her power to put him back into touch with what should have been his own world, the historian found real solace. Unable to keep back ennui shanghaied in this world of rain and intensive family feeling, with Miss Edgeworth he breathed astringent air. This man wrote, in an unfinished Preface:

> I have had no celebrity in my life. But a prospect of posthumous fame pleases me at this moment . . . we are so made that while we are still living we like to think that we shall not be forgotten after our deaths.

He referred to the promise, solemnly given, that his family were to see through the press his *Historical Memoir of the French Revolution*. For this purpose, £500 was set aside; in this was to lie his posthumous fame. It was good that he found the prospect worth so much. For his *Historical Memoir* was never published, though Miss Edgeworth brought up her failing powers and Louisa and the already distracted George Henry did what they could. It was left to the last George, in an access of family spleen, to bring up the fate of the manuscript.

George Henry Moore's problems as landlord and politician occupy later chapters of Mr Hone's book. *An Irish Gentleman* was the title of George Henry's biography, by Colonel Maurice Moore, his second son. Their father's death left George Moore the Fourth, the writer, and Maurice Moore, the soldier, heirs to the family predicament – and to more, to the family *sense* of predicament. The keen British officer and the Catholic patriot ceaselessly struggled inside Colonel Moore's breast. Also, Colonel Moore loved Moore Hall with passion, his wife had lived there, his children were bred to love it – but Colonel Moore was only the second son and George had broken the entail and could do what he liked – a position George did not fail to make more than dear. George himself was martyrized by a divided wish – to be the free artist, to be the *grand seigneur*. He was plagued by Moore Hall worries wherever he went – fateful letters in dogged handwriting, sure to begin inside, 'Sir, I am sorry to tell you . . .' Letters that make the absentee's heart sink at an Irish stamp. Such letters had harried every reigning Moore; they followed George to Paris, to Ebury Street. The debts, the debts, the roof, the tenants, the drains, the trees . . . How continue the page of unmarred prose with the Irish stamp sticking out under the manuscript? If George's mincing shoes and town clothes looked funny to his employees, he was nonetheless a just landlord; he rackrented Moore Hall for sensations only – the lake gave him two books. In essence, he wished to return – the Ely Place years had disabused him of Ireland, but he kept the physical feeling for Moore Hall – his ashes repose on one of the lake islands now. His cruelty – an unnerving sprightly sadism – to his over-sincere brother was, I think, neurotic, fruit not only of their over-intensive childhood but of generations of life before them, rank with the family myth.

Mr Hone's *The Moores of Moore Hall* covers much ground, in years and experiences, and is at the same time admirably compressed. He has dealt temperately with his material. He quotes just fully enough from letters – family letters, letters from stewards, trainers, debtors, neighbours and friends. Small momentous incidents come out – there was the cook, for instance, who could no longer stand heat. The racing chapters could not be livelier, and seem to me well-informed; the sticky political passages are done with clearness and calm. Here is not only a very welcome pendant to Mr Hone's existing *Life of George Moore*, but a picture, put in perspective and generalized, of an Irish landed family's scope and fate.

CHAPTER 2

Wartime Geography
1940–1945

The Big House, October 1940, *The Bell*

Big houses in Ireland are, I am told, very isolated. I say 'I am told' because the isolation, or loneliness, of my own house is only borne in on me, from time to time, by the exclamations of travellers when they arrive. 'Well,' they exclaim, with a hint of denunciation, '*you* are a long way from everywhere!' I suppose I see this the other way round: everywhere seems to have placed itself a long way from me – if 'everywhere' means shopping towns, railway stations or Ireland's principal through roads. But one's own point of departure always seems to one normal: I have grown up accustomed to seeing out of my windows nothing but grass, sky, tree, to being enclosed in a ring of almost complete silence and to making journeys for anything that I want. Actually, a main road passes my gates (though it is a main road not much travelled); my post village, which is fairly animated, is just a mile up the hill, and a daily bus, now, connects this village with Cork. The motor car demolishes distances, and the telephone and wireless keep the house knit up, perhaps too much, with the world. The loneliness of my house, as of many others, is more an effect than a reality. But it is the effect that is interesting.

When I visit other big houses I *am* struck by some quality that they all have – not so much isolation as mystery. Each house seems to live under its own spell, and that is the spell that falls on the visitor from the moment he passes in at the gates. The ring of woods inside the demesne wall conceals, at first, the whole demesne from the eye: this looks, from the road, like a *bois dormant,* with a great glade inside. Inside the gates the avenue often describes loops, to make itself of still more extravagant length; it is sometimes arched by beeches, sometimes silent with moss. On each side lie those tree-studded grass spaces we Anglo-Irish call lawns and English people puzzle us by speaking of as 'the park.' On these browse cattle, or there may be horses out on grass. A second gate (generally white-painted, so that one may not drive into it in the dark) keeps these away from the house in its inner circle of trees. Having shut this clanking white gate behind one, one takes the last reach of avenue and meets the faded, dark-windowed and somehow hypnotic stare of the big house. Often a line of mountains rises above it, or a river is seen through a break in woods. But the house, in its silence, seems to be contemplating the swell or fall of its own lawns.

The paradox of these big houses is that often they are not big at all. Those massive detached villas outside cities probably have a greater number of rooms. We have of course in Ireland the *great* houses – houses Renaissance Italy hardly rivals, houses with superb façades, colonnades, pavilions and, inside, chains of plastered, painted saloons. But the houses that I know best, and write of, would be only called 'big' in Ireland – in England they would be 'country houses,' no more. They are of adequate size for a family, its dependants, a modest number of guests. They have few annexes, they do not ramble; they are nearly always compactly square. Much of the space inside (and there is not so much space) has been sacrificed to airy halls and lobbies and to the elegant structure of staircases. Their façades (very often in the Italian manner) are not lengthy, though they may be high. Is it height – in this country of otherwise low buildings – that got these Anglo-Irish houses their 'big' name? Or have they been called 'big' with a slight inflection – that of hostility, irony? One may call a man 'big' with just that inflection because he seems to think the hell of himself.

These houses, however, are certainly not little. Let us say that their size, like their loneliness, is an effect rather than a reality. Perhaps the wide, private spaces they occupy throw a distending reflection on to their walls. And, they were planned for spacious living – for hospitality above all. Unlike the low, warm, ruddy French and English manors, they have made no natural growth from the soil – the idea that begot them was a purely social one. The functional parts of them – kitchens and offices, farm-buildings, outbuildings – were sunk underground, concealed by walls or by trees: only the stables (for horses ranked very highly) emerged to view, as suavely planned as the house. Yet, in another sense, the most ornate, spacious parts of these buildings *were* the most functional – the steps, the halls, the living-rooms, the fine staircases – it was these that contributed to society, that raised life above the exigencies of mere living to the plane of art, or at least style. There was a true bigness, a sort of impersonality, in the manner in which the houses were conceived. After an era of greed, roughness and panic;

after an era of camping in charred or desolate ruins (as my Cromwellian ancestors did certainly), these new settlers who had been imposed on Ireland began to wish to add something to life. The security that they had, by the eighteenth century, however ignobly gained, they did not use quite ignobly. They began to feel, and exert, the European idea – to seek what was humanistic, classic and disciplined.

It is something to subscribe to an idea, even if one cannot live up to it. These country gentlemen liked sport, drink and card-playing very much better than they liked the arts – but they religiously stocked their libraries, set fine craftsmen to work on their ceilings and mantelpieces and interspersed their own family portraits with heroicized paintings of foreign scenes. Outdoors there was at first a good deal of negligence, but later one planned and planted demesnes . . . All this cost money: many of these genial builders died badly in debt and left their families saddled with mansions that they could ill afford. Then, decline set in almost at once. A more modest plan of living would have made, in the end, for very much more peace: big houses that had begun in glory were soon only maintained by struggle and sacrifice. Sons were recalled from college, or never went there; daughters, undowered, stayed unwed; love-marriages had to be interdicted because money was needed to prop the roof. Husbands and wives struggled, shoulder to shoulder, to keep the estate anything like solvent, or, in the last issue, to hold creditors off; their children grew up *farouches*,[1] haughty, quite ignorant of the outside world. And in this struggle for life, a struggle that goes on everywhere, that may be said, in fact, to *be* life itself, and should not therefore have anything terrible about it, the big house people were handicapped, shadowed and to an extent queered – by their pride, by their indignation at their decline and by their divorce from the countryside in whose heart their struggle was carried on. They would have been surprised to receive pity. I doubt, as a matter of fact, that they ever pitied themselves: they were obsessed, and to a degree exalted. They had begun as conquerors and were not disposed to let that tradition lapse. These big house people admit only one class-distinction: they instinctively 'place' a person who makes a poor mouth.

It is, I think, to the credit of big house people that concealed their struggles with such nonchalance and for so long continued to throw about what did not really amount to much weight. It *is* to their credit that, with grass almost up to their doors and hardly a sixpence to turn over, they continued to be resented by the rest of Ireland as being the heartless rich. Now this myth has broken down: I think everyone knows that life *is* not all jam in the big house. Nowadays, what I hear most commented on *is* the apparent futility of the sacrifice. New democratic Ireland no longer denounces the big house, but seems to marvel at it. Why fight to maintain life in a draughty barrack, in a demesne shorn of most of its other land, a demesne in which one can hardly keep down the thistles, far from neighbours, golf links, tennis clubs, cinemas, buses, railways, shops? 'What do you *do* all day? Isn't it very lonely? Do servants stay with you? Can you keep warm in winter? Isn't it very ghostly? How do you do your shopping?'

To most of these questions it would be hard to give a concrete and satisfactory answer. To some few of the big houses wealth and security have returned – or one should say had returned, for the war attacks these again. But in the majority life maintains itself by a series of fortuities. As I have heard many occupants say: 'I have no idea how we live, but we do.' Such people not only live but enjoy life. To the keeping afloat of the household not only the family but the servants contribute ingenuity and good will. As on a ship out at sea, there is a sense of community. There is also – and this, I think, *is* the strength of such households – a very great feeling of independence: in the big house one does not feel overlooked; one lives by one's own standards, makes one's own laws and does not care, within fairly wide limits, what any body outside the demesne wall thinks. This may tend to exaggerate, to the point of absurdity, the family's individual point of view: there are a thousand legends of eccentricity. But it does also make for a sort of hardiness and absence of social fear. And ennui, that threat to life in Ireland, is kept at bay by the constant exigencies, some of them unexpected, of the house and place. (This was not so in the more prosperous days – 'Beautiful as it is, much as I love it,' wrote one of George Moore's ancestors about Moore Hall, 'I have not been able to exclude ennui from its precincts.') No, life in the big house, in its circle of trees, is saturated with character: this is, I suppose, the element of the spell. The indefinite ghosts of the past, of the dead who lived here and pursued this same routine of life in these walls add something, a sort of order, a reason for living, to every minute and hour. This is the order, the form of life, the tradition to which big house people still sacrifice much.

From the point of view of the outside Irish world, does the big house justify its existence? I believe it could do so now as never before. As I said, the idea from which these houses sprang was, before everything, a social one. That idea, although lofty, was at first rigid and narrow – but it could extend itself, and it must if the big house is to play an alive part in the alive Ireland of to-day. What is fine about the social idea is that it means the subjugation of the personal to the impersonal. In the interest of good manners and good behaviour people learned to subdue their own feelings. The result was an easy and unsuspicious intercourse, to which everyone brought the best that they had – wit, knowledge, sympathy or personal beauty. Society – or, more simply, the getting-together of people – was meant to be at once a high pleasure and willing discipline, not just an occasion for self-display. The big, or big-seeming, rooms in the big houses are meant for just such pleasures of intercourse. They are meant for something more creative, and gayer, than grumbles, gossip or the tearing to pieces of acquaintances' characters. 'Can we not,' big, half-empty rooms seem to ask, 'be, as never before, sociable? Cannot we scrap the past, with its bitternesses and barriers, and all meet, throwing in what we have?'

There are difficulties – expensive 'entertainment,' for instance, cannot be given now. The distances are great – and an impalpable barrier stands between city and country Ireland. But there are buses and there are bicycles; we all eat and drink a good deal less, and would not find it any shame in a host not to offer what he has not got. The world around us is moving so rapidly that it is impossible to be dull-minded; we should all, more than ever, have a great deal to say; every newcomer, with his point of view, becomes an object of quite magnetic interest. Symbolically (though also matter-of-factly) the doors of the big houses stand open all day; it is only regretfully that they are barred up at night. The stranger is welcome, just as much as the friend – the stranger, in fact, *is* the friend if he does not show himself otherwise. But who ever walks in? Is it suspicion, hostility, irony that keep so much of Ireland away from the big house door? If this lasts, we impoverish life all round. Or is it the fear that, if one goes into the big house, one will have to be 'polite'? Well, why not *be* polite – are not humane manners the crown of being human at all? Politeness is not constriction; it is a grace: it is really no worse than an exercise of the imagination on other people's behalf. And are we to cut grace quite out of life?

The big house has much to learn – and it must learn if it is to survive at all. But it also has much to give. The young people who are taking on these big houses, who accept the burden and continue the struggle are not content, now, to live for themselves only; they will not be content, either, to live 'just for the house.' The young cannot afford to be stupid – they expect the houses they keep alive to inherit, in a changed world and under changed conditions, the good life for which they were first built. The good in the new can add to, not destroy, the good in the old. From inside many big houses (and these will be the survivors) barriers are being impatiently attacked. But it must be seen that a barrier has two sides.

Report from Ireland: Ministry of Information, 9 November 1940[2]

MR CHURCHILL AND THE IRISH PORTS

The reaction in this country to Mr Churchill's remark on the Irish ports has been very unfavourable. Even were Mr de Valera to be amenable, he now clearly feels himself placed, with regard to public opinion in his own country, in a position of appalling difficulty.

There seems – I have gathered from talk and the Irish papers – only one basis on which Eire would consider treating for the ports. That is, on some suggestion from the British side that the Partition question was at least likely to be reconsidered. It is felt here (I do not know how correctly) that the Six Counties' intransigence comes from British support.

The flare-up of resentment and suspicion on this side (since November 6, when Mr Churchill's speech appeared in the morning papers) is all the more to be regretted because, since August, pro-British feeling and sympathy for the British cause had been steadily on the increase here. I was struck by this, and impressed by the change of atmosphere, when I arrived in Eire in the middle of last month. (I think I mentioned this, or suggested this, in my notes.) Perhaps I only realise now, by contrast, how propitious things here, till November 6, had been.

(When I arrived over here last July I found this country in a state of alarm and anger caused by an unfortunate British press campaign. During July and August this gradually calmed down and Britain became on the up-grade in popularity.)

The childishness and obtuseness of this country cannot fail to be irritating to the English mind. In a war of this size and this desperate gravity, Britain may well feel that Irish susceptibilities should go to the wall. But it must be seen (and no doubt is seen) that any hint of a violation of Eire may well be used to implement enemy propaganda and weaken the British case. Also, that aggravation of feeling in this country makes one more problem to settle after the war – or rather, is likely to make the settlement of an outstanding problem more difficult.

All sensible people in this country follow the line taken by Mr James Dillon,[3] and point out that Mr Churchill no more than deprecated the loss of the ports as bases, and that he made neither demands nor threats.

In fact, during the recent (comparatively) halcyon period, the solider element in this country has had time to take stock of its position, and has admitted to itself how closely Irish interests are bound up with the future of Britain. To put the thing at its lowest, a row with England would, at the present moment, suit nobody's book. Mr Dillon clearly feels, more strongly than anything, the *inexpediency* of portions of Mr de Valera's speech.

It may be felt in England that Eire is making a fetish of her neutrality. But this assertion of her neutrality is Eire's first *free* self-assertion: as such alone it would mean a great deal to her. Eire (and I think rightly) sees her neutrality as positive, not merely negative. She has invested her self-respect in it. It is typical of her intense and narrow view of herself that she cannot see that her attitude must appear to England an affair of blindness, egotism, escapism or sheer funk.

In fact, there is truth in Mr de Valera's contention. It would be more than hardship, it would be sheer disaster for this country, in its present growing stages, and with its uncertain morals, to be involved in war.

That Eire might lease her ports *without* being involved in war is a notion the popular mind here cannot grasp. I have spoken of the horrific view held here of the Nazi bombing of England. To the popular mind here, 'being involved in war' now conjures up only one picture – a bombing of Eire. The panic caused by this is intense: it is like England before Munich, twenty times more. People say, '*We* could never stand it,' and they are right. One air raid on an Irish city would produce a chaos with which, in the long run, England would have to cope.

I have emphasised since I have been here (I hope rightly) *that England has no wish that Eire should enter the war.*

This wave of panic, plus a severe resentment, will have to be allayed before any negotiations with this country, on any subject affecting a war issue, can be fruitfully entered upon. A tactful broadcast, apparently *to* England, but *at* Eire, might do much. All English broadcasts are eagerly listened to. Also, it would be well – if this were possible – to mitigate the tactlessness, with regard to this country, of the British press. This last is very important.

Contributory, and important, factors to the Irish anger are the allegation that (a) German submarines are refuelling off this coast (b) the 'hostile' remarks, in the House, by British Labour back-benchers (which have, inevitably, been given prominence here) and (c) – inevitably – Lord Craigavon's[4] comment – which in my view should have been suppressed.

I should believe Mr de Valera to be right in saying that submarines are not refuelling here. The coast, as well as the countryside, is being closely and zealously patrolled by the army and L.S.F. These are on eager look-out for 'incidents'. And the Civic Guard, working in connection with the L.S.F., have a close and thorough system of information.

Typical Dublin comments:

(From the pro-British): 'Churchill has certainly dropped a brick this time.' 'It's a pity: the state of feeling here towards Britain had never been better.'

(From the anti-British, or swivellers): 'What right have the British to keep denouncing the Nazis? Haven't they been Nazis to us for centuries, and aren't they trying to be Nazis again now?' 'Churchill timed his speech very cleverly; he waited till he was certain he would get Roosevelt in.' (N.B. These were remarks I heard on November 6 itself: I left Dublin for County Cork that evening. Dublin may, meanwhile, have calmed down.) Typical country comments:

'Oh God, we'll be bombed surely.'

'Something surely must be going to happen: they took down all the signposts on Monday night' (Monday, November 4).

I could wish some factions in England showed less anti-Irish feeling. I have noticed an I suppose inevitable increase of this in England during the last year. The charge of 'disloyalty' against the Irish has always, given the plain facts of history, irritated me. I could wish that the English kept history in mind more, that the Irish kept it in mind less.

EIRE AND THE USA

The Presidential election caused some excitement in Dublin, though not – given this country's interest in the USA – so much excitement as I should have expected. The election results, on November 6 morning, jockied Mr Churchill's speech for the big headlines. The newspapers (other than the *Irish Times*) devoted their leaders that day to Mr Roosevelt rather than Mr Churchill. The press was no doubt glad to reserve comment on the ports question till it had Mr de Valera's riposte.

It seems to be felt here that Mr Roosevelt's election brings the USA decidedly nearer war.

America's increasingly pro-British attitude, and the steps by which she has made this manifest, have undoubtedly influenced this country.

One faction believes (I do not know why) that 'Germany will bomb Eire the day America enters the war.' Apart from this, there seems a general wish here that America should not enter the war. Eire has always expected American support for her own neutrality. She could not expect the same sympathy from a belligerent.

I know nothing of the American 'press campaign' of which Mr de Valera complains. For that matter, I can form no idea of the English 'press campaign' – if any. It is hard to get English papers here in County Cork.

You will no doubt have Irish papers of November 8 to hand. I append the front page of The *Irish Independent* featuring Messrs de Valera and Dillon and Lord Craigavon.

DUBLIN

I regret that my ten days' general view of Dublin was prior to the publication (on the morning of Wednesday, November 6) of Mr Churchill's speech in the Irish press. From October 28 to November 6 I was occupying a small flat in St Stephen's Green. I was able, under these circumstances, to see again, over tea or sherry, people whom I had met elsewhere, and to continue conversations that had promised to be interesting. Ostensibly I was in Dublin on holiday and 'having a rest.' I attempted to meet, and was on the whole successful in meeting, as many people as possible of differing points of view.

Dublin, as a society – or rather as a complex of different societies – seemed to be suffering from claustrophobia and restlessness. The suspension of travel to and from England is being much felt. Socially and culturally speaking, the virtual closing of the Irish Channel is equivalent, for the more intelligent and Europeanly-minded people in Dublin and throughout Ireland, to a closing of the Burma Road. An increasing threat of parochialism in Dublin talk, interests, artistic outlook and social amenities is being recognised, and deplored. As 'someone from the outside' I was kindly met and frequently and hospitably entertained.

There is still, among people of any means, a good deal of good living. I felt there was a general wish to escape, in society, from the general sense of oppression, or depression, caused by the war. At some of the less inspired parties that I attended, this deliberate escapism produced a rather dreary effect. But on the whole I was struck, in all circles, by the intelligence (if not always the wisdom) and the animation of the talk. The stereotyped, or completely conditioned, mind seemed to me rarer in Dublin than in London. (There is also a great deal of bigotry, but this seems to be individual, not mass). Public opinion in Dublin is almost dangerously fluid. It is, at the same time, less homogeneous than in any English city I have known.

The two universities, the medical and legal professions and some of the more popular and socially-minded of the Senators (such as Senator Frank MacDermot[5], Sir John Keane[6], Senator Robinson[7]) seem to form the nucleus of the most distinctive Dublin society. These people cut ice: their traditions are in the English favour: to such people a view of all that is enlightened and progressive in the present British policy could usefully be, and should be, presented. They are, for the most part, strongly conservative. They are conscious of, and they deplore to the point of underlining, any British mistake with regard to this country.

Outside the recognised political circles, political figures (with the exception of the Senators I have mentioned) are very little met. They do not appear to be popular. Thus, there is very little infiltration of ideas between the theorists and the practitioners in politics.

In the same way, the literary people sequester themselves, or are sequestered. With the death of Mr Yeats and the departure of Dr Gogarty,[8] Dublin seems to have lost her only two social–literary figures. No view expressed by any Irish writer (novelist or poet) on the European situation, on Irish politics, seemed to be much listened to, or cut much ice. In fact, Dublin in general holds the Platonic view of the poet. The writer-as-propagandist in any sense seems to be ineffective in this country. This may or may not be a pity: in view of any psychological approach that Britain might wish to make to Eire, it seems to me worth noting.

I did notice in Dublin a more general interest in, and a rather more full information as to, Continental affairs (apart from immediate war issues) than one would find in an English city. I would put this down – I do not know how rightly – to the international element in the Roman Catholic Church. Many men and women I met in Dublin had lived for some time, or had been educated, or had fairly extensively travelled abroad.

RELIGION

I find a great readiness, in talkers of all classes, to stress the 'spirituality' of Eire's attitude towards world affairs. At the root, this is not bogus: that this country *is* religious in temperament and disposition as well as in practice is, I take it, an accepted fact. Unhappily, religion is used to cover or bolster up a number of bad practices. I mentioned in Notes last summer, and still see, a threat of Catholic-Fascism. And officially, the Irish RC Church is opposed to progress, as not good for the people.

The most disagreeable aspect of this official 'spirituality' is its smugness, even Phariseeism. I have heard it said (and have heard of it constantly being said) that 'the bombing is a punishment on England for her materialism.'

The better side, or aspect, is – that it can breed a very genuine charity, that it makes the people capable of imaginative pity and distress. There is no doubt that 'the bad state of the world' is a more than conventional, a genuine source of sorrow to many people, especially to the simpler people, here.

The theory that England is ungodly *is* dangerous: it might be worked upon. Possibilities of an English alliance with 'atheistical' Russia are very unfavourably seen. The idea of a Catholic–Latin block does not seem to have caught on here in the intellectual sense as much as I should have expected. But I believe it to be a latent emotional wish. Sympathy for Pétainist France (idea of spiritual re-birth) if not in the increase since last summer is certainly not on the decrease. The equally reconstructive side of the Free French programme seems to be overlooked. And there is still admiration for Franco's Spain.

Only Italy has (as I stated last week) temporarily lost caste.

The effect of religious opinion in this country (Protestant as well as Catholic) seems still to be, a heavy trend to the Right.

The word 'revolutionary', in whatever context, has a purely sinister connotation here. I found that to say that we younger people in Britain are fighting this as a revolutionary war produced an unhappy effect: hearers' minds seemed to turn immediately to chaos, red flags and barricades. I find 'reconstructive' better, and use that word now.

The English idea of world betterment through (only) social reform will never cut ice here. It is dismissed as 'materialistic'. The Englishman to whom religion is a reality (even though this may make him fanatical or bigoted) will always do better in, or in dealings with, or in overtures to, this country than the most open-minded and liberal agnostic. Good regards towards individual English statesmen seems to be meted out according to whether they are felt to be 'Christian' or not. Lord Halifax[9] is liked. It is remarkable that, though the Tory party in England have seldom shown themselves sympathetic to Irish claims, they are respected, at present, here as being *Christian.* Whereas the Labour Party and the intelligentsia are suspect, as being 'red' (or godless).

This innate religious predisposition, as well as overt religious outlook, must, in any dealings with this country, be taken into account. *Some* hypocrisy goes to it, but it is not all hypocrisy. One reason why one cannot deal with Ireland is that she has this vast super-rational element. In so far as one does, in Ireland, meet the conditioned mind, the conditioning has been done by religion. Though I constantly hear it said that the (RC) Church is losing its hold on the young people, it will be many years before the effect of this (if it is really happening at all) is felt.

I do, however, continue to hear, among enlightened Catholics, considerable criticism of the RC Church for its failure to take up a more positive attitude in this world crisis. This ranges from criticism of the parish priests for their lack of outlook, their ambiguous and teetering attitude ('They tell us to pray for peace, but how are we to work for it?') to criticisms of the Vatican's political feebleness.

EDUCATION

Enthusiasm for the teaching, use and general cult of the Irish language seems to be on the increase. Mr de Valera gives the movement every support. Even the *Irish Times* now prints part of itself in Irish. The Gaelic gathering and festival was in full swing in Dublin last week while I was there: it lasted a week and took place in the Mansion House. Plays, singing and conferences appeared to compose the programme. I say 'appeared' because all reports were printed in Irish, which I cannot read. For the same reason (not knowing Irish) and because 1 was busy, I did not attend any of the sessions. As a gathering of people (largely teachers) from all over Ireland, they would have been interesting to *see*. Outside immediately Gaelic circles, the proceedings did not seem to arouse much interest. No political interest appeared to attach to them. During that week, Irish 'national dress' appeared in the streets.

The Gaelic movement goes with a cult of *Heimkunst*[10] that certainly is not negligible. It is the source of considerable, if limited, sentiment. The German Minister and his wife are said to be liked in Gaelic circles because of their (no doubt) genuine interest in *Heimkunst.*

UNIVERSITIES

George O'Brien, Professor Economics in the National University, has deplored to me the over-production of graduates. A large number of men and women leaving the University apparently fail to find the positions to which their education entitles them – in fact, given the smallness of the country, such positions do not exist. These young people return to the provinces to take (if they are lucky enough to get even that) underpaid and, in view of their aspirations, unsuitable work. They form

(Professor O'Brien says) throughout the country an unhappy strata – breed discontent, spread depression and are apt for political mischievousness.

It is Professor O'Brien's view that a large number of students who pass through the National University are unfit for, and unable to profit by, higher education. Every year, they leave to augment the 'unsettled class' . . . Exodus to, and hopes of expansion in, England and America having been stopped; the problem of these young people (able or otherwise) is becoming acute. Temporarily, the Army (Irish) may absorb some of the young men.

I spent an evening with three Trinity College young men. Given their intelligence, which was marked, they seemed to me unexpectedly detached about European affairs. They denied having any political point of view, and professed no interest in politics. TCD's most extreme move to the Left appears to be the existence of a Fabian Society. TCD seem to feel – though I do not know how far it consciously suffers from – a certain Protestant-Unionist isolation. Many of them are not joining the LSF as the fear of 'having to fight England' still prevails. The young men I met said, 'We are all feeling depressed about the future.' I asked, 'What future?' and they said, 'Our own: the British Empire has always supplied us with jobs, and what will we do if the British Empire breaks down?'

(It is interesting that the worst defeatism, on behalf of Britain, that I have met, and tried to counter, in this country has been among the Protestant Anglo-Irish. A far more optimistic view of 'England's chances' is taken by the Irish-Irish.)

That this gulf between the two Irelands – Anglo-Ireland and Irish-Ireland – should continue to be felt by young people seems to me a pity. In fact, the Anglo-Irish would be doing much better service to both England and Eire if they would not so zealously represent themselves as England's stronghold here. (Though it is interesting that even these Southern would-be Unionists have little liking for and no patience with the Six Counties.) If the Anglo-Irish would merge their interests with Eire's, they could make – from the point of view of England – a very much more solid and *possible* Eire, with which to deal.

Mr Erskine Childers[11] interested me by saying that he proposes to send his sons to school at St Columba's College (Protestant, ex-Unionist, built to be 'the Irish Eton'). St Columba's is apparently on the up-grade and is felt to be doing all it can to effect the merger that seems (to me) desirable. Its present Warden, an Englishman, is on friendly terms with

Mr de Valera. Irish is being soundly taught, and outstanding Irishmen are invited to lecture at St Columba's on subjects of national as well as European interest. At present the religious distinction is preserved: several Catholic families are said to be anxious to send their sons to St. Columba's (and the College is willing to receive them). Irish RC public schools are, in some cases, felt 'to be too hard on the character'.

MR JAMES DILLON

I had a long and very interesting talk, over tea, with Mr James Dillon. He had struck me for some time as being one of the ablest, and at the same time, least spectacular, figures in Irish politics. At the same time, he is very much disliked, and I must say that, though liking him very much personally, I see why. He holds some views which even I distrust, and which are abhorrent to many Irish people whose integrity I respect. In talk he is equable, rational and shows the kind of intellect that can make fullest use of any experience. He is less parochial in outlook than most Irishmen: in fact, not parochial at all. His personality is at once monkish and worldly. Superficially, Mr Dillon would be (from the English point of view) a very much easier man to deal with than Mr de Valera. I say superficially, because while Mr de Valera's fanaticism is on the surface, Mr Dillon's, which exists quite as strongly, is deep-down: it exploded once or twice towards the end of our talk – religious fanaticism of the purest kind I have met. This streak in Mr Dillon might be strongly felt in this country, if he ever came into full power. It would not, I think, affect his external policy – at least, where England was concerned.

If the de Valera Government were to fall (which does not at the moment seem at all likely) I have no doubt that Mr Dillon would emerge as leader of the so-called Cosgravites.

Mr Cosgrave[12] seems (these days) to be negligible. Mr Dillon is said to be the ablest speaker (in fact, the only orator) in the Dáil. I could gather Mr Dillon's own strong feeling for power from his speaking to me of his mistrust of it. In the material sense he is in the position to be disinterested: he is well-off (owing to a business in the West of Ireland) unmarried (and therefore clear of the domestic influences that count for so much in the middle-class Irishman's life) and shows a contempt for 'society'. His nature seemed to me concentrated, and his intellect powerful and precise. I give this note on Mr Dillon at some length because, both as a person and as a factor in Ireland, he struck me as important. He is important now, if only as a counterpoise to Mr de Valera. In any dealings with Eire, he is a man with whom one would have to deal.

He may, on the other hand, be a man who is better in Opposition. This, time may or may not, show.

I have heard Mr Dillon labelled a Fascist – which is I am afraid at least partly true.[13] I have also heard him accused of pro-Germanism – which is, I think, 'wild'. He showed a truer sense than most Irishmen of the British mentality: his attitude towards England struck me as guarded, calculating, satirical-respectful, not hostile in even the oblique sense. In his almost morbid interest in Hitler's personality, he struck me as following a private bent of his own. We discussed the histrionics of oratory. Mr Dillon told me that he decided to get rid of O'Duffy[14] when, standing behind O'Duffy on a Cork balcony, he heard the General passing over into Hitlerian convulsions of speech. Mr Dillon felt something dangerous was getting loose.

Mr Dillon said that his fear for the world was, that we should be left, at the bitter end of this war, with the idea ('fallacy', Mr Dillon called it) that it was the *form* of government that mattered. Forms of government (said Mr Dillon) do not matter: all forms of government amount, in effect, to the same. What matters, what determines the state of a country, what makes, in the long run for good or bad legislation, is the good or evil in men's hearts. Mr Dillon then explained to me what he felt to be the constitutional importance of the spiritual-moral. So far as I could see, Mr Dillon believes in government by Divine inspiration. Given his hard-headed point of view, both in conversation and in the Dáil, this theory of Mr Dillon's, and the sort of explosion that he permitted himself, was a surprise to me.

MR JOE WALSHE

Mr Joe Walshe, Secretary for External Affairs, I met twice and should have liked to have met more often. But he is not popular and seemed to be out of contact with any of the other people I met. He struck me as having a good intellect (he is a 'spoilt' Jesuit) and he has a personality you could cut with a knife. His judgment might well be questionable. His person is uncouth and his past (apparently) sinister. I was frequently told he was a pro-German. It would have interested me to discover if this were really the case, and, if so, why.

I noticed that anti-Semitism in Eire is considerably on the increase. It is said to arise from business jealousy – plus the inevitable results of campaigns abroad. It has ugly manifestations in the business world.

James Joyce, by Herbert Gorman, 14 March 1941, *The Spectator*, Review

James Joyce, European writer owed to Ireland, remained during his lifetime a rather aloof figure. He enveloped himself in no mystery, took up no poses and had no part in promoting the foolish legends that came to settle about his name. After a protracted poverty and obscurity, due to his refusal to make concessions, he became a person almost everyone talked of and many people were anxious to come and see. He sustained, with a simplicity that was disconcerting and that appeared cryptic, the prominence into which he had been thrust. He had desired no more – and no less – than the consummation every writer desires: the consummation of his books finding their mark. In his prominent, as in his obscure years, he stood clear of those heated intimacies in which so many writers lose or imperil virtue. He loved his family, liked good company and was subject to the sort of solitary humour that made him dance by himself in a cloak on a Paris bridge; but the atrocities of human communication were unknown to him: he did not hand himself out to disciples in small change. The circle of people with whom he grew familiar was broken up by this present war, and a winter silence hangs over his death.

In days when there is a bad name for detachment, it is hard to assess the detached man. As to the bare circumstances of Joyce's life there has been, up to now, ignorance: by a number of people he has been vaguely seen as an aesthete piqued with his own country, choosing to live abroad. Actually, the detachment Joyce did achieve, the detachment that made it possible for him to go on writing, was a continuous heroic act of the spirit. Nothing was spared him: extreme poverty, repugnant work for a living, frustrations, humiliations, physical pain, sense of exile were by him felt to the full – but they were surmounted. He was reared and educated in a religion from which a deep nature does not without crisis secede, and from which a lonely nature dreads to detach itself. He was adolescent in a provincial capital, Dublin, that ignored or vituperated his vision, a capital whose intelligentsia devoted itself to, as he saw it, a petty and local myth, a national sentiment. In a Paris indifferent to his eager presence, the boy of twenty hanging over his notebooks was excruciated by toothache – he had not a franc for a dentist – that at least did him the service of reconciling him to hunger: he would have been unable to masticate the food he was for days unable to buy. Recalled to Dublin, he for five months watched his mother die in an agony only made supportable by the consolation of a Church he knew she knew he had forsworn. Early fatherhood made acute, in a series of foreign cities, that struggle for the very barest subsistence that, apart from art, he accepted as being life. The vacillations of publishers and the *pudeur* of printers blocked, year after year, the publication of his finished works – in fact, the dealings of Joyce's publishers and putative publishers with him could have opened gates to dementia. And his writing, with its immense exactions, could only be done at the weary end of a day: when, in Rome, he wore out the seat of his only trousers, this was not on the writer's chair but on the high stool of the bank at which he worked overtime; in Trieste the precise and burning lover of words drummed commercial English into Berlitz pupils at the rate of tenpence an hour. Landlord after landlord threatened evictions from the minute grilling foreign apartments that were the Joyce homes; he saw his wife humiliated; financial quandaries spoilt his relationship with his brother. All his life he was hampered by eye-trouble, and just when poverty slackened its extreme grip, blindness was found to be imminent – blindness held off him by operations that were ordeals to his whole frame.

To pile up these facts, from the Gorman biography, might seem to be recruiting for Joyce a pity that he certainly never asked, or felt, for himself. Never was there a less pitiable man. The facts should be known, only, because they make his life-history as inspiring as any history of conquest. Also, they invalidate once and for all any foolish idea about an Ivory Tower – how many reputed ivory towers would stand the test of an examination of fact? Joyce's equanimity triumphed, through everything: it was a combination of an unmoved belief in his art with a Jesuit-instilled rule of self-discipline. Joyce had that kind of *hauteur*, independent of circumstance, that Stendhal calls *espagnolisme*. He had the Irish qualities shaped and steeled. If his imperturbable manners irritated the bully, they could disarm the bully as well. His gusto for life, his love of round roaring pleasure dictated, during his youth in Dublin, his choice of medical students as his allies: with this pack he ran the city and knew Nighttown.

Mr Gorman's Joyce biography is exciting. I suppose almost every biography *could* be better done: in this the first forty pages descriptive – move rather heavily, and a few repetitions and *longueurs* come later on. Mr Gorman's writing, however, is admirably impersonal; he is not intrusive and he makes no claims. The Dublin environment and the foreign scenes are well rendered. The book is documented with Joyce's letters – the letter to Ibsen on his seventy-third birthday, written when

Joyce was eighteen, is a superb salutation from youthful to aged genius. There are Joyce poems – everything from the doggerel to the lyric – and excerpts from early essays and, most valuable of all, Joyce's notes on his own aesthetic, departures from Aquinas and Aristotle, worked on through that first Paris winter of toothache. Joyce's father, that grand old unstable stalwart John Stanislaus, civil servant and tenor, stands out excellently. The vicissitudes of the books with the publishers, the Babel and almost Bedlam years in wartime Zurich, the inauguration of the first cinema in Dublin, are fascinating matter. Through all, Joyce's love-hate relationship with his own city, Dublin, and the crystallization of Dublin inside his art, appears.

Eire, 12 April 1941, *New Statesman and Nation*, Essay

Difficulties arising from the position of Eire have been on the increase since the start of the war, without being, on either side of the water, at all comprehensively understood. It has been difficult for the people of Britain to see Eire's declaration of neutrality, and resolute abiding by her neutrality, as anything but a passively hostile and in some senses rather inhuman act. They are puzzled by Eire's apparent failure to realize the magnitude of the issues at stake, and puzzled to find a country that cared so much for freedom refusing to add her effort to freedom's war. Pigheadedness, ostrichism, childishness, apathy as to the fate of civilization and even a dishonourable timidity have been charges levelled at Eire from this side. Pictures of Eire existing in indifferent comfort, under a British protection she does not recognize, cannot, as the rigours of war heighten, fail to present themselves to the British mind. The British popular press does not allow such pictures to lapse: the blaze of Dublin city lights (almost Broadway, after the darkness here) suggest an unfeeling ostentation, and hams, steaks and butter are given luscious prominence by journalists who, on flying visits to Dublin, failed to obtain the desired interviews. The number of Germans at present in Eire, their social acceptability and their power were, until lately (when exact figures were given) exaggerated with a good deal of busyness. That the effect of all this has not been more inflammatory is only because Britain, at this juncture, has not much idle angry feeling to spare. But misstatements about Eire, in irresponsible columns, have a serious aspect: they hamper those responsible men who, at both sides of the water, work to maintain an equable atmosphere in which negotiations between the two countries may be carried on. If Anglo-Irish relations stand, as they must stand, this present strain, there are great hopes of something pacific and durable. Time and tact, on which there are many demands already, must go to disposing of rumours hostile to this.

Britain – that is to say, the mass of people in Britain – is not only in the dark as to Eire's intentions, but doubts, apparently, the validity of her will. It is true that a thinking minority in Eire holds that the country would, in her own interests, have done better to enter the war, on the British side, in the autumn of 1939. This reflective opinion, quietly held, is distinct from the emotional opinion of former Unionists, with their tradition of service under the British flag. But this minority recognizes its own extreme smallness. It also holds that Eire, having declared for neutrality, is at this stage in no position to alter her policy. So this minority has to be ruled out: it does not now hope or wish to effect a change. That the overwhelming wish of the people of Eire was in 1939, and is still, for neutrality is an indisputable fact. In Mr de Valera's declaration sounded the almost unanimous voice of his people – a people to whom the *positive* aspects of peace were newer, and seemed more essential, than Britain may realize. The decision – of which the momentousness was recognized – was made on behalf of a people young in political life, not yet adult in citizenship, now only just on the upgrade after internal strife and in no sense fit or ready to enter war. But the decision was not wholly grounded in weakness: it had one aspect of an assertion of strength. It was Eire's first major independent act. As such it had, and keeps, a symbolic as well as moral significance – a significance that identifies, for the people, Eire's neutrality with her integrity. Eire feels as strongly, one might say as religiously, about her neutrality as Britain feels about her part in the war. She has invested in it her natural consciousness. She has taken a stand – a stand, as she sees it, alone. All this should be kept in view when one asks oneself how the Irish, given their disposition, can embrace what seems from the outside such a colourless, timid and negative policy.

Hopes of immunity – and among the unthinking people, which means most of the people, these at the start were many – have been dashed with a sureness that ought to satisfy Eire's most savage critics at this side. Any hopes of war-profit were early dispelled. The country grasped slowly the fact known to its Government – that not only would no one be richer for all this but that one would need all one's energies to survive at all. At present Eire suffers, in all senses, and while her deprivations are far less than Britain's, they have to be met without the heroic stimulus that comes from participation in war. She is outside every circuit; she has not an admirer; she is conscious of a cold draught of disapprobation from what she has taken to be America's friendly shore. The suspension of travel between Eire and Britain sets up an abnormal isolation, of which the effects are felt in all departments of life. Accustomed, whether as Eire or Ireland, to being much visited, not only by sportsmen and tourists but by people of cultural sympathies and enquiring mind, the country does not like segregation. Eire's immense sociability, her natural bent to the stranger makes this loss more vital than it might appear. And Eire is as hard to leave, just now, as she is to enter: claustrophobia is the threat to every civilized mind. Society, localized, becomes very intensive: opinions rapidly come to boiling-point. On top of this, the countrysides have been immobilized and the cities slowed down by the disappearance of petrol: private cars – other than those of priests, clergy and doctors – are off the roads; and in the bus services that join up whole tracts of trainless country there have been severe cuts, and threats of more. More adjusted than she had realized to modern tempo, Eire finds it hard to go back to the old.

If this isolation, of and throughout Eire, results in an apparently arrogant hardening of attitude, who can wonder? It is in Eire's power, in the long-term sense, to justify her neutrality: she well may. But, temporarily, some of the measures she takes to guard it are having a rather dwarfing effect. The Censorship is an outstanding example. There is freedom of public speech, but no freedom of reporting. No home criticism of Eire's neutrality, or suggestion that this ever could or should be abandoned, is allowed mention by the press. No award or honour to any Irishman serving with HM Forces is allowed to be mentioned – in newspapers – so that, virtually, the hero's country is debarred from its natural pride in him. (The exodus of young Irishmen to enlist, across the Border or across the Channel, has not been stopped; it is officially ignored. The numerous Irishmen serving with the Army, Navy or Air Force may re-enter Eire on leave, in civilian clothes.) Leading articles on the course of the war have to affect a cautious colourlessness – one may deplore no outrage and praise no victory. This does not, one is bound to admit, impair the dispassionate shrewdness of many comments: there have been times in Britain when one could have wished for a more dispassionate press. But the general effect is – the sense of a ban on *feeling*, in a country in which feeling naturally runs high. And, more serious, there is an inhibition of judgement that cannot be good for human development. No fact (with regard to Europe) is withheld, but facts are denied moral context. In the cinemas, the omission of all war scenes from the newsreels gives one the feeling of an invented world – one may watch social functions (not connected with war effort), trotting-races in the sunny Dominions, and one may still watch America drill, and the American warplanes take to the sky. No film drama featuring or hinging on the present war (or even, I understand, the 1914 war) may be shown. And, inevitably, *The Dictator*[15] is not on view. Exception having been taken by the French and German Ministries to Mr Lennox Robinson's[16] dramatization of *Boule de Suif*,[17] the play was withdrawn from the Gate Theatre. As against this, English books on the war and on wartime political theory are available at bookshops and libraries, and English newspapers and periodicals can be obtained on order. *Picture Post* is in constant demand. Shortly, a watch is kept on anything that could be taken as propaganda. But, owing to the (still) common language, the British view of the war is represented, while the German, except in random talk, is not. On the whole, Eire's sequestration from Europe is (for her) the principal ill of her neutrality: it may go to create a national childishness, a lack of grasp on the general scheme of the world.

Compassionate feeling towards war victims there has been no attempt to check: this not only finds all but official expression, but has a number of outlets. The bombing of British civilians inspires horror and pity that are a good deal more than perfunctory. The Coventry raid, in particular, made a profound impression: one southern county raised, by subscription, a mobile canteen for Coventry. (It must be remembered that the name of Coventry has stood out in Eire ever since the IRA bomb affair, and the executions that followed.)There is a wish, particularly in country places, to receive children from England – and this wish extends beyond the children already received – who have been, so far, limited to those of Irish connections or birth. The wish to house British children is more than purely compassionate; it embodies the hope for a future better relationship. 'If the children grew up together,' a countryman said, 'the two countries might grow to be better friends.'

Any German influence in Eire has, very largely, a cultural source. The Nazi encouragement of folk culture runs parallel to activities in Eire that date from the start of the Gaelic League, and the Nazi revivals of racial history and myth, the organizations of *Heimkunst* and song and dance are sometimes held up as a model. Educationists wishing for progress on these lines are impressed. The cultivated middle-class Irish traveller has tended to overshoot Britain: one meets an impregnable ignorance of any advance in British social conditions. To many serious people of the new Eire, at odds with the fatalism of their own land, the Nazi briskness, race-culture and application of method showed (at least until recently) only its admirable side. Also, to the obstructed youth of Eire, the idealization of youth makes its appeal. (As against this, there is the temperamental dislike of regimentation in any form.) Again, the Nazi sweep-forward in the first year of the war had, for the imagination of an inactive country, Martian impressiveness – though against this stood the stigma of cruelty. I have met no one who entertained the idea that Eire could really profit from Axis victory – to most minds it seems clear that she would in the end suffer. Factions who might expect to gain for Eire from a severe limitation of Britain's power do not seem to welcome the idea of the concomitant – extension of Axis power to the Irish shore.

Materially, neutral Eire in wartime is far from being the home of comfort and ease. Shortage and insecurity are felt everywhere. Any original fools' paradise is being rapidly broken up. The de Valera government is not unrealistic with regard to home affairs; Mr Lemass, Minister for Supplies, and Dr Ryan, Minister of Agriculture, have issued a succession of biting home truths, directed at self-delusion in any form. Eire has been, and continues to be, warned: not only are luxuries out of the question, but she must look to herself only for her necessities. It is the last hard application of Sinn Féin. The situation is grave, and may become desperate if there is not a response in solid national effort. Outside the huge extension of compulsory tillage there is a drive for digging. The acute coal shortage has raised the slogan 'Cut more turf' – but there is a danger that one may strip the bogs. Lack of raw material for the industries threatens unemployment on an alarming scale. The cost of living goes up. Tea is to be closely rationed – and one has to know Eire to know how much this is felt. Butter is (in fact) short – owing to a severe drought in the summer and to reduction, for tillage, of grazing lands. The crowning threat to the country is the outbreak of foot-and-mouth disease – the worst in this century. The stoppage of petrol, by emptying shopping towns, hits trade all round. Everywhere there is sombreness, and anxiety. But there is, with this, a growth of the sense of responsibility, an abandonment of the idea of privilege. Parish Councils work for co-operation, for emergency action, for mutual aid. Factions have come together, and national unity is more than a phrase. The Army shows, with regard to the size of the population, imposing figures; the size and zeal of the Local Security Force – whose junior group has been taken over for training by the Army command – shows citizen readiness to defend the land. While the rights of Eire's neutrality may be questioned, the conviction behind it must be believed.

James Joyce, March 1941, *The Bell* 16, Essay

The death of James Joyce was felt by few in his own land as a personal tragedy. He died, as he lived the later part of his life, outside Ireland. Those of us who met him, met him in Paris, where he was almost an object of pilgrimage, or during his last shy, brief appearance in London. His Dublin days are so long ago, now, that his personal legend – idiosyncrasies, humours, habits, addictions, gestures, weaknesses – lives for very few people. His youth in Dublin remains for us inside the crystal of his art: to those of us who have read *Dubliners, A Portrait of the Artist as a Young Man* or *Ulysses*, he is forever walking the Dublin streets or looking with us along the wet sands of the Bay. But how many Dubliners still in Dublin actually remember the man passing, or look at a stretch of railing, a bridge parapet, a street corner, and say: 'That is what I always connect with him?' It is surroundings that tie us closely to people, that are the earth of friendship. And that physical, associative tie with his countrymen Joyce broke when he went to live abroad.

Yet he was before all an Irishman. All the cerebral complexity of his later art went to reproduce the physical impressions that he had received in Ireland, in youth. These obsessed him – and all the more, perhaps, because he had withdrawn from them, as though in fear. Of his life abroad we have no record of his at all – it is as though that life no more than flowed over him. Ireland had entered him: it was the grit in his oyster shell. Great linguist, he explored and discarded language after language because of the, to him, final inefficacy of any language at all. Sensation was, above all, his subject, and the sensations that were his fever and pain are common – what remains extraordinary is the length he travelled in his efforts to put sensation into words.

Is it not Joyce's fundamental Irishness that has defeated, and in some cases antagonised, the critics forced into pronouncement by his death? The English can never know us – and are we ready to know ourselves? To challenge our view of ourselves, I should say that it is more academic than we realise. Our talk and writing, and most of all when it is about ourselves, is more full of conventions than we know. Joyce was unacademic, and by not a single convention did he save himself from his awareness of life. What he laid bare, or what he scorned to conceal, has been repugnant first of all to his countrymen.

He was a great buffooner, a great scorner – in that, is he not like most of us? Only, his scorn and buffoonery admitted no stop. His early work is inundated with pity – and it is in our power to feel pity that we, as humans, are at our greatest. If there seems in the later work to be less pity, that came, I believe, in Joyce from the natural human refusal to suffer too much – to suffer, in fact, to that extent of which he was capable. (For the thing about pity is that it *does* make us suffer: it is much more than an imaginative act.) Pity for the frustrated dreams of the living, pity for the finished dreams of the dead – gradually, Joyce withdrew from pity, as he withdrew from Ireland.

This is part of the end of his longest short story, 'The Dead', from the collection *Dubliners*, published in 1914. Gabriel Conroy and his wife have been to a party, on a winter night: the evening stirs up strange emotions in them, and on their return she tells him about the young man, Michael Furey, who had loved her when she was a girl, and had died. She lies on her bed weeping, then falls asleep.

> She was fast asleep . . .
>
> A few light taps upon the pane made him turn to the window. It had begun to snow again. He watched sleepily the flakes, silver and dark, falling obliquely against the lamplight . . . Yes, the newspapers were right: snow was general all over Ireland. It was falling on every part of the dark central plain, on the treeless hills, falling softly upon the Bog of Allen and, further westward, softly falling into the dark mutinous Shannon waves. It was falling, too, upon every part of the lonely churchyard on the hill where Michael Furey lay buried. It lay thickly drifted on the crooked crosses and headstones, on the spears of the little gate, on the barren thorns. His soul swooned slowly as he heard the snow falling faintly through the universe and faintly falling, like the descent of their last end, upon all the living and the dead.

This could not be gentler: there is the sound of snow in it. And Joyce the man kept, as I understand, this gentleness with the people he loved. In the foreign countries he was to live in, his home life was dear to him. But as a writer he was, too, to develop that wayward and jeering cruelty that is either the inverse of pity or a reaction against it – cruelty that is a rigid abstention from feeling of any kind. It is never brutality: it is too full of nerves. I do not say we are often cruel, but when we are, is it not like this? Joyce's portraits – some of the figures in *A Portrait of the Artist* and *Ulysses* – are drawn with a mercilessness more shocking to many people than any of his obscenities. At last he turned from character: in *Finnegans Wake* all human forms disappear.

Was Joyce irreverent? I think not. His apparent irreverence is a sort of despair – the outcry of a reverence that has thwarted itself. All through *A Portrait of the Artist* there is a man asking too much – an *attacking* nature –

> His throat ached with the desire to cry aloud, the cry of a hawk or eagle on high, to cry piercingly of his deliverance to the winds. This was the call of life to his soul not the full gross voice of the world of duties and despair, not the inhuman voice that had called him to the pale service of the altar. An instant of wild flight had delivered him and the cry of triumph which his lips withheld cleft his brain.
>
> . . . What were they now but the cerements shaken from the body of death – the fear he had walked in night and day, the incertitude that had ringed him round, the shame that had abased him within and without – cerements, the linens of the grave?

And Joyce had another gigantic faculty – laughter. His laughter, after some rumbles and false starts in *Dubliners*, after a check throughout the taut and burning *Portrait*, breaks out in the course of *Ulysses* into a sustained roar, and it sobs and wheezes and almost dies of itself behind the obscurities of *Finnegans Wake*. His laughter is disconcerting; people have edged away from it, as from a man laughing all by himself. When one was a child one used to be told: 'It is bad manners to laugh for no reason, without telling people what you are laughing at.' Joyce's attempts to tell us what he was laughing at produced the more contused passages of *Ulysses* and the almost lunatic reaches of *Finnegans Wake*. He pounded language to jelly in his attempts to make it tell us what he was laughing at. One may say that he ended by laughing so much that he could not speak. At the end of his solitary burning first phase, at the end of the racking ordeal of his long adolescence, the joke of the universe suddenly dawned on him, and, adult, he broke out into laughter so adult that it has been too much for most of us. He was, most of all, solitary in his mirth. And yet, it is in Joyce's own country that this cosmic devouring laughter is most heard. A door swings, and it hurtles out in a gust. Remember, in *John Bull's Other Island*, how shocked the Englishman was when they all laughed when the poor pig died in the motor-crash.

In short, the contradictions of Joyce's nature ought not to perplex his own countrypeople: we have them all in ourselves. In the state of uneasy politeness caused by his death, British critics, these last weeks, have been circling around him. *Was* the man kidding? What was he getting at? Had he, for the last twenty years and more, been leading young intellectuals up the garden path? The earnest cautiousness of the approach is marked – and from behind this emanates a relief that Joyce, the reviewers' nightmare, is now honourably hushed and will not make trouble again. Joyce has, by implication, been accused of having imposed himself craftily on the inter-war neurosis and disorientation of the young, of being a writer purely about the limbo for the too willing and desperate dwellers in it. To *Dubliners*, with its feeling objectivity, clearness, and strain of unhappy beauty, and to *A Portrait of the Artist as a Young Man*, with its universality and burning seriousness, all honest critics give praise. But waves of hostility can be felt breaking against the two later, obscure and in themselves 'hostile' books, *Ulysses* and *Finnegans Wake*. Wartime England is in a state of reaction against what seems to her febrile or over-cerebral: she has only room, now, for the primary feelings, for plain speech and properly drilled thought. France is, at the moment, tragically silent, and slow mails hold up, for us, what America has to say.

An article in the *Times Literary Supplement* most fairly puts into words the general charge against Joyce. It speaks of him as 'shirking his job of communication.' Did he? Or was it that, as his years went on, he increasingly overstrained language, himself and us in the very efforts he made to communicate? I have (with *Finnegans Wake* in mind) spoken of him as (impatiently) pounding language into a jelly – strictly, the effect on our minds is that that was what he was doing. In fact, we know that Joyce had no impatience, and that his attitude to language was mathematical. He used authority to vary the formula. We know that every line of *Finnegans Wake* was the product of minute and exhausting care, and that, more than half-blind, he, for sixteen years, hung and hung again over every word.

Was this (as Arnold Bennett said, after *Ulysses)* a writer 'playing the lout to the innocent and defenceless reader?' Or was it, this half-blind fumbling over a foreign writing-table, the end of the vision at which young Stephen Dedalus had wanted to cry aloud like a hawk or eagle, the 'hawklike man climbing sunward above the sea . . . the end he had been born to serve and had been following through the mists of childhood and boyhood . . . the artist forging anew in his workshop out of the sluggish matter of the earth a new soaring impalpable imperishable being'?

Almost all of *Finnegans Wake* is, in the ordinary sense, unintelligible. It is unintelligible to the part of the mind that expects statement or narration. We are used to receive, from a page of print, *information*, of one or another kind, information that we could, if necessary, pass on to a friend in our own words: even a love-lyric is informative – as to the lover's emotion, as to his mistress's charms. We do not, on the other, expect *information* from a symphony or the sound of a waterfall. *Finnegans Wake*, like music or a long natural sound, acts on us. We are affected, profoundly, instead of being informed. Sense has been sacrificed to sensation. Is this wrong? – to the greater number of people it offends every morality of the mind. There seems no doubt that Joyce, in writing *Finnegans Wake*, used the whole of his, by then, complete mastery not only of language but of its associations against the defences of mere intelligence. The associations that reinforce his language are super-intellectual and sub-infantile. The esoteric levity of the scholar fuses with the trance of the young child chanting non-words to itself in the half-dark. The punning is packed with intellect; the school man swoops off into Jabberwocky tongue. The maddening, watery book has a river theme; the images cast on it, as on a current, bend. There are names in it, and speakers, but no forms.

In fact, what happens in *Finnegans Wake* is that Joyce *does* communicate, but does not inform. To identify communication with information is to take a narrow view of communication. If art is not to stop, we shall have to widen communication. If art is not to stop, we shall have to widen our view. Joyce saw this widening as possible.

The charges against the Joyce of *Ulysses* have been more diverse. They have been serious enough to have, in this country, removed the book from our ken. Compared with *Finnegans Wake* the greater part of *Ulysses* is easy reading, though it has been found fatiguing because of its extreme length. Passages of it – notably the Dublin Bay sequence at the beginning – are so beautiful, and so in every sense inoffensive, that I wish they could be extracted from the rest of the book and made available to the public in Ireland. The theme of the book is well-known – the convergence, throughout the course of a Dublin day, of Stephen Dedalus upon Mr Bloom, the puzzled and cheery little Dublin Jew. There are scenes in the tower overlooking the Bay, in the National Library, in a hospital, at a funeral, in an eating-house, in a low haunt, in Mrs Bloom's solitary bedroom, scene of her monologue. Living Dublin figures appear. The middle of the book (after the hospital) is turgid with the first of those communication-experiments that were to culminate in *Finnegans Wake*. To be brief, the language goes funny, and undergoes a number of style-changes – we get a page or two of Olde Oake-ish archaisms, and a page or two of Ethel-M-Dell-ese.[18] Most of all, the stomach-turning physical ugliness of parts of *Ulysses*, and the failure of the internal narrative to be deflected by indecencies, have been denounced.

But – here is Stephen Dedalus on the seashore:

> Turning, he scanned the shore south, his feet sinking again slowly in new sockets. The cold domed room of the tower waits. Through the barbicans the shafts of light are moving ever, slowly ever as my feet are sinking, creeping duskward over the dial floor. Blue dusk, nightfall, deep blue night. In the darkness of the dome they wait, their pushed back chairs, my obelisk valise, around a board of abandoned platters. Who to clear it? He has the key. I will not sleep there when this night comes. A shut door of a silent tower entombing their blind bodies, the panthersahib and his pointer. Call: no answer. He lifted his feet up from the suck and turned back by the mole of the boulders. Take all, keep all. My soul walks with me, form of forms. So in the moon's mid-watches I pace the path above the rocks, in sable silvered, hearing Elsinore's tempting flood.

With Stephen Dedalus we go back in time to *A Portrait of the Artist as a Young Man*. This has been in the exact (not in the vulgar reviewer's) sense, Joyce's most powerful book. By those who do not like it and do not like adolescents, it has been called the bible of adolescents. But one might say the same of *Hamlet*. When Joyce perceived in himself and immortalised Stephen Dedalus, he defined not only the burning of one spirit, the desperate revolutions of one brain; he defined and seemed to create a type. He gave to male intellectual adolescence its lasting prototype in art. The sons of Stephen are many; he may be said to have bred a whole generation – but in Ireland they are most truly his sons. Across the quadrangles of old English universities, through the streets of London, New York, Paris have walked many self-seen Stephens, since *A Portrait* appeared. But to be truly Stephen one must be a born Catholic and Irish city-bred man.

'Crying aloud in the rain on the top of the Howth tram' – Stephen is undetachable from his place.

The writing of *A Portrait of the Artist* is straightforward, un-elliptical. The 'stream of consciousness' writing that Joyce perfected – and with which he did much to infect Europe – has not begun yet. This is the one pure – or, one might say, classic – novel he wrote, and as such alone it would be admirable. The narration is direct, the dialogue telling, the characters three-dimensional. Here is Joyce in full daylight, and in the first phase of his strength. Why, we may ask, could Joyce not be content to use again this novel-form he had found that he could perfect? (For, here, he communicates fully, but *through* information.) I cannot believe him to be so fractious an artist that he despised whatever he could command. Nor was he so much of a virtuoso that he must seek new form for new form's sake. It was, simply, that he could not be static. As he found more and more to communicate he found, for this, the means that seemed to him best.

Europe and America have acclaimed Joyce. But it is in our power, as his people, to know him as other countries do not. His death, since he went away so long ago, need not estrange him from us, but rather bring him back. We have given to Europe, and lost with Europe, her greatest writer of prose. The shy thin man with the thick spectacles belonged to us, and was of us, wherever he went. He has not asked us for a grave – we have too many graves already. It is not with his death that we need concern ourselves, but with the life (our life) that, still living, he saved for us, and immortalised, line by line. In Ireland we breed the finest of natures, then, by our ignorance, our prejudice and our cruelty drive those finest of natures from our shores. Let us strip from Joyce the exaggerations of foolish intellectual worship he got abroad, and the notoriety he got at home, and take him back to ourselves as a writer out of the Irish people, who received much from our tradition and was to hand on more.

Truths about Ireland, *Ireland–Atlantic Gateway*, by Jim Phelan, 5 September 1941, *The Spectator*, Review

Mr Phelan's book is, on one sense, topical: it discusses that aspect of the Irish question that is now most immediately in the British mind. But a permanent value is given to the discussion by the way he has placed an immediate problem – that of the future of Eire's Atlantic bases – in its relation to lasting facts. These facts are the outcome of a long-lived but not incurable psychological difficulty between two countries: accepted wrong ideas on the subject of Ireland have, in the long run, made for more trouble than wrong acts. Wrong acts can be cancelled, but wrong ideas, if they persist, must continue to generate fresh mistakes. Mr Phelan makes the important point when he shows that a hangover from unhappy history is not, actually, as operative in the present Irish attitude towards England as many English people are resigned to believe. In so far as the hangover does exits, it operates – or rather is able to be exploited – only when some fresh blunder makes a context for it. And blunders arise, from the English side; from an ignorance that, in this writer's view, it is in one faction's interest not to disturb. The ordinary English person's ignorance not only of Irish history but of Irish mentality, hopes, conditions may be said to be natural – there is no reason why the peoples of two very different islands should be presupposed to have true ideas about each other. But now, when every trend of events shows that only understanding can make a possible world, the maintenance of such ignorance and its exploitation, becomes unnatural and begins to look sinister. Mr Phelan writes as an Irishman who, both for the sake of his own country and in the general interests of Western peace, desires good understanding between Eire and Britain. He addresses himself, in good faith, to the English reader, who is in equally good faith willing to be informed. *Ireland–Atlantic Gateway* will, I hope, be read. It is realistic, balanced, informative, and takes the long view. Having declared his position, the author shows no bias in his statement of facts. And the facts are stated not in the esoteric or *nous autres* language in which the Irish too often write about Ireland, but in common terms. For instance, the peasant mentality – a phenomenon if you like but an ancient and very powerful one – may have been understood in relation to France or Russia without being, in relation to Ireland, her past or her present-day policy, either recognised or given its proper place. Again the semi-imperial relationship of Ireland to Irish-America, although this had so many analogies, has not, to the English mind, very much come to light. The Atlantic remains for Ireland very much narrower than the Irish Sea – and the psychological geography should be recognised now that wartime geography puts Ireland so vitally on the map. 'The Irish Empire' chapter is one of the most important in the book. And the chapter on Ulster contains truths that, fairly speaking, English people should know. One may say that the aim of the book is to combat fallacies that Mr Phelan rightly considers dangerous to the British conduct of the war. Though in no undue sense an alarmist, he gives alarming accounts of attempts (to which, as an Irish journalist he has been subjected) on the part of gentlemen sufficiently influential and beyond this claiming a further august authority to 'inspire' articles with just this fallacious note. As an Irish reader of the English press, one has learned – with concern, to know such articles well: the mischief they do is incalculable – they are the remaining blunders towards Ireland of our own day. Indeed – as Mr Phelan shows in his valuable chapter on Nazi propaganda in and towards Eire – it is, as much as anything from the British journalistic faux pas that the Nazi propagandist is waiting to take his cue. Beyond this, given the inherent temperamental anti-Nazism of Ireland, the Nazi propagandist is not on hopeful ground; having committed himself to a number of promises (to specifically different factions) whose inconsistency has already appeared. A final note on *Ireland–Atlantic Gateway*: it is a first-rate analysis of the nature of Eire's neutrality. Without suggesting that this should be abandoned, Mr Phelan does suggest how it not only could, but urgently ought to be approached.

Report for the Ministry of Information: 9 February 1942, by Elizabeth Cameron

NOTES ON EIRE: GENERAL IMPRESSIONS

I arrived in Dublin in the middle of the afternoon of Thursday last, February 5. I find that the London–Dublin journey, which *is* by about eight hours longer than it used to be, has assumed fantastic proportions to the mind over here. I was congratulated several times on my 'courage' in undertaking it. The effect of this is, to increase the impression of isolation in this country. Rumours of weather-conditions in England – any references to which have been cut out of letters by the censor – are greatly exaggerated: the impression appears to be that most of England has been lately paralysed by frequent and heavy falls of snow.

The winter in this country has been exceptionally mild. This, in view of the acute shortage of fuel, has been seen as one of Eire's very few bits of good luck. Individually, the people of all kinds to whom I have talked seem very depressed. Causes for this seem to be:

1. Supply difficulties: acute fears of further shortage. Rising food-prices, absence of price-control. Mistrust of the Government's hold on the supply situation. Acute cigarette-shortage – producing a neurosis in Eire's high percentage of heavy smokers. Reduction of sweets – sugar sweets still fairly plentiful, but expensive, but chocolate very rare and said to be giving out. (Dublin restaurant-prices – in the better class restaurants – are still markedly lower

than London prices. Wines still plentiful (at least in hotels and restaurants) and still at pre-war prices. But this is of course an advantage only felt by a few. In the (formerly) cheaper and more popular restaurants, prices are perceptibly *up*.)

2. War Fears: there is a renewed wave of bomb-nervousness. I am told that 'everyone feels it in their bones that Dublin is soon to be bombed again'. This wave of physical apprehension – which with some people seems to have reached a neurotic point – may be due, more than people realise, to the time of year, physical low vitality, waves of illnesses ('flu, etc.). But the fear is most often rationalised by the statement that the presence of USA troops in the Six Counties will attract punitive bombing to the *whole* of Ireland – South as well as North. (NB I believe that expressions of ill-feeling against America are being exaggerated with a view, among other things, to averting this.) There is also a heightening of the fear that Eire is on the verge of 'being dragged into the war', I believe that with many people there is a nebulous fear that war is *infectious*: the more belligerents accumulate in the Six Counties, the more likely it is that the 'germ' will spread. War, in fact, is not *entered* but 'caught' – or picked up – just as, passively and unwillingly, one catches or picks up measles.

   (Bomb-nervousness is, according to Mr James Dillon – see my conversation with Mr Dillon, later – being deliberately stimulated, at this juncture, by the de Valera Government for its own purposes. Also being stimulated through plugged talk by German agents in Eire. As Mr Dillon says, these recurrent waves of nervousness are always to *someone's* interest, and can be traced to a source.)

3. Economic Fears: bad trade position, closing of small shops. Intense fears for their investments among the *rentier* class: 'no money seems safe these days.' Feeling of financial insecurity seems to be penetrating, and general. Fear of *increased* unemployment, further rise in cost of living. Great envy expressed of the good employment, owing to war, in England. Wages received by factory and other employed people in England are fabulously exaggerated, at this side.

I meet, everywhere, the feeling that the average Irish worker is suffering from – and is likely to suffer further from – the effects of war without reaping any of war's benefits. I have met no one of any class (except a few Unionists) who says that Eire should enter the war *now*. But the number of people who say (or at least imply) that Eire would have done better to enter the war in 1939 seems to me to have markedly *increased*. I note a spread of the feeling that Eire has reached, or is on the point of reaching, an impasse. The 'desertion' of Eire by America (for as such it seems to figure) contributes immeasurably to this bad morale.

My main – psychological – impression of Dublin, after five days here, is that the air is full of rhetorical questions – questions either (a) incapable of being answered, or (b) to which an answer is not really desired, as being likely to be too unpalatable.

AMERICA

Feeling against America does run high. Apart from everything else, I still (I mean, after the lapse of what has been nearly two months) notice a sort of hangover from what must have been a sharp emotional shock. Eire, besides being morally indignant, is *upset*. Pro-American feeling, and certainty of American support, is as much and as deeply part of this country's make-up as anti-British feeling and traditional suspicion of British motives.

There is no doubt that, however temporarily, the severe reaction, in Eire, against America has had the effect of sending Britain's shares up. (The ovation accorded, in a big way, to the British Representative, at the pantomime at the Gaiety Theatre, Dublin, some weeks ago, at the invitation of Mr Jimmy O'Dea, has I know already been reported. Mr O'Dea is a genius at tapping popular feeling. The incident, of which I have been told many times, still seems to represent Dublin's mood.) To say that, in Dublin's present mood, Britain could not at present put a foot wrong would be an obviously dangerous and mischievous overstatement. But at the moment Britain is not being watched with the usual suspicious semi-hostility, and the Irish persecution mania does not seem to be operative in her direction. All this has, for the time being, diverted itself towards America.

In his present attitude towards America, Mr de Valera is in perfect touch with popular feeling. In representing himself as the spokesman of this he is correct. But he is also heightening popular feeling – which is more his creation than his public realises.

One can see that America's entry into the war *could* have been made to operate, on Irish feeling, in an entirely different – in fact, the reverse – way. December 1941 was a crux, for this country. I do not know yet how completely the people realise the increase, thanks to Mr de Valera, in their isolation.

The attitude of the American press to Eire has, of course, been resented. Its attacks are *not* (in so far as I can see) taken as being inspired by Britain. American journalists travelling south to Eire from the Six Counties after the arrival of USA troops there obtained interviews with Mr de Valera and by their (apparently unexpected) uncompromising and 'hustling' attitude gave Mr de Valera great – and more than impersonal – offence. As Mr Dillon says, when America decides to shift from one foot to the other she does not do so either silently or with regard for anyone else's feelings. The American press in general, and American journalists in the course of their visits here, seem to have been at pains to make clear to neutral Eire that they now regard her as a nuisance, an anachronism and an impediment. It is arguable that more tact, and what one might call more 'wooingness' could have done no harm. At present, everything goes to aggravate anti-American feeling here.

The idea that America is either (a) negotiating for the Ports (b) putting *hard pressure* on Mr de Valera for the Ports (c) preparing to seize the Ports at any moment is prevalent, and on the increase. 'Those troops have been sent to the North to intimidate us.' I have been asked several times if I know (from information in England) 'what America is up to in this country'.

I have not (so far) met the idea that Britain is making a catspaw of America in the matter of the Ports. The Irish (or at least the Dublin) mind seems to be as single, or one-ideaed, as it is vehement.

American atrocity-stories (in the Philippines) are, I am told, being put into circulation in the Dublin streets. 'Did you hear what the Americans did to the natives in the Philippines?' Query: is this German plugged talk?

Whether, in spite of strict army orders to the contrary, American soldiers from the Six Counties *are* actually crossing the Border, in small parties, in mufti, on pleasure trips – I find it hard to make out. A good many 'likely' stories, to this effect; are in circulation: I cannot check up on any one of these. The Americans are said to be talking big and throwing their weight about. One 'likely' story – much in circulation – is that a party of Americans, in a pub, dive or some other resort in Dublin declared noisily that the Irish need now no longer be frightened; '*we've* come to look after this little island of yours.' To which some Irish present riposted, 'You're not much good at looking after your *own* little islands, are you?' Upon which a scrap ensued and the police were called in.

Actually, if there *have* been any Irish-American 'incidents' of a nature at all likely to cause trouble, these would seem to have been discreetly suppressed. 'American stories' that I have heard have been circulated largely by irresponsibles.

MR JAMES DILLON

I had a very interesting afternoon's conversation with Mr James Dillon.

Mr Dillon appears to be regarded by the older, more static members of his own party with considerable alarm. He is seen as the *enfant terrible* of the Cosgravites. I notice that in Dáil debates his colleagues are at some pains to disassociate themselves from his more positive and dynamic remarks. I have heard, however, on almost all sides (the exception being extreme de Valerites) expressions of admiration for Mr Dillon's *courage*. If anything, he is seen to err in too extreme disregard for that general mass of opinion that, in most cases, inhibits Irishmen.

Were there more young, young middle-aged or even young-minded men in Irish politics, Mr Dillon would probably have collected more of a following. As it is, he and Mr Erskine Childers are the only two prominent young men in politics.

One could wish to see – and apparently, from conversations that I have had, a number of people in Eire are beginning to wish to see – the formation of a third party, which should no longer show the effects of the division left by the Civil War. Such a party, were it to show a constructive attitude to internal affairs and a realistic outlook on external affairs, might do much to rally intelligent opinion in Eire. It might break down the present cynicism with regard to *all* Irish politicians. At present, the country seems to be lacking in political self-respect. (There is a tendency to belittle members of the Government – with the – occasional – exception of Mr de Valera – and to circulate petty scandals about them. It would appear to be the accepted idea that a man cannot at once hold office and keep his integrity. As for the Cosgravite party, they are in the main seen as old fogeys, players-for-safety and ineffectuals.)

Mr Dillon's uncompromising attitude is said to have lost him a good deal of support. The country is frightened of him. There is a widespread idea that Mr Dillon would bring Eire into the war. He is anathema to the people in this country – at present about 85 per cent – who prefer in all matters a cagey and negative attitude.

Were this negative attitude, with its attendant nervousness, to abate, there seems no doubt that Mr Dillon could ably head a reaction against the present Government's policy. He seems to have all the qualities of a leader. He comes of almost the only family in Ireland that has a continuous political tradition. He is – which might commend itself to a reaction – as impersonal in his dealings with people as Mr de Valera is personal. He is very much more European in outlook – sympathies, culture and social tastes – than other political Irishmen (of today). In many ways, he would strike me as being as fanatical a character as Mr de Valera, but he is more objective and has wider terms of reference. Is capable – in the psychological sense – of speaking and understanding languages other than his own. The fervour of his Catholicism is apparent whether he is bigoted I cannot say. It is obvious that, in external affairs, Catholic affiliations would always weigh with him. One of his objections to Mr de Valera is, that Mr de Valera 'affects religion'.

Mr Dillon anticipates serious evils for this country from Mr de Valera's mishandling of the situation. He deprecates the present unfriendliness to America – and the Government's exploitation of the unfriendliness – as likely to throw the country into the arms of German intrigue. He believes that German agents, acting more and more openly, are likely to cash in on Eire's disillusionment with regard to American friendliness to her. On these lines: 'The one friend you always trusted has let you down. Perhaps you will now learn who your true friends are.' As Eire increasingly feels the draught, Mr Dillon fears that she may slip into an acquiescence with the German idea.

On the subject of Irish neutrality, Mr Dillon states that he believes Mr de Valera to be insane. That is to say, he believes the neutrality idea to belong, in Mr de Valera to the region of sheer obsession – incapable of being related to outside facts. In this region (he says) Mr de Valera's otherwise able intelligence does not operate. (He instanced asylum patients who, on all but the obsession-subject, are amenable, well-informed, amiable – in fact, sane.)

Mr Dillon believes that the pros and cons of Irish neutrality should be open to fair and reasonable debate. The rights of maintaining neutrality *could* be fairly argued. But he objects to the *noli mi tangere* on this subject that Mr de Valera maintains.

He holds Mr de Valera to be a deep-dyed, but unavowed, Machiavellian. He says that Mr de Valera has Machiavelli by heart and, by sheer reflex, corrects any misquotation.

Mr Dillon accuses Mr de Valera of having broken the country's spirit by the exploitation of fear. He compares the crossing of the line into avowed terror with the crossing of the line into mortal sin. Once the line has been crossed, the degrees of further commitment become indifferent: the original integrity has been lost. He also believes that Mr de Valera has exploited the Irish anti-realism.

Mr Dillon says that the position of his own party – at present the Opposition – were they to become the Government, would *not*, at present, be tenable. For this reason: that the de Valera party, were they in opposition, would resort to methods of sabotage. They would rather (he says) see Eire in chaos than in course of constructive growth under other rule. Mr Dillon is therefore alive to the danger of a major attack on de Valera *made too early*. He said: 'We must let go a little nearer the precipice. He is near enough to it now. The position is desperately dangerous. But possibly *one* moment will come.'

Mr Dillon deprecates the loss of Eire – a loss which, unless there can be a change in her attitude, he foresees as inevitable – of Commonwealth position and advantages after the war. He believes, also, that Eire has *not* (in spite of her emotional predisposition towards America) ever at all fully realised how dependent she has been upon American regard and support, e.g. – she has not realised that the so-called 'victory' over Britain was, actually, the outcome of Britain's deference to opinion in America . . . In fact, she is at present due to sustain much graver losses than she actually knows.

These were, roughly, the headings of my conversation with Mr Dillon. The substance of it I could, further, fill in by verbal report.

On my return to London, at the end of this week, I will complete and send in a second batch of Notes. I have already a good deal more to say, but think it better to give my time, while I am here, to collecting as much further material as I can.

Report for the Ministry of Information: 20 February 1942, by Elizabeth Cameron

LONDON, MR JAMES DILLON'S RESIGNATION

The news of Mr Dillon's resignation from the Fine Gael Party does not come as a surprise to me – nor will it have come, I imagine, as a surprise to anybody in Eire. During my last days in Dublin, people spoke of almost nothing else but his speech at the Mansion House on the morning of February 10. Almost unanimously, opinion had it that 'Cosgrave would be afraid to keep him in the Party.' Personal supporters of Mr Cosgrave praised the tolerance that he had shown towards the 'dangerous' Dillon up to now.

I was fortunate enough to be present at the Mansion House meeting, and to hear Mr Dillon make the memorable speech. – I had, in fact, previously just completed a batch of Notes to be sent to the Ministry of Information (MOI) via 50 Upper Mount Street. In these, as you may remember, I summarised Mr Dillon's views on the situation – these got from a long conversation that I had previously had with him.

Mr Dillon (naturally) did not, in the course of our conversation, give me any idea that he was on the point of 'exploding' these same views (and still more forcefully than he had put them to me) from the Party platform at the coming Fine Gael meeting. I entered the Mansion House knowing that he was due to speak, but having only a general idea what he was to say.

His speech, delivered with a virtuosity – or, should one say, calculated dramatic effect – that did *not* detract from its effect of impassioned sincerity, had the effect of a bomb. There was a reaction of excited, and highly emotional applause – an applause that seemed so general that I could have believed for a minute that Mr Dillon had carried the room with him. His shots – references to the Irish tie to America – had been nicely placed. I should say that of the people there, one-third were strongly with Mr Dillon, one-third were neutral (temporarily swayed but due to react against him later) – one-third definitely hostile.

There was evident, first of all, a very definite pleasure in his speech (a) as a piece of courage (b) as a *tour de force*.

The most bitter attacks on Mr Dillon were to come, I was sorry to note, from the *younger* members of the Fine Gael Party, at the back of the room. These struck me as being definitely terrified for their skins.

Mr Cosgrave and the rest of those on the platform preserved, during Mr Dillon's speech, resolutely expressionless faces. Not an eyelid was batted. One elderly occupant of the platform (whom I did not recognise) took the still more cautious line of feigning sleep.

En masse, I did not care for the looks of the Fine Gael Party. The main effect of them was at once cagey, and muddled. They struck me as being likely (as I saw them that day) to put forward no positive policy for the country. Their main function appeared to be, to carp at the de Valera government and this, as a function appeared to content them.

I did, however, see one or two honest and vigorous faces – among the older men and women. And I heard one or two speeches that, though not ambitious, seemed expressive of honesty and good sense.

The general social level was *petit bourgeois.*

Among the younger men – who attacked Mr Dillon after his speech – there were one or two crypto-fascists: nasty pieces of work. Their complaint that the Party needed *younger* leaders (though these were to be other than Mr Dillon) did, however, seem justified.

DUBLIN VIEWS

In Dublin, after February 10, I found practically no support for Mr Dillon. Not even among the people who had (to me) deplored Eire's present ignominious position, and said she 'would have done right' to enter war. Even ex-Unionists, with their vehement sympathies for the British cause, either deplored or ignored Mr Dillon's speech. A few tepid expressions of admiration for his courage was as far as anybody seemed prepared to go. I may say that I felt particularly out of sympathy with those people who wished at once to indulge their fine feelings and save their skins.

Few people, in the general excitement, seemed to have taken Mr Dillon's exact point. Which was, *not* that Eire should immediately and gratuitously declare war on the Axis, as a gesture of support to America, but simply – that Eire should make a stand (with regard to German demands) at a point past which she could not, consistently with her honour, continue to yield.

His contention, in fact, had been that one can reach a point where dishonour is worse than war.

My general impression of Eire – or rather, Dublin – on this visit was that the country was morally and nervously in a state of deterioration. Intimidation was having malign effects. In general, people seemed to have lost face – with themselves, with each other.

That, I imagine, was why Mr Dillon's speech stirred up an almost neurotic anger and fear. *Toute verité n'est pas bonne a dire.*

I should prefer to expand these points in conversation.

Report for the Ministry of Information:12 July 1942, by Elizabeth Cameron

I have been just over a week in Dublin, having arrived on the evening of July 3.

HOLIDAY TRAVEL

On that day – as, I understand, during most of this season – there were an exceptional number of passengers on the Mail – Irish workers in

England returning on holiday. The amount of these people, and their possible effect, while on holiday, on an Eire otherwise cut off from news from England, impressed me. In Dublin, I have followed the subject of these 'returned Irish' up.

On the whole, I should say their effect on Eire was bad. They are great carriers of defeatist rumours, and tend to exaggerate to their Irish listeners, any stories of disaffection in British factories. They are irresponsibles, with no particular axe to grind, but with the usual Irish love of talking for effect's sake. Inevitably, they are quoted (here) as authorities.

I merely note this – cannot suggest how it is to be checked. Can only suggest that any propaganda directed to Irish workers in *England* would reach, and have an effect on, the Irish in Eire.

Apparently, an effort is being made (from this end) to organise and provide social amenities for Irish workers in England through the RC priests. I feel that the RC authorities here are not altogether wrong in taking a dark view of the possible bad effects on young Irish workers, of both sexes, of high pay, a more or less disorientated existence in English industrial towns and total lack of normal responsibilities, outside work. On their return here, *en masse*, after the war, they are likely to be a problem, and a nuisance, to Eire. If they continue to find work in England, and therefore remain in England, they are likely to make irresponsible citizens. If they should fall out of work they would be, I suppose, automatically returned to their own country. Otherwise, they would be an additional charge on an already burdened British community.

In any event, I wish that these Irish workers in England – of a number too large to be negligible – could be contacted, and something done about them. – But possibly this is in hand already? – I do not know enough about industrial England (especially under present conditions) to know whether they are unpopular with their English fellow-workers.

It is a pity that Irish of this kind should in most cases qualify for, and therefore receive, return permits for holidays in Eire, while many Irish of a better type fail to qualify (through not having parents, etc., alive) and are therefore unable to return for the duration. Responsible and intelligent Irish people, in genuine sympathy with the Allied war effort, could do untold good over here. I think I have stressed, in all my Reports, the immense importance, in this country, of personal impressions and personal talk.

At present, the disparity in numbers between what I could call 'bad' and 'good' Irish returning to Eire is deplorable – and opinion and morale in this country suffer accordingly.

At this juncture – when the British and Allied war position, is to the Irish eye, bad and unpromising – the need for unofficial and unostentatious 'ambassadors' becomes greater than ever.

While it is obviously not possible to check the return to Eire on holiday of 'workers' qualifying for permits, I wish that its effects could be counteracted by the admission, also, of more serious people.

Report for the Ministry of Information: 19 July 1942, by Elizabeth Cameron

Later – July 19

'INVASION' OF DUBLIN

In this last week, I find that Dublin has been invaded by a very large number of workers from the Six Counties, on Holiday. Bookings on the Great Northern, from Belfast to Dublin, have apparently exceeded all records.

The main impression left on Dublin, by these holiday-makers, is that Ulster's much vaunted war effort is not very serious. The fact that Harland and Wolf closed, for the usual week's holiday, round the 12th of July, has been a good deal commented on – and with some derision.

'Hitler could walk into Belfast on the 12th of July and none of the fellows up there would raise a finger.'

Otherwise, the visitors from the North are tolerated, as having money to spend. They are some compensation to Dublin for the loss of the money usually taken in Horse Show week. They frequent the cheaper hotels, crowd the shopping streets and crowd the cafés and restaurants. Dublin is undoubtedly flattered to find herself in the role of a pleasure city. They are said to be down here chiefly to eat.

Officially, the shopping of these Northern visitors has been restricted by the introduction of the (Eire) coupon system for clothes. There is, however, a great traffic in coupons. (I was told, on my arrival in the country, that I could buy a book of clothes-coupons for 15/-. Later, the offer was repeated to me, but the price had risen to £2. I took it that this rise in price was accounted for by the July 12 week immigration from the North, and the brisk trade in coupons that had succeeded it.)

The daughter of a friend of mine – a girl on leave from service with the ATS – reports that, having travelled down on July 15 from Belfast to

Dublin in a train packed with holiday visitors, she and her fellow-traveller were accosted at Amiens Street station, Dublin, by touts openly offering sheets from coupon-books for ten shillings a time.

As her information was definite, her father has reported the matter to the Ministry of Supply in Dublin. Whether steps have been taken I do not know.

BLACK-MARKETING

The feeling against black-marketing in this country, even among the 'steady' people, is still much less strong in Eire than it is in England. The love of evading or circumventing 'the law' in any form is, of course, traditional. But chiefly, there does not exist the same patriotic stimulus to conformity. 'The Emergency' is not a very inspiring flag around which to rally.

Though decidedly, the Government *is* making an effort, and in many ways a far from poor effort, to rally the people round this flag. I observe a new outcrop of posters – much on the English lines. 'Help in the Emergency!' posters are much used by the transport services, especially the city and country-going buses. Form queues – tender exact fare – put used tickets in boxes – etc. I have *not yet* seen a 'Is Your Journey Really Necessary?' In fact, the discomforts of travel, by bus as well as by train, might well make anybody think twice.

No restrictions seem to be well received. Every cut is attributed to mismanagement on the part of the Government.

I have heard more grumbling in Dublin, in trains and in the country, on this present visit than on any other. 'We'd be better off if we were in the war!' is a remark I must have heard a hundred times. I should describe Dublin as thoroughly out of temper – more this than actually depressed.

Given its position the Government seems now to be showing considerable common-sense. But it is handicapped by the grumbling mistrust of the majority of the people. In Eire, common-sense is not popular. And it is not easy to 'sell' Austerity in the name of anything so negative as Neutrality.

Black-marketing is, *in fact*, I think, being checked by investigations and very severe penalties. (By the people, it is seen as increasingly impracticable, though not shocking.) Price-control is being enforced fairly rigidly. Prosecutions for offenses against this are given wide publicity by the Press.

TRANSPORT

Cars *are* really off the roads and the streets. The Dublin streets are quite startlingly empty (of traffic). As someone remarked, 'The town now looks like Sunday every day of the week.' It does.

I was surprised to find that any new law in Eire could be at once so quickly and so strictly enforced.

In Dublin, a few taxis are for hire, but these have not the petrol to travel far. The hire of taxis (or 'hackneys') for attendance at race meetings is now strictly forbidden. There are a few elderly horse vehicles (both private and for hire) on the streets. I had expected to see more of these, as they had only so recently disappeared. But apparently many had been destroyed.

One now pays £100 for a (strong) pony and trap, or a pony and float. Traps, carts and carriages are at a premium. So are bicycles. Second-hand, these are fetching high prices. There are many cases of theft. The bus services have been very much cut. The buses serving suburban areas in which workers in Dublin live, are now said to be insufficient. One hears many complaints from 'stranded' people – sometimes workers, sometimes pleasure-seekers. Dubliners are learning the queue habit (for buses). The electric tram service appears to have been increased – to relieve strain on the buses.

Where Dublin and its environs are concerned, I should say that the transport situation was much the same – certainly not worse – than the public transport situation in and round London. But the public are still less well organised, or 'conditioned'.

Trains seem to be running better. I had been told fantastic stories of breakdowns and delays – for instance, a twenty-two hour journey between Cork and Dublin. These, until recently, seem to have been true.

Now, a remedy has been found in improved fuel. The Great Southern Railway is making, at Inchicore, *briquettes*, which it feeds to the engines of main line passenger trains. Consequently, the one train a day from Dublin to Cork is now running more or less up to time. Early this week, I made the journey from Kingsbridge as far as Kilmallock in Co. Limerick. We were only half an hour behind time. On the return journey from the same station to Dublin, we were forty-five minutes late – which was considered not bad. The 'up' journey, I am told, is generally slower, as when and if the *briquettes* give out they have to be supplemented with unsatisfactory coal.

The goods trains and side-line trains still use coal and are still subject to grave delays. The time of arrival of any object by goods trains is – acceptedly – incalculable.

The reduction and slowing of trains has, inevitably, affected the postal services. Posts from the country to Dublin now take two days. I notice, all round, a slowing up of the country's life – though at no time was this conducted at high speed.

CONDITIONS IN DUBLIN

Dublin struck me as, on the whole, surprisingly prosperous. One unlikeness to London is the continued prosperity of the small shops – grocers, greengrocers, confectioners, general stores. On the North (the poorer and more populous) side of Dublin, this is particularly remarkable. Of course, it takes only a small turnover to keep such shops going: rents in the poorer streets cannot be high, and in most cases these are family businesses, run by the family, not employing assistance and therefore with no wage problem.

The Irish lower standard of living makes the disappearance of 'luxury' groceries less noticeable. The severe tea-rationing and the bacon shortage are the two most usual causes of complaint. Lack of tea is more felt than anything. It looks like creating a neurosis. Also, there is now a habit, bad from the health point of view, of stewing and re-stewing the used leaves. The (surprisingly large) number of people who had laid in reserves are at, or in sight of, the end of their reserves. So far, only the improvident or the over-honest have really felt the extremity of the tea rationing.

Small shops that *do* suffer are the newsagents and tobacconists. The cigarette situation is much worse than in England. Supplies of pipe tobacco are uncertain. The severe (and apparently, on the part of the public) unforeseen paper shortage has cut down periodicals. Daily papers make such small printings, that, in many cases, readers arrange to 'share'. The random purchase of a morning newspaper is at present more difficult than in London. Many people now seem to depend for their news on the evening papers, to be bought in the streets if you are on the look out for them.

In the cinemas, the supply of new films has been greatly reduced since Hollywood 'went war'. (No films featuring, whether fictitiously or otherwise, this present war are allowed to be shown in Eire.) Most British films are disqualified for this same reason. The larger Dublin cinemas *used* to be up to date – the releases being often simultaneous with London. Now, there are only 'escape films'. Cinema-goers – of whom there are many in Dublin – are beginning to feel the draught. One hears grumbles against the 'militarisation' of Hollywood.

The film *Day in Soviet Russia* had been announced, and much publicised, as a big attraction at a Dublin music hall. About a day before the film was to appear came the announcement that the film had been 'officially' withdrawn. This caused much comment, and more excitement in Dublin than the actual showing of the film could have done. Suggested reasons for the withdrawal were (i) that the film would annoy the Germans (ii) that it was 'Communistic', and that therefore the RC Church had intervened.

The moral effect was (as far as I could judge) that Soviet Russia, because forbidden to the Irish view, became magnetically attractive. I heard much discussion of Russia, and speculation about Russia, in the days following the withdrawal of the film.

In general, I think this country surprisingly apathetic on the subject of Russia – people seem to have few feelings either for or against. I believe I am right in thinking that the RC Church keeps sympathy for Russia (as a country fighting for her own land against the invader) banked down. There also maintains, among the middle-class business element, an almost fanatical dread of Communism. And the farmers dislike what they know of Soviet interference in land tenure.

In the country, objectors to the Government's enforcement of tillage say, 'We might as well be under the Soviet.'

Report for the Ministry of Information: 25–31 July 1942, by Elizabeth Cameron

JULY 25, CLOTHES RATIONING

At present, objection to the clothes rationing seems to be much livelier in the shops than with the purchasing public. Many of the public seem to derive a mild self-importance from being 'like England' – in fact, in the movement. The purchasing-power of coupons being higher in this country than in England, most people seem to feel that they have enough coupons to cover their usual needs. If they have not, they easily and quietly do a deal with their poorer neighbours who would not be buying clothes.

At any rate, where purchasers are concerned the matter seems to have adjusted itself. My impression is that (in this quarter) the clothes-rationing is less grumbled about than any other restriction since 'the

Emergency' was declared. As in England, it provides a welcome topic for dull days.

But some of the shops continue to feel bitterly. Particularly the larger Dublin shops, accustomed to a large turnover, to a repetitive claim to 'the latest fashion' and to renewing their stocks. These shops, also, had customers who spent fairly lavishly. (The customers of the smaller Dublin and of the country shops probably never spent more on clothes than their coupons could still continue to make possible.)

The larger Dublin dress-shops had boomed in the last two years. The travel restrictions played into their hands – well-to-do Irish people shopped in Dublin instead of London, and this same class of people, deprived of travel, used to flock up to Dublin and spend their money. Random and often extravagant shopping had been one of the few amusements left.

Also, and as importantly, the large Dublin shops had done very well with customers coming down from the North. A great trade was said to be done with British officers' wives from the Six Counties. Also with well-to-do Northerners, rationed at home.

The Eire coupon system has stopped all this.

I have heard that one main reason why clothes rationing was introduced here was the need to stop clothes leaving the country. (Irish workers back from England on holiday had been, also, supplying themselves with clothes.)

The country shops, having not had this 'foreign' market, with its advantages, are less thrown out. In the country, the elder people make few clothes-purchases, other than necessities. Country girls have shown, lately, an increasingly high and sophisticated standard in dress. But they meet the situation by using their parents' coupons.

JULY 27

I have confined this first batch of Notes, as will be seen, to a more or less general report.

In my next Notes, I hope to give an account of conversations I had with the RC Archbishop of Dublin, Mr James Dillon, Mr F. Gallagher, Dr O'Brien and others. My rough notes on these, made at the time, are still to be put in order.

I have also, still in the rough, a report on *country* conditions.

I hope to send my next Notes off at the end of this week. My visit to Eire, on this occasion, has been the most interesting and profitable I have had.

JULY 31, WAR NEWS IN THE COUNTRY

In this rural part of Eire (Co. Cork, approximately 135 miles from Dublin), which is, I suppose, typical, I notice a very much greater degree of cut-offness, since last year, with regard to up-to-date war news. This for two reasons – (1) The scarcity, and late arrival of newspapers; even the local paper, the *Cork Examiner*, does not reach the village until the late afternoon of each day. (2) The difficulty, nearing impossibility, of obtaining new high tension batteries for wireless sets. Wireless sets, other than those run on electricity (ESB or the plants of the big houses) are gradually going out of commission. Almost all the cottage wireless sets are now silent, and likely to remain so.

The break in the habit of listening in is energetically regretted by the country people. Cottages that had wireless were much frequented by neighbours after working hours. Young men and boys who did not possess a wireless had the habit of walking miles in the evening to listen in at a friend's house – always to the war news.

The virtual suspension of wireless, and the greater difficulty in obtaining newspapers, only bring into prominence the keen interest felt by rural South Irish people in the progress of the war. I have gathered opinions on this from many people – employers of labour. All are struck by the intelligence, the grip and the up-to-dateness shown, on the subject of war news, by country working men. The interest would appear to be keener than in many parts of rural England.

In this, I notice a contrast between the Irish country and Dublin. Dublin was more apathetic. In the country, the men (though not, I think, the women) are keen readers of newspapers – even when these are, owing to present conditions, a day or two out of date. The increasing uselessness of country wireless sets is felt as a deprivation and injury. At those informal gatherings of country working men that go on in the evenings, at the crossroads and bridges, I am told (and can gather from what I have overheard) that 'they talk of nothing else but the war'.

As people from England, my husband and I are constantly, eagerly questioned by everybody we meet. It becomes impossible to transact any business, in an office or shop, until there has been about ten minutes conversation about the war.

The pros and cons of the second front question are eagerly debated. I would say there was passionate interest in the war as a topic; and at the same time, there is a dispassionate tone to discussions, as few people are willing to declare themselves *parti pris* on either side.

I have met, and heard of, almost no explicit pro-German feeling in this part of Eire. But there continues to be manifest an almost superstitious admiration for the German fighting technique.

One psychological explanation of this interest in the war is that it is a form of escapism. With regard to Eire domestic affairs, the country people are at once bored and depressed. A sense of immediate dullness, fretted by deprivations, seems to cloud life here. 'The war' stands for drama, events in a big way, excitement. All this appeals to the Irish temperament.

The leader in today's (July 31) *Cork Examiner* appears to give point to this theory of mine. The leader, headed 'The Uninformed Citizen', rebukes Irishmen for substituting war interest for interest in his own local affairs – particularly, the forthcoming local elections.

It says:

> The average man nowadays can give quite a good account of himself in any argument concerning the military possibilities in Europe, Africa or the Far East, whereas in matters nearer home he remains dumb and uninformed unless they directly and obviously affect himself or his livelihood. The bend of the Don, the commanding heights of the Ruweizat Ridge, the sinkings in the Caribbean, are everyday topics, and subjects of self-instruction from the daily Press, while the conduct of affairs in the citizen's own town, or his country, is followed with only a hazy interest by no means comparable to the avid consumption of communiques and the outpourings of military correspondents . . . The man who turns his back to glance at the map of Russia and wheels around to discover that in the interim some of his personal rights have been whittled away by some order or other, has nobody to blame but himself. It is his duty to himself and his neighbour to keep in touch, as well as he can, with what is going on around him at home, and to make his voice felt in the Government of the nation. He can do so by paying as much attention to the reading of reports of the meetings of the Dáil, Senate, and local councils as he does to the plans and deeds of foreign generals and soldiers on fields thousands of miles away. Very shortly he will be given one of the very rare opportunities afforded to citizens of voicing satisfaction or dissatisfaction, when he will be asked to go to the polls in the local elections. We wonder whether he will be too busy, engaging in discussions about the Caucasus or the Suez Canal, to spare time to inquire into the qualifications of the candidates and to vote for the man he thinks best fitted to preside over the general conduct of local government in his borough, county, or urban area?

It is to be noted that the *Cork Examiner* is a Cosgravite, or Opposition newspaper. All Opposition people that I have met are suspicious of the devices used by the Government to distract attention while they put something across. (Overtly, the forthcoming local elections are to be non-political in character – or rather, candidates are expected to disassociate themselves from Party issues outside the local field – but a general consensus of opinion seems to regard this as, for Eire, Utopian. The local elections are, therefore, likely to serve as a straw ballot, and their outcome is being keenly awaited by politicians, who are anxious to stimulate all the interest possible. I subscribe to the *Cork Examiner's* view that the *ordinary* man, so far, regards the elections with apathy. There are many grumbles at their having been fixed for the middle of harvest time. This, the countryman regards as a bit of typical 'Dublinism'.)

The prominence given to war news in the *Irish Press* (the official Government paper) might support the Cosgravite contention that the Government is exploiting the people's interest in 'foreign generals and soldiers on fields thousands of miles away', in order to distract attention from the management (? or mismanagement) of affairs at home.

MR JAMES DILLON

Mr James Dillon, whom I saw twice in Dublin, on July 18 and 20, gave it as his opinion that Irish fervour on the subject of Eire's neutrality is beginning to lapse. He believes that this fervour was rooted first in national vanity, secondarily in fear. The first is (he believes) at present on the decline; the second at present (comparatively) dormant.

Mr Dillon told me that he made another of his 'anti-neutrality' speeches in the Dáil, on Thursday, July 16. It was of some length and, as usual, forcible. It was not only not reported but not referred to in any of the Irish newspapers. (Censorship) Mr Dillon was only quoted as having made in the Dáil, on July 16, a remark on the pig situation.

Mr Dillon's speech, I gather, continued his former line, re-iterating Eire's obligations to America, and recalling the protestations of gratitude to America that her spokesmen, especially Mr de Valera, had from time to time made. Features in Mr Dillon's speech were quotations from speeches made, on behalf of the Irish nation, by Mr de Valera when in America. Mr Dillon said he gave these quotations full force. He believed they were not without effect on the Dáil. Mr de Valera, he said, made no reply or comment, and did not. once, while Mr Dillon was speaking, raise his head from his hands.

(I must observe, however, that from my own attendance at the Dáil I formed the impression that this attitude of Mr de Valera's, during *any* debate, is habitual. He remains with his head supported inside his hands, his fingers laced over his forehead. The attitude implies intellectual weariness, and the very barest degree of tolerance exercised towards most of the speakers. I must say that in most cases the prolixity of the speakers, and their inability to keep to the point, was remarkable. Some were barely audible – at least, from where I sat, and I should imagine from any part of the house. Possibly the acoustics of the Dáil are not good. I understand that a good deal of incorrect reporting comes from the pressmen's difficulty in hearing what is said.)

Mr Dillon said that the Dáil's reaction to his 'anti-neutrality' speech was noticeably less hostile than formerly. He said that when he had made such another speech, this time last year, he had had reason to doubt whether he would leave the Dáil without being assaulted. He said that on this occasion he was listened to with what he would call passive interest. It is possible that Mr Dillon's ideas are beginning to make some little way for themselves. Or, at least, that they are less in advance of general ideas than they were. It may merely be that the Dáil is becoming accustomed to Mr Dillon, and expects diversions of this nature from him.

His vitality, and his terrier-like alertness, are good antidotes to the sluggishness of the Dáil. He appears never to fail to harry the Government, even on small points. His attitude towards vagueness and procrastination is merciless, and obviously embarrassing. His new position, as an Independent, gives him a freer hand. In some matters, he had been inhibited by fear of embarrassing the Cosgrave party.

General opinion has it that Mr Dillon has still, in the country, very little support. The reputation of being a war-monger clings to him. He is criticised for not keeping enough in touch with real feeling – for, in fact, advancing too rapidly without keeping in touch with his base.

All the same, it is possible that he may anticipate the Irish feeling of tomorrow, if he does not express the Irish feeling of today. As a speaker as well as a personality, he is in the dynamic tradition. In another country, he would be the young men's leader. But in Eire it is the young men who are the most timid.

Mr Dillon said to me that Mr de Valera was the victim – and was likely to make Eire the victim – of his own mania about consistency. He said that Mr de Valera was unable to admit that he could ever have been at any time, wrong – either in a prediction or a decision. He said that Mr de Valera showed, with complete absence of principles, an (almost) admirable political virtuosity. In fact, that Mr de Valera would be capable of reversing even a major decision (such as neutrality) *could this be done without loss of face*. No statement of his must ever *appear* to have been gone back on, and no decision must ever *appear* to have been reversed.

For instance, Mr Dillon said, hypothetically – should Mr de Valera reach the conclusion that his position as neutral was untenable, and should he therefore decide to abandon this position and come into the war on the British side, he would be first concerned to make this act unchallengably consistent with all his former statements. He would isolate some possibly quite small incident between himself and the German Minister in Dublin, and describe this as an aggression which had become intolerable, and which therefore must be resisted. He would, in fact, take the line of – 'My patience is exhausted.'

Mr de Valera's view of *what* constituted aggression would remain (according to Mr Dillon) a completely personal one – one in accord, solely, with his policy. While he still saw no reason to change his present policy, the Germans might drop bombs on Eire with impunity.

Mr Dillon regards the country, especially the young people, as being demoralised by the acknowledged 'timidity' of Eire's attitude. He believes that the national character will suffer. He says that the children and young people already have less respect for their leaders, because they detect in their elders, at this world-crisis, signs of havering, of dishonesty, of turning the blind eye.

SELF-CRITICISM

Mr Dillon's criticisms of his country-people, however tonic, are probably delivered rather too harshly and ruthlessly. Accordingly, they are resented. At the same time, I do notice that the Irish, both in Dublin and in the country, are becoming more self-critical. I notice this change even since this time last year. Self-complacency has waned with self-confidence. People are inclined to say, 'We are getting slack.' This is given point to by the droppings off, and increasing slackness, in the Local Security Force (LSF). Also, to an extent, among all voluntary workers for 'Emergency' services. (Though, Dublin continues to man its Air Raid Precautions (ARP) posts night and day.) The original inspiring sentiment has lapsed. What is more important is, that the people seem to be conscious of, and ashamed of, its lapsing.

At the beginning of the war, Eire, prepared to defend her neutrality, claimed the right to regard herself as a land of heroes . . . Now, most of the heroic illusion has been stripped from Irish neutrality. (Possibly Mr Dillon's speeches may have done something towards this.) Now, neutrality seems to be seen as a dreary and negative state – the sheer negative of 'not being in the war'. Its glory – as being Eire's first autonomous gesture – appears to fade.

The people are candid enough, with regard to themselves, to admit this drop in height. Hence, a good deal of self-dissection has gone on lately. The atmosphere reminds me a little of the atmosphere in England in the year after Munich.

It would be much too much to say that the people would feel relief if they were to be precipitated into the war. But participation in the war is not regarded with the same superstitious horror as it was two years ago.

THE ARCHBISHOP OF DUBLIN

On July 10 I had tea with the RC Archbishop of Dublin, Dr McQuaid, at his house in Glasnevin Road. I had, and have, heard it said that Dr McQuaid is anti-Protestant. But he seems to have taken trouble to keep in touch with Protestant friends of his in Dublin. It was through one of these – Professor Constantia Maxwell, of TCD – that I met him.

Miss Maxwell proposed our visit to the Archbishop on the grounds of my being interested in social work. Dr McQuaid takes a keen interest in technical schools, housing, clubs, people's restaurants, etc. Part of our conversation was on these subjects. The municipal school of cookery (on the North Side of Dublin) he strongly supports. He is anxious to raise the Irish standard of living, to improve the amenities of the home. He showed me the curricula of the cookery school, and other technical schools; unfortunately, these had just closed for the vacation, so that, though I could have seen over the premises, I could not have seen the classes at work.

Dr McQuaid said that the Irishwoman had (as a housewife) much to learn from the Frenchwoman. He appeared to believe that she might learn it . . . He is an enthusiast on the subject of France: has lived there, has many French friends. The greater part of our conversation was, in fact, about France.

The Archbishop said that, much as he had felt for the French humiliation he could not regret (for France's sake) the fall of the Third Republic. As a form of government for France, he had regarded this as pernicious because it was not representative. He is in favour of Marshal Pétain's work, first of all, as a movement of de-centralisation – one calculated to return to the different French provinces their integrity. In which lay the health of France as a whole.

Dr McQuaid said that he would wish to see Eire more decentralised. He believed Eire and France to be much alike. He believed in the provincial spirit, in both countries. Would wish to see the Irish provincial cities – Cork, etc. – asserting themselves, expressing themselves and become centres of life, instead of being drained of their best, most ambitious men, who at present all went to Dublin.

(I heard it said in Dublin that the Cork men run Dublin now. The Archbishop did not refer to this. But he evidently feels strongly that Cork men should run Cork, Waterford men Waterford, etc.)

Dr McQuaid's reputation as a man of intellect, and as a live wire, is established – I need not discuss it. In the course of our conversation, that afternoon, I was struck by the balance he kept, in his point of view, between the mystical (we discussed visions) and the practical – belief in good cooking, intelligent domestic life, etc. I was aware that the Archbishop was being both courteous and diplomatic: he made every allowance for my point of view in any matter we talked about. This, however, made his few assertions of his own point of view – such as his defence, in passing, of M. Laval – all the more interesting.

I shall be sending further Notes in the middle of next week.

Weeping Earl, *The Great O'Neill*, by Sean O'Faolain, 6 March 1943, *New Statesman and Nation,* Review

Hugh O'Neill was the second Earl of Tyrone. The title had first, in 1542, been granted by English patent to his grandfather, the limping Conn, who, with the formalities proper to 'The O'Neill's' person and to centuries of O'Neill independence behind him, came to Greenwich Palace to make formal (time was to show how purely formal) obeisance to the ruling English monarch, Henry VIII. Conn's predecessor in this act, thirty-one years before, had been his Ulster neighbour and kinsman by marriage, Young Hugh O'Donnell (son of Red Hugh, that 'full moon of the hospitality and nobility of the north') who left the presence at Whitehall as Sir Hugh. What had preceded, what was to follow, what was the motive for and who profited by the interchange of these equivocal courtesies? That lesser Gael, O'Conner Sligo,[19] who deemed it wise to come in more or less entirely under Henry VIII's system of 'Surrender and Regrant,' was to provide a warning sinister enough to stick in the O'Neill and O'Donnell minds. The weak Earl of

Desmond,[20] after miserable years in London, still had his apotheosis – the Munster rising – ahead of him; he had been back again where his forefathers started before his head was hacked off in the wet woods. From Desmond, the second Earl of Tyrone, who rode Munster with the English who rode him down, had also something to learn. Ultimately, it was Tyrone (Hugh O'Neill) and Red Hugh O'Donnell the second who were the double kernel of the resistance to English expansion in Ireland in Elizabeth's reign.

Mr O'Faolain's *The Great O'Neill* is a study of the man and his time – a time of which he was considerably ahead. As a character, Hugh O'Neill was and is inscrutable; he gave away little and left little behind. As general, as statesman with no defined State behind him, he was recognized by his contemporaries abroad. At home, patriotic myth has not only blurred but falsified his figure: from these however heroic mists it becomes his biographer's purpose to rescue him. As uncertain successor to the O'Neill lordship, he was occupied, till well on into maturity, with playing his own hand – and it was to the English interest that he should continue to be so occupied; hence the English flirtation with his successive rivals. The Elizabethans, as Mr O'Faolain shows, were adept at giving slight tips to the rocking stone. The Anglo-Gaelic lord's lust for personal power looked like making him an amenable man – but were power once acquired, it could not fail to spell trouble. It was acquired, and did. O'Neill knew how to play up to the English idea that he was being kept banked down. He used years of quiescence to extend his domination and to multiply and to build up his men. Increasingly reluctant to fight the English, he became increasingly able to do so at any time. It took the climax of a series of English blunders to make Hugh O'Neill a patriot *malgrè lui*. Elizabethan England had instructed O'Neill, if it had not – or had it at all? – impressed him. For seven years of his boyhood he was allowed to view, from close up, the more august side of that civilization to be imposed on his own country, soon, by fire and sword. Sir Henry Sydney's taking of the boy of uncertain future back with him to his home in England may have been either an act of private compassion, or, equally, an experiment in policy. The English wish to civilize Ireland was as keenly felt as the Spanish wish to civilize Mexico, and was at least no less disinterested. Each Gaelic lord, on his brief appearance in London, looked shocking, with his air of contrary hauteur, 'his escort of gallowglasses, armed with battle-axes, bareheaded, their curls long, their shirts bright saffron, their sleeves flowing, and their tunics brief beneath their furry cloaks,' and rumour found him worse than he looked. Each was the apex of his own tribal system, into which, since Strongbow, the Anglo-Norman feudalism had seeped. Carew[21] was to write to Cecil[22] of 'the great desire of the Irish lords to keep justice out that they may tyrannize with absolute power, confiscating both goods and lives at pleasure.' As for the creatures tyrannized over, they were savages by such unmistakable showing that their reclamation would not have been worth the gesture had it not excused the annexation of land . . . To civilize young O'Neill, to return to a place of power in Ulster a perfected Elizabethan gentleman, would not be a bad idea – if that *were* Sydney's. The lad knew Ludlow Castle, Penshurst, where he was allowed to play with young Philip Sydney, London (on a leash) and – under Leicester's patronage[23] (which was to prove more enduring than Sydney's) – Kenilworth.

Here, however, was a Renaissance character with whom Elizabethanism did not take. For one thing, the subject was glowering with a strong sense of family wrong: his uncle Sean, 'The Proud,' had successfully murdered his (Hugh's) father, Matthew – beloved bastard and named heir of Conn O'Neill. Over there in Ulster, Sean the usurper had now the field to himself. Pleached alleys, fishponds and graceful converse would, under the circumstances, seem very unreal. To tolerate them could be no more than a policy. Hugh O'Neill, upon his return to Ireland at seventeen, had already begun to embrace those humiliations attendant on playing for English support. He was Baron of Dungannon, but not, for years more, Tyrone. The satisfaction of seeing his uncle's head on a pike was to be mitigated for him, too soon, by the emergence of his second cousin Turlough, who not unfavourably caught the English eye.

Hugh O'Neill was a man who knew how to behave – but knew when not to. His public tears and his bawlings may have been unstrategic: their effects could not have been bettered by calculation – they embarrassed his English peers; they gained time. He had the knack of setting a scene his way: one crucial interview had to be shouted across a stream; his talk with the second Essex (a turning-point) took place with O'Neill on horseback in a river, water up to the horse's neck; Essex high and dry on the bank. Mr O'Faolain's study must stand or fall by the importance he succeeds in giving its subject – and to my mind it stands triumphantly: shrewdness and a perception on the poetic level are equally present in the interpretation. The art and the artfulness of the novelist have been both used and subdued here. As to the history – the point of view, with its here and there almost blighting detachment, gives the record, *qua* record, still more point. The Elizabethan campaigns in Ireland do not make pretty reading – though it still becomes evident, in some contexts, that they are reading to recommend. Mr O'Faolain, as an Irishman, shows unusual power to photograph this country's attitude to his own. Evidently it is the extra-Europeanism of Ireland, the lack of common memories based on Roman rule, that has been and still may be found repugnant. All the same, O'Neill, the 'savage,' could reach round England to entertain lively relations with Rome and Spain. He spoke a language, he acted in a tradition that Europe, if not England, was able to understand. He was not only Catholic and patriot; and not only as Catholic and patriot has he been studied here. He was the last of the barons – across the water, in England, the Tudor new order, raised over the fall of the barons, could still not be indifferent to his threat. In England, the overt Shakespearean tussle, the threat to the throne, was over: power-politics kept men jockeying outside the Queen's door. Is one to wonder that this last of the barons – this red-eyelashed, peering Gael, this salmon-fisher, this honeymooner disdaining the gallant word – tried Elizabeth's temper to frenzy, and, in the end, finished her? He was the fly in the ointment, the crack in the mirror, the thorn in the flesh. When he made his final submission to her Deputy, Mountjoy, O'Neill had not yet been told that she lay dead.

The Desire to Please: A Story of Hamilton Rowan and the United Irishmen, by Harold Nicolson, 22 May 1943, *New Statesman and Nation*, Review

At the end of July, 1806, Hamilton Rowan came home in style. Killyleagh was *en fête*. 'The bells of the church,' says his agent, Archibald Hamilton, 'which had lately tolled his father's funeral, now rang for joy at the son's arrival.' Spectators, waiting for miles along the road, were gratified by the length of the cavalcade. The four elegant bays were removed from the shafts of the carriage, and townspeople competed to take their place, so that 'the carriage and all the family were drawn triumphantly into the town – except Mrs Hamilton Rowan, who very sensibly observed that she would not be drawn by human creatures who could debase themselves to the rank of beasts.' There were, in fact, demonstrations of just that kind against which Mr Hamilton Rowan had been advised by his cousin and neighbour, Lord Dufferin. Himself, he was out to discourage nothing: all this was exactly after his own heart. He became, upon approaching the Castle, 'very much affected indeed. The scene was impressive to an extreme. After so long an absence – an absence which but a short time ago he thought was to be for ever – after so many years of exile and misfortune – once more to enter the seat of his ancestors and to enter it as its proprietor and lord-absolved-restored-renewed-triumphant – 'twas not easily to be borne. He melted into tears.'

The end of the exile – which had been, from the start, one long slow graduation in disenchantment – marked the official end of Hamilton Rowan as rebel, hero and patriot. It was the inconvenience of a long-standing death sentence – this only remitted in Dublin the other day – that had kept the master of Killyleagh from home. As for the 'misfortune' – you could trace the use of that word to the agent's typical tactful Irish obliqueness, but actually it goes pretty near the mark. There *had* been one consistent misfortune: temperament. From this had sprung (as the world saw it) aberrations of every possible size. Hamilton Rowan, whose mother had made a special journey to London that her child should not see the light on Irish soil, had been born, in 1751, to an age and into a society in which the moon was the enthusiast's only proper friend. His parents' marriage had been of the kind that is unpropitious most of all for the children: the English Rowans deplored the Ulster Hamiltons; in Rathbone Place the boy was reared with a bullying sternness intended to weed out every Hamilton trait. Could Ireland fail to become the magnetic alternative to the detestable, daily English regime? Could nobility fail to be queered into silliness, daydreams into obsessions, courage into bravado, in a youth made heir to his English grandfather's fortune on condition he changed his father's name for his mother's and not visit Ireland at younger than twenty-five? Apparently, he both had his cake and ate it: while drawing, to meet his Cambridge and other debts, on his expectations under the Rowan will, he paid secret flying visits to his father and Killyleagh. But if this duplicity kept both parties quiet it aggravated the conflict inside the man. Hamilton Rowan (whose surname at birth was Hamilton, and whose children reverted to that name) was Mr Harold Nicolson's great-great-grandfather; *The Desire to Please* is Hamilton Rowan's story. The book has a sort of double structure: there is direct biography and there is speculation. The biography covers the years and scenes – Ireland, London, Ireland, France, America, Ireland again – at an even pace; the speculation is static and works down, like a drill. The action is very clear, being part of history;

but the actor is, at times, a blurred, looming close-up, made more rather than less mysterious by being almost too near the eye. This placing of Hamilton Rowan just out of focus I take to be not a failure but a deliberate intention of Mr Nicolson's art. The underlying subject of *The Desire to Please* is the feeling of a descendant towards an ancestor. The suspicion of being implicated, the over-susceptibility to certain traits, the sense of guilt, the touches of harshness (such as one might feel towards oneself), the wary search for the ulterior motive – all are there. That this analysis of the sense of being descended is fascinating, I need not say. It might, however, seem to the outside person that Mr Nicolson has overshot the strong latent naivety in Hamilton Rowan, and that he has either ignored, or abandoned as too simple, explanations of his character and his conduct that might be clear to another eye.

The story of Hamilton Rowan, as told in *The Desire to Please*, begins, not with his birth in Rathbone Place in 1751, but with his emergence – out of the family past, out of a disregarding silence and awkwardness – into his great-great-grandson's youthful consciousness. Mr Nicolson, as a boy on visits to relations in Ireland, became aware of an ancestor who for some reason had not been quite the thing. This was the man whose face came to be printed, together with faces of other patriots, on handkerchiefs into which the Dublin crowd wept, outside a prison, during a 1920 political execution. How was he to be reconciled with the great houses? The child's first wish to drag anything awkward up gave place to intellectual curiosity, to the will to assimilate Hamilton Rowan, even though this might mean having to know the worst.

The worst does not seem so very bad. Hamilton Rowan's behaviour was impolitic. The failure of the projects he espoused made him appear mistaken. He threw his personal weight and, through everything he remains an impressive man – behind causes without enough calculation. The American Revolution and the French Revolution were two dawns that, for him, lost their colour late. He identified England with oppression, as he had had reason to do in youth. The sobriety and the vehemence of the Ulster Whigs, of the United Irishmen, rallied in him all those faculties that he had always, really, hated to dissipate. Acting with the United Irishmen, he conspired with France against England, in Ireland's interest. His adventures were, on the whole, ignominious; his troubled life held not one explicit heroic moment. His tastes were simple: he loved dogs and boating and his on the whole rather bleak wife. *Did* anything so consistent, so calculating, so fundamentally cold as 'the desire to please' really dominate him and determine the course he took? I see in him rather the desire to *be* pleased, to believe in masters, to release the waiting floods of his admiration. The ideas to which he had sacrificed, from which he recanted in order to return as master to Killyleagh, no longer drew any force from his nature: it was his tragedy that they had died in him. He was the principal sufferer from his own guilelessness.

The Most Unforgettable Character I've Met, 1944, *Windmill*, Essay

A great cold grey stone house, with rows upon rows of windows, ringed round with silence, approached by grass-grown avenues – has life forever turned aside from this place? So the stranger might ask today, approaching my family home in Ireland. It is miles from anywhere you have ever heard of; it is backed by woods with mountains behind them; in front, it stares over empty fields. Generations have lived out their lives and died here. But now – everybody has gone away?

No: not quite. A low wing runs out at the back of the house, and from its chimney you see, winter and summer, a plume of wood smoke rising against the trees. And through one window, as dusk falls, the glow of firelight welcomes you. This fire never goes out; it is Sarah Barry's – or was Sarah Barry's until last spring, when she died. Since then, her son Paddy keeps it alight: he sits beside it in his chair, looking across at hers.

When Sarah, then Sarah Cartey, first arrived at Bowen's Court, County Cork, she was a girl of fourteen. She left her home in County Tipperary to become a kitchenmaid in my grandfather's house. Taking her place in the trap beside her new Master, she had set out one morning upon the fifty-mile drive. She did not know when, if ever, she would see home again. Ireland looks so small from the outside, it is hard to realize how big the distances feel: for the simple people, each county might be a different continent – and way back in the last century this was even more so. Young Sarah, face set towards County Cork, might have been driving off into Peru. Mr Bowen,[24] towering beside her in his greatcoat, and keeping his horse along at a saving trot, was for her the one tie between the old and the new – she already knew him by sight, and by awesome name, for the Master owned large estates in both counties, and drove to and fro weekly between the two. It was on the return from one of these trips that he was bringing back with him Sarah Cartey. In his part of Tipperary, as in his part of Cork, everyone went in dread of Mr Bowen. He was a just man, but he was hard: to his wealth was added the weight of his character – choleric, dynamic and overbearing. In those days, the Protestant Irish landlord exercised more or less absolute power, and was, if he misused it, hated accordingly. Tall and heavy, bearded, genially ruddy but with rather cold blue eyes, my grandfather was typical of his class. Unlike some, he ran his estates like a man of business. Few loved him, but he was a big gun.

But so, in her way, was Sarah. From the first, it seems, they recognized this in each other, which was the reason why they got on so well. Driving along that day, she sat fearlessly upright. When he spoke she answered, cheerfully and forthright. The tears that kept pricking her violet-blue eyes were blinked back: she did not let one fall. At home, her mother and all the neighbours had told her she was a lucky girl, to get such a start – legends of Bowen's Court grandeur were current in Tipperary. So she kept her chin high, as befitted a lucky girl. If this were life, she was going to live it well. It was in the dusk, at the end of the day-long journey, that Sarah saw Bowen's Court for the first time.

When Sarah, as an old woman, told me this story, she looked at me with eyes that had never changed. Their character and their colour were set off by jet-black lashes. Laughing and ageless, these were the most perfect Irish eyes in the world. They were, I suppose, strictly her only beauty – though Sarah was as comely as you could wish. Her complexion kept into old age its vivid bloom. Her hair, curling generously round her forehead, lost no vitality as it turned white – in youth it was, like her vigorous eyebrows, dark. She was short and, since I remember her, broad and stout: she must have been thickset even as a young girl.

The Bowen's Court in which she took up her duties was unlike the silent house of today. Lavishly kept up, it was at the height of its Victorian prime. Mr and Mrs Bowen, their nine children, eight indoor servants and frequent visitors more than filled it. The eldest Bowen daughter was also called Sarah. Perhaps it was something in the tie of the name that made the two girls friends from the first, then lifelong allies. The young Bowens had been rigidly brought up: in the heart of this countryside they led formal lives. Handsome, but overgrown and pale, they lived in fear of their father. They might well have envied Sarah her spontaneity. They adored their gracious mother, but her they too seldom saw. Under the Mistress's calm rule, the household ran like clockwork.

Of the upstairs rooms – with their damasks, marbles, mirrors, mahogany – Sarah Cartey at first saw little: the basement claimed her; over the dark stone-flagged floors she hurried to and fro. At first she was like a kitten, under everyone's feet, but her wits soon gave her command of the situation. Clean, strong, quick, friendly and willing – she was approved. The Bowen's Court servants, from the butler and cook down, were a hierarchy, but a good-humoured one. Some, like Sarah, were Catholics, others Protestants – 'But', Sarah told me, 'we all got on so well together, you'd never know which was which.' In that case, tempers must have been doughty, for the kitchen worked at exacting pressure: if a meal were not on his table up to the minute, the Master would 'roar aloud', at which the whole household quaked.

Except Sarah. She never quaked at the Master: she understood him. He had been out early, poor man, so needed his dinner *now*. As a rule, he ignored the servants, who for their part gave him a wide berth. But whenever he came across Sarah – staggering with her pail from the well, perhaps, or running an errand out to the garden – he would stop and ask her how she was getting on. Was she learning to like her work, did she miss her home? Looking up, she assured the Master that she was happy. The fact was, she refused stoutly to be anything else. Therefore, she kept those dear Tipperary memories locked away in her heart. But there, as a part of her inmost being, they grew in strength and power as years went by. As an old woman, she ached to go back *home*. What kept her? She stayed with us to the end. It was to Bowen's Court that she gave her genius – her genius for making all that she touched live.

Though hers was the most independent mind I have known, Sarah did not question the social order. The injustices (as they would appear now) of my grandfather's household did not strike her. Out of what might have been servitude she made for herself a creative career. Her whole personality went into what she did. I believe that 'class' to Sarah meant simply this – the division of people according to their different duties. Thus, she worked alongside the Bowens, rather than for them. She respected the Bowens because, as she saw it, they played their allotted parts in the proper way. She perceived that the Master, in his estate management, spared himself no more than he spared his men; that the Mistress's life, with so many demands upon it, was selfless; that the young gentlemen lived under discipline like cadets; that the young ladies studied, and practised the piano, as industriously as she, Sarah, scrubbed at the pots and pans. If downstairs you worked like a black, upstairs you had to 'behave' like a Spartan. Life evened up, in the long run. She envied no one, and only pitied those to whom God had given nothing to do. When she was nearly eighty, I told her she worked too hard. 'Thank God, I always enjoy myself!' she flashed out.

Clouds gathered over Bowen's Court. First, the Mistress died of smallpox – her eldest son had brought the infection home from abroad. Then, the Master married again, and his growing-up children resented the woman who had taken their mother's place. Strife and estrangements followed: all over the house one now heard angrily raised voices, or encountered sullenly shut doors. Worse was to come – it became evident that the Master was going out of his mind. The estate, lacking his grip, suffered: it began to run at a loss. When the Master died, it was found that severe retrenchments must be made; labourers were turned away from the farm, and most of the indoor servants were sent away. My father, who as eldest son had now succeeded to Bowen's Court, was hard put to it, even so, to keep things going at all. His sister, Miss Sarah, kept house for him. Need it be said that Sarah Cartey became the new young Mistress's lieutenant?

Together, the two Sarahs schemed and worked to make home what it ought to be for the others. This was always a hard and sometimes a thankless task. Miss Sarah, sensitive to the criticisms of her younger brothers and sisters, relied upon Sarah Cartey to keep her spirits up. The sorrows and terrors of the last few years had left their mark on the young Bowens; also, left will-less without their father's authority, they now hardly knew where to turn. They needed to be rallied, inspired, cheered – and it was here that Sarah Cartey came in. She became the steady dynamo of the house. From her they learned the meaning of zest for life. Her esteem built them up in their own eyes. And she understood them – her devotion was never blind. Short of money, and isolated in the great shabby house, they could easily have dropped out of society. But Sarah insisted that this should not happen; the old Master's children must keep their place. She encouraged the brothers to bring home their friends from college, and compelled the sisters to entertain. She loved to hear laughter. Meanwhile, she was doing the work of six, turning her hand to everything – cooking, laundering, scrubbing. I don't know how many times a day she plied up and down between the basement and attics. But she always had time to joke with the young gentlemen, or to help the young ladies to dress for balls. She, who had left her own mother at fourteen, never ceased to pity the motherless Miss Bowens: she supplied, in her own way, motherly pride and love. It was a lasting disappointment to her that none of the four married.

She herself did not marry till she was over thirty. Her comeliness and her fame as a cheerful worker could not fail to bring many suitors around – but she had literally no time to listen to them. When at last she did give her heart, she chose worthily. This marriage went only in one way against her dreams – it won her away forever from Tipperary. The Barrys were County Cork people: living on the estate, they were trusted employees and friends of the Master's household – and more, between Bowens and Barrys existed the foster-tie, then very strong in Ireland. One after another, the Bowen's Court babies had been sent out to nurse with Mrs Barry, who raised up alongside them a numerous family of her own. I have always heard, and can well believe, that the Barrys were descended from the Kings of Ireland – their ancestors must have been mighty over this very land before my own, Cromwellian settlers, arrived. Certainly, Patrick Barry, who became the husband of Sarah, was tall and distinguished-looking. And he was upright in character as he was in build.

The young couple set up in a colour-washed cottage on the outskirts of the estate: it faced across the road towards distant mountains, but its back window overlooked Bowen's Court, down the fields. So Sarah, even at the height of her own happiness, could still keep an eye on us – and she did. I only hope that calls from the helpless mansion did not break in too often on Sarah's years as a wife. For these, had we only known it, were to be as few as they were ideal.

At Bowen's Court there had again been changes. My father had married; his brothers and sisters had gone their different ways into the world. My mother – charming, dreamy and totally inexperienced as a housekeeper – found her new home an alarming proposition. She had been left by Miss Sarah a parting word of advice – 'Go to Sarah Barry if you are in any trouble.' At this point, I come on the scene – and as far back as *I* can remember, Sarah was with us more or less every day. To escape downstairs to the laundry where Sarah worked became my dominating idea. Happiness stays, for me, about the warm smell of soapsuds. I remember her short strong arms red from the heat of water, and the hilarious energy with which she turned the wringer – as though this were some private game of her own. Under her hand, the iron sped effortlessly over the steaming linen. I suppose all children delight in seeing a thing well done – the craftsman is their ideal grown-up. Sarah, I can see now, was divided between her love for 'the Baba' and her love for her work – one could hardly fail to get in the other's way. When I flopped into her baskets of new-bleached linen, she would haul me out with – 'Come on, now: you're too bold for me altogether!' On the best days, she used to let me 'help'. One of the pleasures of growing older was that of growing more fully into her confidence. And I grew tall fast – it was not so long before her laughter-creased eyes were on a level with mine.

Her vivid plumpness was fascinating – it went with her abundance of warmth and wit. Time was to teach me how comprehending her love could be. In those first years, as the child of a happy home, I suppose I took love for granted – it was, rather, Sarah's *amusingness* that attracted me. Her repartee could be lightning-quick – at that nobody got the better of her. And almost every day she had something for me: a surprise, a story, a secret – only for her and me.

Sarah's cottage home – with the lustre mugs on the dresser, the new-baked bread, the speckless hardwood furniture – seemed to me paradise. But, looking round it again, I found one thing missing: after that I began asking my mother, 'But why hasn't Sarah got any baby?' Other friends must have wondered the same thing – Sarah childless meant a sort of loss to the race. She herself never ceased to believe that God would see to the matter – and so He did. I shall never forget the morning when Sarah called me to her in a particular tone. I could feel at once that something was in the air. She put her arms close round me; her dear breath tickled my ear as she whispered, 'Now here *is* a secret for you – God is going to send me a little parcel!'

We were away when her son was born. My father's illness kept us from Bowen's Court, so that I did not see Paddy till he was two years old. Any child of Sarah's would have seemed beautiful, but this one really was so. The sunshine of her nature seemed to have found its way into his eyes, his glowing cheeks and his golden curls. Her womanhood had been crowned as it deserved. It would have been understandable if Sarah, after her years of waiting, had been unable to bear her darling out of her sight. But in this, as in all, she was generous – she let me make off with this miracle-baby for afternoons together, climb with him up to the tops of hay-ricks, carry him off to the stream to sail paper boats. In our absence – and our visits during those years were brief – she was acting as caretaker at Bowen's Court: with small Paddy clutching her skirts she patrolled the deserted rooms. It seemed unnatural to her, then as always, that 'the Family' should be away – but she could fill the emptiness with her own summer – the radiance in which she lived with husband and child.

Then, while Paddy was still a small boy, Patrick took sick and died. I do not know how she faced out her desolation: she to whom so many had turned could now only turn to herself. Sarah was never meek; there was always a touch of fire about her goodness. Her whole being cried out against this loss. In the end she triumphed; she did not let it warp her. Only, as I grew old enough to be able to read her eyes, I could see behind their gaiety an eternal wound. For a while, her thoughts turned to Tipperary – should she not go home again, taking her child with her? But no; she was wanted at Bowen's Court – she stayed. She continued to live in the roadside cottage, though there were times when its loneliness frightened her. Often, the mountain winds roared through the trees at the back; after holidays, drunken people lurched past her door. One terrible night, she heard one man kill another – as key-witness, she had to attend the trial. Agitation made her evidence contradictory: both the victim and the prisoner had been her neighbours. 'I pitied both the poor fellows,' she said to me.

Sarah's sense of justice was strong, but personal. She felt the law's aim should be the same as her own – good treatment for as many people as possible. What she detested in crime was its unkindness. The killing at her gate had been exceptional in being a *crime passionel*: most violence in Ireland had a political source. Her girlhood had been in the days of the Land League; she was to live through the repercussions of the 1916 Rising, through 'the bad times' that followed the Great War, through the Civil War after the Treaty, when the British had gone. Lorries crashing along with armed men rocked her house in the night; she saw horizons scarlet with burning mansions and farms; she heard reverberations, from blown-up bridges. You never knew what might happen, from day to day. Through all this, Sarah never took sides. Thinking in terms of people, not of ideas, she never examined the ethics either of landlordism or British rule. When, after the Treaty, Ireland was split in twain, it was simply against *all* foolishness that she shook her head. She loved life's decent pattern of love and work – anyone who destroyed this became her enemy.

Through it all, no faction raised its hand against Sarah. Since her widowhood, she had kept herself to herself – on civil terms with all neighbours, she was on close terms with none – and she never talked: her discretion stood her in good stead. In the thick of it all, she did say, 'It would break your heart to see good time squandered away like this.'

I grew from a schoolgirl into a young woman: I married, travelled, became a writer, and enjoyed my fill of big city life. But, each time I returned to Bowen's Court and to Sarah I found that she, who had never in her life left the South of Ireland, could still make circles round me. Nothing I told her surprised her. She liked to hear about London, and, of course, about Rome – I was able to bring her back a rosary blessed by the Pope. She was alarmed when she heard I planned to go to America, for fear I should not come back – so few Irish people did. I don't think she saw much point in travel, really: why should anyone wish to move from their own place? Sarah's scepticism was good for me – like most young people, I bolted ideas whole simply because they were the ideas of my own day. Attempting to argue with her, I was forced to think.

I know that my having no children disappointed her deeply, though she was too delicate in her feeling ever to speak of this. When my father died, at the end of weeks of illness that had been agonising for him and for all of us, it was to her that I turned. Leaving his room, when it was over, I found the staircase full of spring evening light and Sarah standing there looking up, waiting for me. We sat down side by side on the stairs, and she put her arms round me – as she had not done since the day when she whispered to me about her 'little parcel'. 'The poor Master . . .' she said. Her memories of my father, reaching back, made his life complete. I had only known my father as my father. But she, as we sat there, saw the red-headed schoolboy, the anxious young head of the house, the proud bridegroom, the lonely man fighting breakdown for many years. Her sense of his triumphant dignity as a human being passed, without a word spoken, from her to me. It was she, a few hours later, who did the last work for him – 'You must come and see him,' she said proudly, 'He looks lovely.' She took me to see – he did. Her fingers had fluted the linen over his body into a marble-like pattern, a work of art.

I had been the only child: Bowen's Court was now mine. I could not live there altogether; our married home was in England, near my husband's work. So, in order that everything might be taken care of, Sarah and Paddy shut up their cottage and took up their quarters at the back of the house. When we *could* be there, she took charge of us and of everything. What summer holidays she gave us, and what Christmases! And what meals she cooked – once again, the big kitchen range roared, and she stood over it royally. Into those visits of a few weeks on end she helped us pack the feeling of an unbroken home life. Each time, the rooms to which we returned might have been left only yesterday. Fires burned, flowers were in the vases, and our beloved possessions (preserved by Sarah as might be the toys of children) lay where we had put them down last time.

As of old, she was all for company: to please her we could not invite too many guests. Beaming, she watched me re-open what had been dismantled bedrooms at the top of the house. She declared, 'We're like a palace again!' Sarah's idea of company, I remembered, had been formed in the stately days of my grandfather – gentlemen in tailcoats and high collars, ladies whose rustling silks swept the ground. What would she make of my friends – creatures of a changed society, of an outside world that she did not know? But at bare-limbed young women in brief skirts, at young men in slack and colourful country clothes – sunning themselves on the steps, calling out of the windows, playing wild games on wet days – she did not bat an eyelid. They were happy, they liked the house and us and her cooking – so they were all right with her. Because she loved human nature, she could move with the times. Each new guest, on arrival, came downstairs with me to be introduced to Sarah – and there were few who did not find their way down again. One was safe in tracing a missing guest to the kitchen. As one of them said to me, 'She's an education.'

What Sarah felt in her heart of hearts about my becoming a writer I do not know. Books could teach her nothing, and played no part in her life. She was used to seeing a gentleman at his desk – my grandfather at his accounts, my father over his legal documents – but she might well have considered a typewriter inhuman company for a woman. I think it was always a shock to come on me, rooted there, indoors on a fine morning or late on into the night. But her philosophy with regard to work held good: happy in hers she could not begrudge me mine. Also, I had explained to her how my affairs stood – since my grandfather's death finances had not improved: I could only afford to keep Bowen's Court if I earned money. So she saw that what I did, along with the much that she did, followed the same ideal – to keep things going.

Sarah refused to believe that this war would come. She still held that the Great War had taught us the needed lesson – she was not a student of European affairs. Her optimism had kept so much trouble at bay that I think *I* almost believed it could stop Hitler. After Munich, she was all triumph – 'Didn't I tell you, now?' When, on that sunny Sunday morning, 3 September 1939, I switched off the radio after Chamberlain's[25] voice, I hesitated at the head of the kitchen stairs. How was I to tell Sarah she had been wrong? When I had done so, she shrugged her shoulders, opened the front of the range and poked the fire. The she flashed round on me – 'Well, it won't last!' I wish she could have lived through it. Shadows of change, anxiety, deprivation crept up on the house in her last years. I don't think she set much store by Ireland's neutral safety while my husband and I were in London, 'among those bombs'. She knew I knew she would have given the world for me to have stayed at Bowen's Court, out of it all. But her comprehension of things was too fine to allow her once to suggest that I should do so. My husband's work was in London, and my place was beside him: people she loved did not desert their posts. Beyond that, this war had for her no definable rights and wrongs, any more than a senseless family quarrel. She hated war as unkindness; she mourned it as waste.

Our visits were shorter, fewer: no friends came with us. From rooms no longer in use Sarah packed away the hangings and pictures – 'Till the good times come back.' The wing behind Bowen's Court, in which she lived with Paddy, is a row of rooms overlooking the grass-grown yard. From them in the old Master's day one had heard the clatter of horses; in my day cars being run in and out of the garage. Now all was silence. Sarah's parlour had been my grandfather's estate office: with its barred window and iron safe in the wall it was not home-like – but somehow she made it so. She hung it round with pictures that had been in my nursery, and on the hearth kept burning that constant fire. Again, she patrolled the empty block of the house, on the watch for any suspicion of damp or damage. Every day Paddy switched on the library radio, and, among sheeted furniture, he and she heard the news. Paddy, now grown up into a clever man, explained the war to his mother – but could not explain it away. Things began to run very short – coal, tea. And you had to think twice before you lit a candle.

It was in the fourth year of the war that the final assault on her came. A growth formed in her body. To her, who always had been sound from top to toe, this at first seemed a nightmare from which she must surely wake. It was weeks before she nerved herself to tell Paddy. When she did, she bound him to secrecy: *I* must not be worried – wasn't the war enough? Things got worse: she consented to see a doctor. Radium treatment in Dublin was his urgent advice. Very well: she would go, she would try it. She was not in pain, thank God.

Sarah, now nearing eighty, left Bowen's Court in the spirit in which she arrived there at fourteen – chin up, heart high, ready for what might come. Before she left she was busy: she had a great deal to see to. She went over every inch of the house – yes, it was fit for us to come back, if we chose, tomorrow. In the larder, she checked over the bottled fruit, and re-covered some dozens of jars of jam. She wished she could have made more strawberry, that was our favourite kind. The evening before she started, friends from far and near came in to bid her Godspeed.

Sarah, the Tipperary woman who had always kept her heart a little detached, had to realize how well County Cork loved her. Even those who only knew her by sight, driving her donkey trap up the hill to Mass on Sundays, sent good wishes. Everyone, shyly, promised Sarah their prayers. *She* – as they all remember – was in great spirits. 'Oh, I'll be back,' she laughed, 'before you can miss the time. And too grand for you altogether, after my trip to Dublin.'

She had only once – and that years ago – been to Dublin before. She said she would be a poor thing if she couldn't enjoy a journey. She and Paddy made their way down the train to the tea-car, where they declared a feast. The line, as though specially laid for her, runs through County Tipperary – all the way she sat entranced, looking out of the window at the landscape flying past in the spring light; also, she had all the fun in the world observing her fellow-passengers and their ways. But the journey's end held pain: at the Dublin hospital she and Paddy had to say goodbye. I reached Dublin from London two days later. Sarah's treatment, with its alarming strangeness, had started – but as I walked down the ward to her bed her smile came to meet me, gay as ever. Lying there in a striped jacket, with sun falling on to the fluffy curls round her face, she looked young, almost schoolgirlish. At the same time, she was already the queen of her surroundings. She sent me up and down the beds, distributing the flowers and fruit I had brought her among the other patients. From left and right, I saw poor exhausted faces turned her way, as though imbibing strength. 'Mrs Barry's a treat for us all,' said the nurse to me. Sarah praised the hospital, saying she could not have run it better herself. During my daily visits we never, by her clear wish, spoke of her ordeal: instead, we chatted and laughed over little things. She said, 'Don't you want to know how I like Dublin?' I reminded her I still owed her a Christmas present, and she said she'd like a length for a new dress – 'with a nice little clever pattern; not too bold'.

I brought the stuff, but she never wore the dress. Just when everyone was most optimistic, when plans for her return journey had begun to be made, her heart gave out under the treatment: Sarah died. It was now, at last, that she realized her wish to return forever to Tipperary. As she had asked her son, she was buried there. Her funeral drove past the farms and gates and hedges whose picture had always been in her heart. Through Paddy's mind, as he followed, ran all those Tipperary stories she had told him over their fire in County Cork. At the start, I pictured Bowen's Court standing empty. But that is not the picture Sarah would want you to see – and more, it is not a true one. Her presence is still to be felt there, and from no place where Sarah reigns can life turn away for long. I believe in her power to magnetize people home again: in the rooms will be heard again the laughter she liked to hear. You may say she gave her genius to a forlorn hope – to a house at the back of beyond, to a dying-out family. But I think no gift goes for nothing. She never lowered her flag; and by that she alone could make me believe in greatness. If we can play our parts in building a better world in Sarah's spirit, we shall not do too badly.

Mainie Jellett, 3 December 1944, *The Bell* 9, Essay

I first knew Mainie Jellett when we were both little girls: her mother and mine were friends, and neighbours in Dublin; and Mainie and I first met and looked at each other solemnly before we were either of us able to speak. The little Jelletts and I used to meet on our schoolroom walks through the streets and squares, and we were often in and out of each other's homes. And I was one of the children who went to the painting classes which, held by Miss Elizabeth Yeats[26] in the Jellett's Fitzwilliam Square diningroom, saw the opening of Mainie's life as an artist. I remember the excitement of that free brushwork, the children's heads bent, all round the big table, over crocuses springing alive, with each stroke, on the different pieces of white paper. If she and I shared, as children, the same burning wish, it was in those says an inarticulate one. My wish has taken me down the path of another art. During our working lives, we worked in different places, and met, where I am concerned, too seldom. But I have never lost the proud sense of being at least a contemporary of Mainie's, and a friend in the sense that distance and separation do not damage. To have worked *with* her must surely have been a great thing.

I saw her last, last October, in the quiet back room of the Leeson Street nursing home, where she lay with her bed pulled out under the window. A fire burned in the grate, and brick buildings in October sunshine reflected brightness into the room. The eager, generous little girl of my first memories was now a thin woman, in whom the fatigue of illness, mingling with that unlost generosity and eagerness, translated itself into a beauty I cannot forget. The greatness of Mainie Jellett was to be felt in many ways; but not least in her simplicity. She was not only easy but, which is rarer, easing to be with: she not only calmed one but re-lit lamps which seemed to be going out. I felt very much her junior, in vision, in virtue, in experience of what is truly life. Among other things, we talked about the book she had been reading, which had been in her hands when I came in, and about its author, Dorothy Richardson,[27] a woman unknown personally to both of us, whose strain of genius has not yet been enough recognized by the world. Mainie recognized it: she talked to me about writing with a pure comprehension of which, I think, few actual writers are capable. I know, now, that for her all the arts converged: they are different manifestations of something single. For a long time, Mainie studied the piano, which, up to the time of her last illness, she played often and beautifully. Her music is palpable in her painting . . . In that October hour, we talked about many things, and discovered (where I was concerned) so many new things, that this for me was almost like a first meeting. It had certainly none of the character of a last one. And it was not a last one. Mainie's death has been a deprivation for so many people that I can only with humility speak of my own sense of it. But for her it can have been only another step on. The immortality of what she did and was remains.

I have begun this memoir in a simple and personal way because I cannot write about Mainie Jellett in any other. Her affections were vivid, and I think it would seem to her natural to be spoken of first in terms of ordinary human memory. There was something about her that would discountenance 'sought' phrases and carefully chosen words. But also, I have her own authority – the authority of her essay, 'An Approach to Painting', published in the *Irish Art Handbook* of two years ago – for my idea that an artist's natural place is in the heart of human society.

> I believe (she says) in the necessity of a sense of craftsmanship being highly developed in every professional artist; they should be capable of executing whatever job they are commissioned to do adequately. An artist should be a competent worker as in the periods when the Guild system operated, have an honest standard of workmanship like any competent worker in other walks of life. The idea of artist being a special person, an exotic flower set apart from other people, is one of the errors resulting from the industrial revolution, and the fact of artists being pushed out of their lawful position in the life and society of the present day.
>
> Artists as a whole are people with certain gifts more highly developed than the general majority, but for this very reason their gifts are vitally important to the mental and spiritual life of that majority. Their present enforced isolation from the majority is a very serious situation and I believe it is one of the many causes which has resulted in the present chaos we live in.

> The art of a nation is one of the ultimate facts by which its spiritual health is judged and appraised by posterity . . .

Mainie Jellett's place in the art of Ireland is beyond discussion: what is not less striking is the advance she has given to Ireland's art's place in the art of the world. Could one say that, her nationality being part of her temperament, internationalism was part of her discipline? One of her pupils, Stella Frost, writes: 'Her gift to Ireland was a rare one. Being national in her outlook, no small accomplishment in the circles in which she was born, she was at the same time international. By her specialised knowledge of the art of other nations, both ancient and modern, she was able to link up the best in all art and to weld it into the living expression of her own work and into that of her pupils. Her vision knew no bounds, whether of art or religion, the only necessary passport to her sympathy was sincerity of spirit.'

First, her life as a pupil. In Dublin, after Miss Yeats' classes, she worked with Miss Celia Harrison, then with Miss Manning, in the Merrion Row studio; then, about 1915, went to the Orpen[28] class in the Metropolitan School of Art in Kildare Street, to study from the life. Early in 1917, she went to London, to work under Walter Sickert,[29] at the Westminster School. (At the same time, during those London years, she was a piano pupil of Miss Landers' – herself a pupil of Leschetitzky[30]: it was not until Mainie Jellett was twenty-two that she decided that she must, wholly, concentrate upon painting.) In 1919 she left London, to go, in 1920, with her friend Miss Hone[31] to Paris, where they both worked in André Lhote's[32] studio. It was in 1923 that both Irishwomen became pupils of Albert Gleizes[33]; and after Mainie Jellett returned to live, to paint and to teach in Dublin, yearly visits to France for study with Gleizes, in Paris or at his house in the Rhône Valley, continued up to 1933. During those years, she exhibited paintings in Dublin, London and Paris . . . In 1922, on a visit to Spain with Miss Hone, she was profoundly impressed by El Greco's work, as seen in its natural ground of the Spanish landscape. Months in Lithuania, in 1931, gave a fresh wave of impetus, mingled with her delight in what she called, to her sister, 'Hansel and Gretel' surroundings. Her last visit to France was in 1939. War clanged a gate shut between her and the Continent. But she had reached her maturity. Learning days would never be over, but now she learned for herself – learned, perhaps, even in teaching, for is there not in teaching, at the height to which she brought it, some blessed endless reciprocity and exchange?

Teaching took time, drew steadily on her psychic powers as on her physical strength, and made less, if in the quantitative sense purely, the body of her own directly creative work. Her selflessness with regard to art showed itself in her selflessness with regard to younger artists, who might (from the outside) have been felt to stand between the art and her. I think, too, that what might be called her family sense – the most sweet and human, surely, of Irish traits? – appeared in her attitude to her pupils, these younger brothers and sisters of the brush. Talking, before she died, to her friend Miss Hone, about her teaching, she said: 'I suppose I had a desire to impart the little I had to give. I felt it was not given to me just for myself.'

Mainie Jellett's essay on her own painting (already quoted) is startling in its objectivity. It is at once an analysis and the statement of a creed. 'In recent years,' she says, writing two years ago, 'my work roughly tends to divide itself into three different categories:

- (i) Non-representational painting based on some emotional contact received from nature or experience, but first born in the mind.
- (ii) Non-representational work based on Christian religious subjects treated symbolically without realism.
- (iii) Realistic landscape treated in a manner inspired by Chinese Art, and direct realistic studies for exercises and reference.'

She speaks of having gone through three major revolutions in her work, style, and ideas, and of, after each of these, starting more or less afresh. The first came with study with Walter Sickert – revolution in composition and use of line, realism, new understanding of the Old Masters. Sickert, being in the direct line of French impressionist painting, was the stepping stone towards the next revolution – Paris and Lhote's studio, with its work on modified cubist theories. 'With Lhote I learnt how to use natural forms as a starting point towards the pure creation of form for its own sake . . . and to produce work based on a knowledge of rhythmical form and organic colour, grouping towards a conception of a picture being a creative organic whole, but still based on realistic form.' Lhote was, in his turn, to be a stepping stone to the third revolution: as a student of Albert Gleizes. With him 'I went right back to the beginning, and was put to the severest type of exercises in pure form and colour . . . I now felt I had come to essentials, and though the type of work I had embarked upon would mean years of misunderstanding and walls of prejudice to break through, yet I felt I was on the right track.'

So it was that Mainie Jellett brought back to her native city a dynamicism that at first, as she had expected, was found unfriendly, destructive, even repellent. She had gone so far as to go, it seemed, out of view. A mystique without her familiar softness, expressing itself in the ice of abstract terms, and the apparent subjugation of the soul to the intellect, took some accepting. A whole force of opinion clings strongly to the idea (or superstition) of art's *spontaneity*, and believes that in theory and discipline, past an accepted point, the artist can do himself nothing but injury. Such opinion she was very slowly and very quietly to confound. (Humanly she was of the type that obeys Christ's injunction to offend none of these little ones.) It became apparent that her spirit had only gained in fullness through its recognition of intellect. Her poetic spontaneity, her human apprehension of life round her, had been strong enough to 'take' the cold discipline. This spirit, which knew its own needs, had had nothing to fear – and, more, it could allay fear in others. Always, her attitude to her art had been a religious one – as, indeed, in the human part of her life appeared self-abnegation and humility. The most profound element in her painting was – from the very fact of its *being* the most profound – the slowest to emerge; many of the pictures painted in the last three or four years of her life were religious in feeling as well as subject. We have *The Ninth Hour* and *The Madonna of Eire*. And not from a less deep, in fact from the same source, came the vision that gave us her Irish pictures – for instance, the *Achill Horses*, whose growth I had seen in her studio, from sketch to sketch.

Mainie Jellett expressed in her talk to friends, states in her essay and made felt in her painting, her consciousness of her own, and our own, time, with its death throes and birth pangs, its agonising transitions. She ignored nothing. Art to her was not an ivory tower but a fortress. We could have wished her beside us, on into the growing days. But she leaves us with a spirit fortified, and fortifying, by its belief.

CHAPTER 3

Prints on the Landscape
1945–1950

Post script to the US edition of *The Demon Lover and Other Stories*, 1945

The stories in the collection entitled *The Demon Lover* were written in wartime London – between the spring of 1941 and the late autumn of 1944. They were written for the magazines or papers in which they originally appeared. During these last years, I did not always write a story when I was asked for one; but I did not write any story that I was not asked for. For at the same time I have been writing a novel; and sometimes I did not want to imperil its continuity. Does this suggest that these *Demon Lover* stories have been in any way forced or unwilling work? If so, that is quite untrue. Actually, the stimulus of being asked for a story, and the compulsion created by having promised to write one were both good – I mean, they acted as releases. Each time I sat down to write a story I opened a door; and the pressure against the other side of that door must have been very great, for things – ideas, images, emotions – came through with force and rapidity, sometimes violence. I do not say that these stories wrote themselves – aesthetically or intellectually speaking, I found the writing of some of them very difficult – but I was never in a moment's doubt as to *what* I was to write. The stories had their own momentum, which I had to control. The acts in them had an authority which I could not question. Odd enough in their way – and now some seem very odd – they were flying particles of something enormous and inchoate that had been going on. They were sparks from experience – an experience not necessarily my own.

During the war I lived, both as a civilian and as a writer, with every pore open; I lived so many lives, and, still more, lived among the packed repercussions of so many thousands of other lives, all under stress, that I see now it would have been impossible to have been writing only one book. I want my novel, which deals with this same time, to be enormously comprehensive. But a novel must have form;

and, for the form's sake, one is always having to make relentless exclusions. Had it not been for my from-time-to-time promises to write stories, much that had been pressing against the door might have remained pressing against it in vain. I do not feel I 'invented' anything I wrote. It seems to me that during the war the overcharged subconsciousnesses of everybody overflowed and merged. It is because the general subconsciousness saturates these stories that they have an authority nothing to do with me. These are all wartime, none of them *war*, stories. There are no accounts of war action even as I knew it – for instance, air raids. Only one character – in 'Mysterious Kôr' – is a soldier; and he only appears as a homeless wanderer round a city. These are, more, studies of climate, war-climate, and of the strange growths it raised. I see war (or should I say feel war?) more as a territory than as a page of history: of its impersonal active historic side I have, I find, not written. Arguably, writers are always slightly abnormal people: certainly, in so-called 'normal' times my sense of the abnormal has been very acute. In war, this feeling of slight differentiation was suspended: I felt one with, and just like, everyone else. Sometimes I hardly knew where I stopped and somebody else began. The violent destruction of solid things, the explosion of the illusion that prestige, power and permanence attach to bulk and weight, left all of us, equally, heady and disembodied. Walls went down; and we felt, if not knew, each other. We all lived in a state of lucid abnormality. Till the proofs came, I had not re-read my stories since they were, singly, written. When I read them straight through as a collection, I was most struck by what they have in common. This integrates them and gives them a cumulative and collective meaning that no one, taken singly, has by itself. *The Demon Lover* is an organic whole: not merely a collection, but somehow – for better or worse – a book. Also, the order in which the stories stand – an order come at, I may say, casually – seems itself to have a meaning, or to add a meaning, I did not foresee. We begin with a hostess who has not learned how with grace to open her own front door; we end with a pair of lovers with no place in which to sleep in each other's arms. In the first story, a well-to-do house in a polite square gives the impression of having been organically dislocated by shock; in the last, a pure abstract empty timeless city rises out of a little girl's troubled mind. Through the stories – in the order in which they are here placed – I find a rising tide of hallucination. The stories are not placed in the time-order in which they were first written – though, by chance, 'In the Square', placed first here, *is* the first in the book I wrote, in a hot, raid-less patch of 1941 summer, just after Germany had invaded Russia.

The hallucinations in the stories are not a peril; nor are the stories studies of mental peril. The hallucinations are an unconscious, instinctive, saving resort on the part of the characters: life, mechanized by the controls of wartime, and emotionally torn and impoverished by changes, had to complete itself in *some* way. It is a fact that in Britain, and especially in London, in wartime many people had strange deep intense dreams. 'Whatever else I forget about the war,' a friend said to me, 'I hope I may never forget my own dreams, or some of the other dreams I have been told. We have never dreamed like this before; and I suppose we shall never dream like this again.' Dreams by night, and the fantasies – these often childishly innocent – with which formerly matter-of-fact people consoled themselves by day were compensations. Apart from them, I do not think that the *desiccation*, by war, of our day-to-day lives can be enough stressed. The outsize World War news was stupefying: headlines and broadcasts came down and down on us in hammerlike chops, with great impact but, oddly, little reverberation. The simple way to put it was: 'One cannot take things in.' What was happening was out of all proportion to our faculties for knowing, thinking and checking up. The circumstances under which ordinary British people lived were preposterous – so preposterous that, in a dull way, they simplified themselves. And all the time we knew that compared with those on the Continent we in Britain could not be said to suffer. Foreign faces about the London streets had personal pain and impersonal history sealed up behind the eyes. All this pressure drove egotism underground, or made it whiten like grass under a stone. And self-expression in small ways stopped – the small ways had been so very small that we had not realized how much they amounted to. Planning fun, going places, choosing and buying things, dressing yourself up, and so on. All that stopped. You used to know what you were like from the things you liked, and chose. Now there was not what you liked, and you did not choose. Any little remaining choices and pleasures shot into new proportion and new value: people paid big money for little bunches of flowers.

Literature of the Resistance has been steadily coming in from France. I wonder whether in a sense all wartime writing is not resistance writing? Personal life here, too, put up its own resistance to the annihilation that was threatening it – war. Everyone here, as is known, read more: and what was sought in books – old books, new books –

was the communicative touch of personal life. To survive, not only physically but spiritually, was essential. People whose homes had been blown up went to infinite lengths to assemble bits of themselves – broken ornaments, odd shoes, torn scraps of the curtains that had hung in a room – from the wreckage. In the same way, they assembled and checked themselves from stories and poems, from their memories, from one another's talk. Outwardly, we accepted that at this time individual destiny became an obsession in every heart. You cannot depersonalize persons. Every writer during this time was aware of the personal cry of the individual. And he was aware of the passionate attachment of men and women to every object or image or place or love or fragment of memory with which his or her destiny seemed to be identified, and by which the destiny seemed to be assured. The search for indestructible landmarks in a destructible world led many down strange paths. The attachment to these when they had been found produced small worlds-within-worlds of hallucination – in most cases, saving hallucination. Writers followed the paths they saw or felt people treading, and depicted those little dear saving illusory worlds. I have done both in *The Demon Lover* stories. You may say that these resistance-fantasies are in themselves frightening. I can only say that one counteracts fear by fear, stress by stress. In 'The Happy Autumn Fields', one finds a woman projected from flying-bombed London, with its day-and-night eeriness, into the key emotional crisis of a Victorian girlhood. In 'Ivy Gripped the Steps', a man in the early 'forties peers through the rusted fortifications and down the dusty empty perspectives of a seaside town at the Edwardian episode that has crippled his faculty for love. In 'The Inherited Clock', a girl is led to find the key to her own neurosis inside a timepiece. The past, in all these cases, discharges its load of feeling into the anaesthetized and bewildered present. It is the 'I' that is sought – and retrieved at the cost of no little pain. And the ghosts definite in 'Green Holly', questionable (for are they subjective purely?) in 'Pink May', 'The Cheery Soul' and 'The Demon Lover' what part do they play? They are the certainties. The bodiless foolish wanton, the puritan other presence, the tipsy cook with her religion of English fare, the ruthless young soldier lover unheard of since 1916: hostile or not, they rally, they fill the vacuum for the uncertain 'I'.

I am sorry that my stories do not contain more 'straight' pictures of the wartime scene. Such pictures could have been interesting: they *are* interesting in much of the brilliant reportage that exists. I know that, in these stories, the backgrounds, and sometimes the circumstances, are only present by inference. Allow for the intensely subjective mood into which most of the characters have been cast. Remember that these impulsive movements of fantasy are by products of the non-impulsive major routine of war. These are between-time stories – mostly reactions from, or intermissions between, major events. They show a levelled-down time, when a bomb on your house was as inexpedient but not more abnormal than a cold in your head. There was an element of chanciness and savageness about everything – even the arrival at a country house for Christmas. The claustrophobia of not being able to move about freely and without having to give account of yourself – not, for instance, being able to visit a popular seaside resort, within seventy miles of London, between 1940 and 1944 – appears in many: notably, in 'Ivy Gripped the Steps'. The ghostly social pattern of London life – or, say, the conventional pattern one does not easily break, and is loath to break because it is 'I'-saving – appears in the vacant politeness of 'In the Square', and in the inebriate night-club conversation, and in 'Careless Talk'. These are ways in which some of us did go on – after all, we had to go on *some* way. And the worthless little speaker in 'Pink May' found the war made a moratorium for her married conscience. Yes, only a few were heroic purely: and see how I have not drawn the heroic ones! But everyone was pathetic – more than they knew. Owing, though, to the thunder of those inordinate years, we were shaken out of the grip of our own pathos.

In wartime, even in Britain, much has been germinating. *What*, I do not know – who does, yet, know? – but I felt the germination; and feel it, here and there, in these stories now that I read them through. These are received impressions of happening things; impressions that stored themselves up and acquired force without being analysed or considered. These, as wartime stories, are at least contemporary – twenty, forty, sixty years hence they may be found interesting as documents, even if they are found negligible as art. This discontinuous writing, nominally 'inventive', is the only diary I have kept. Transformed into images in the stories, there *may* be important psychological facts: if so, I did not realize their importance. Walking in the darkness of the nights of six years (darkness which transformed a capital city into a network of inscrutable canyons) one developed new bare alert senses, with their own savage warnings and notations. And by day one was always making one's own new maps of a landscape always convulsed by some new change. Through it all, one probably picked up more than can be answered for. I cannot answer for much that is in these stories, except to say that I know they are all true – true to the general life that was in me at the time. Taken singly, they are disjected snapshots – snapshots taken from close up, too close up, in the middle of the *mêlée* of a battle. You cannot *render*, you can only embrace – if it means embracing to suffocation-point – something vast that is happening right on top of you. Painters have painted, and photographers who were artists have photographed, the tottering lace-like architecture of ruins, dark mass-movements of people, and the untimely brilliance of flaming skies. I cannot paint or photograph like this – I have isolated, I have made for the particular, spot-lighting faces or cutting out gestures that are not even the faces or gestures of great sufferers. This is how I am, how I feel, whether in war or peacetime; and only as I am and feel can I write. As I said at the start, though I criticize these stories now, afterwards, intellectually, I cannot criticize their content. They are the particular. But through the particular, in wartime, I felt the high-voltage current of the general pass.

Ireland Makes Irish, 15 August 1946, *Vogue*, Essay

Ireland makes Irish, there is no doubt. It is impossible, for any length of time, to be *in* this small vivid country and not *of* her. For centuries she has been drawing strangers to her, absorbing them, kindling something in them, and moulding them into replicas of her own stock. Look back at the past, at history – how first Strongbows,[1] Anglo-Normans, then the Elizabethans, then the Cromwellians came to conquer and seize, and stayed to possess and love. In about two generations, we reckon here, the non-indigenous family has begun to show all the native traits. No country, probably, has taken a sweeter or by the end more gentle revenge upon its invaders.

What has proved so winning, so holding, is, I think, the manner of life here – life infused with a tempo and temperament bred of the magic Irish light and the soft air. Inevitably, I speak of the manner of Irish life I know best: that of the country houses. Many of these were built by former invaders who struck roots: the blending of their stone faces into the green surround, so that the houses look like a natural part of the landscape, seems to symbolise the acclimatisation of their owners' spirits to the adopted land. Indoors, something at once grandiose and nonchalant seems at once to lull and to animate the rooms. Inherited from the old native lords of Ireland, who kept open house, there is a high tradition of sociability – here, there is no halfway: you must either enjoy this flux of people coming and going or adopt the other extreme and announce yourself a recluse. Neighbourliness – unchecked by the sometimes extreme isolation of country houses – is a habit. Then, there is the enormous, encircling element of the out-of-doors, which begins to beckon you from the moment you open your eyes in the morning. What a great part of this life is spent in the open air! All the year round – if you stay all the year round – sport, the farm, the garden, a dozen other calls and duties and pleasures set up a hardy indifference to the capricious weather.

And even indoors, the rooms themselves never have a totally indoor feeling: all day, through their many big windows, they are pervaded by the sky's light and the rustle of trees. In their grates, log fires blaze with their pale flame most of the year round – for in Ireland really hot spells are few – and these fires are magnetic during brief indoor interludes of the day. As evening approaches, more logs are piled on; the warm light flickers through the dusk of the room. And these ever-burning hearths symbolise, too, I think, a genuine intensity of home life, a centring of interests, a democracy of the old and the young – a sharing of whatever may be afoot by the children and the many dogs. Children ride hard and, given their heads, run wild: the school room is an unwelcome alternative to the river, the woods and the stable yard. Above all, as part of this scheme of things, the Irish servant is not to be overlooked: from the patriarchal butler, with his Old Testament vocabulary, down to the young 'mountainy' kitchenmaid with her bog-water eyes, there extends a benevolent attitude to 'the Family' tempered, I ought to say, by an extreme shrewdness. Less numerous, it is true, than they used to be, Irish country house servants, indoor and outdoor, remain a host in themselves. What they do not know about what is going on is, you will soon discover, not worth knowing. In trouble they are allies, in an emergency fellow clansmen; and nobody enters more thoroughly into the spirit of a party.

Much in this way of life is uniquely Irish, a carrying on of self-sufficiency and feudalism from the long-ago days when the Irish lord's castle was a little state or court in itself. But much, also, is unique chiefly in its survival: there are, or used to be, affinities everywhere. I have heard Irish country houses likened to those in Poland and pre-Revolutionary Russia – and indeed, the life on country estates described in nineteenth-century Russian novels, Tolstoy's and Turgenev's, has always seemed more than half familiar to me. Also, I have been given to understand that these Irish houses – or rather, perhaps, the way of life that they stand for – are not unlike some in the Deep South of the United States.

Few of these Irish houses are, by European reckoning, very old – the mullioned, quadrangled Elizabethan pile of England and the peach-pink brick manor are equally unknown here. The majority of our houses are Georgian, and are anything from modestly to magnificently Italianate, according to their owner's rank and wealth and their own size. Very often the settings are of a dreamlike beauty: there was always a tendency to build overlooking rivers and in rivers this country is rich. Gleaming curves of water, clifflike rocks, the varying tapestry of woods and supple outline of mountains are to be seen from windows.

Our ancestors' love of the scenic had, however, to be kept in check by their desire for shelter and dread of gales – in some cases, caution won, and we then have mansions sunk deep in lush green saucers of park and wood. I should make clear that the 'park' of the English big house is here, in Ireland, known as the 'demesne.' Demesnes are, usually, encircled by mile upon mile of grey stone wall; these having been built, in many cases, to give employment during the distress of the famine times. The appearance of such a wall along the roadside indicates to the traveller that he is approaching a house: were the wall not enough, he could note the planting of trees – the screens, knolls, groves and, running in from the gateways, the apparently endless avenues of beech, chestnut, or lime. If our ancestors' *folie de grandeur*[2] embarrassed us, their descendants, with mansions of sometimes preposterous size, we owe to their large view and foresight these lordly trees.

Yes, the time-colour of this way of Irish country living *is*, decidedly, eighteenth-century. Each country gentleman, no less than his neighbour the duke, was an authoritarian and, to the last inch, a character. On the single, square block of the gentleman's seat, inhabited by himself and his family all the year round, as on the colonnaded, salooned, and terraced mansions of the peer of the United Kingdom, visited for only a few months in each year, one finds reflected the influence of the Grand Tour, the classic engraving and the liberal days when Europeans of culture were one great family.

Humanism stocked little or large libraries with books which their owners, drunk with the open air (and not, I fear, always, with that only), respected but were too drowsy to read. Cellars and stables, extensive, were built to be kept stocked. Now coach-houses have become garages, but the yard trees still cast their shadows over mounting-blocks, and the old rich smell comes from harness rooms. Courtyards of out-buildings – dairies, meat and game larders, 'wool rooms,' storerooms of all kinds, carpenters' sheds – show how each of these houses used to function as the self-supporting unit it once was – when the nearest town lay at the end of a day's journey and roads were not lightly set out upon. The walled garden, large enough to provision a small army, lies often some distance from the house.

All our architecture is not Italian-square: in the decades around 1800 Gothic romanticism, also, invaded Ireland, giving us our sense of famous castles. Some (as, for instance, Lismore, County Waterford) were raised on old Anglo-Norman fortified sites – the 'modern' castle incorporating ancient wells, deep-sunk networks of rock passages, battlements, and keeps with walls eight foot thick. And inevitably, many inherit ghosts. With the theatricality of the nineteenth-century crenellations, turrets, pointed windows and polished, dusky galleries and corridors, only the purist would quarrel. It should be said, at the same time, that not every self-styled 'castle' in Ireland *is* a castle: the possession, anywhere in its grounds, of a darkling old Norman fortress-tower (and of these there are many), entitles to this dignified appellation the more modern, unassuming and sunny house.

Gardening, in this country, rapidly becomes an infatuation – and, indeed, what gardens there are to show! The alluvial soil round the river houses, the steamy, moist, sheltered heat of the valleys, produce a luxuriance that is almost frightening. The conformation of the ground, so often, above rivers, in natural terraces, tempts the gardener on and on into further landscape effects. Ruined towers are niched and draped with bloom. The walls and yew or beech hedges of the enclosed gardens make ideal backgrounds for deep herbaceous borders. From peaty soil, azaleas and rhododendrons blaze through the early summers. Tropic speed and richness of growth, here, of course, cut both ways – allow a few months to elapse, and Nature, with her own inordinate beauty, has obliterated all marks of man's, or of woman's, hand.

Land of bogs and rivers and woods and banks and wide fields, how can Ireland be anything but a sporting country? Deep in the tradition, inseparable from the idea of life here, are the horse, the rod, and the gun. Of the Irish hunts, it is not necessary that I should sing the fame: they have great histories and propitious futures. And our trout streams and salmon rivers, equally, hold their place in the memories of great men all over the world. I think it one virtue of Ireland that sport and sportsmen are not isolated; they enjoy the goodwill, approval and interest of the countryside as a whole. Not here are hunting, shooting, and fishing regarded as the preserve of a special class: no particular snobbery, for instance, surrounds hunting: anybody who possibly can turn out does so, and everyone else is glad to see him do so. Households, great or small, down tools and rush to the windows to watch the hunt cross the land: rare, even in cities, is the black-coated worker who does not from time to time handle a gun or rod. Sport, here, is the mighty equaliser, the great solvent – in it, any difficulties or differences of race, politics or religion are forgotten, merged. There is no what one would call 'attitude' towards sport in Ireland; it is in the very air, as natural as love or death.

This way of life has its documentation and its literature. Arthur Young, for instance, that eminent and sociable eighteenth-century agriculturist, leaves us, in *A Tour in Ireland,* the record of a round of visits he paid to Irish country houses in the summer of 1776. Much that he had to say is still to the point. Young's *Tour* has lately been edited by Dr Constantia Maxwell,[3] to whose own pen we owe the contemporary but not less interesting *Country and Town in Ireland under the Georges*. Then, we have the vivacious *Retrospections of Dorothea Herbert* – a late eighteenth-century young lady[4] whom nonstop party-going, throughout the south of Ireland, coupled with love trouble, sent mad. These three books picture the past – things have sobered down since the days when Miss Herbert danced, Arthur Young took coach, and the four first Georges reigned over their Irish kingdom. None the less, a thread of psychological truth knits up Ireland's yesterday with her today. Equally, the mirror which Irish fiction has held up to Irish life does not tarnish: the novels of Maria Edgeworth and the stories of Somerville and Ross[5] show us an Ireland that still, in essentials, lives.

Are we, then, in Ireland, unchanged – perhaps too wonderfully unchanged – in a changing world? Are these houses, with all that they stand for, anachronisms? Fairy-tale retreats from the harsher realities of the twentieth century? Play-houses? No, surely, I, who love these houses, would rather see the last of them razed to the ground than believe that true; and I do not believe it true. Inherent in this way of life, as in all others, is responsibility; the sense of one's debt to society. Ireland, so free with her good times, is none the less no place for the professional good-timer; she has a salutary, rigorous, harsh streak. Her very weather – those gales from the sea or mountains, those foggy dripping silences of mid-winter, those days upon days, at all seasons, of binding and blinding rain – searches out the weak places in your morale.

And her weather is only one of the tests which Ireland applies to character. Her people, themselves, are great summers-up: they soon know what you or I am worth – and by that, I do *not* mean, worth in money. Money, here as elsewhere, can buy much, but not everything – and in Ireland, it is just what money cannot buy that is most worth having: affection, fidelity, respect. The good feeling that has kept Irish houses going has been, always, a matter of reciprocity: 'the Family' in the big house has its part to play; and that part may call for everything that one has. Courage, dignity, fair mindedness, and a willingness to understand and help in other people's troubles are expected. And, what is due to one's employees and neighbours is no less due to the country in which these houses stand.

These Twenty-six Counties of which I write are not merely romantic old Ireland; they are young Eire – and Eire working out her destiny, grappling with her problems, hoping to take her place worthily in the world of today. She has a right to ask for the understanding – and, should she need it, also the help – of those who by birth or choice live within her shores. Domestically, we are managing to adapt these great rambling houses to both the needs and restrictions of modern living – simplifying and cutting at every turn, using electricity to save manpower. In the same sense, I believe it is possible to bring these beautiful legacies of the old world into line with the more arduous ideals of the new.

How They Live in Ireland, Conquest by Cheque-book, 1946, *Contact*, Essay

Ireland – the Twenty-six Counties, Eire – is again in the throes of invasion.

'How many times, let me see, did they conquer us with the sword?' says my friend, rhetorical in a bar in Dublin. 'This time, they come to conquer us with the cheque-book.'

I hope it may not come to conquest: there is bound, however, to be a stiff battle between indigenous old values and imported new. The Ireland of peasants has always moved slowly: the climate has made for fatalism, the Catholic religion for a mystique. A time lag is to be felt in the atmosphere: for the first few hours after the arrival from England (such a short journey!) one experiences a dizzying sense of strangeness.

The Irish standard of living has been, up to now, low. Look at Mick Mac's wages: in the towns his people would not do much better. The secure class, but in a small way, are the civil servants. The teachers have, with reason, been agitating for higher pay. There *is* big money in the country, but it does not travel out of the middle class: the 'strong' farmers, the shopkeepers in the towns, the merchants and the professional people have it. The gentry are, in relation to their liabilities, as poor as the peasants and as behind the times.

Money having all run into one deep narrow pocket, its effect on the general Irish idea of living has on the whole been small. That is what I mean by a low standard – 'simple' would, perhaps, be a better word. A very much smaller percentage of people keep motorcars. Taste – in dress, furnishings, food, entertainment – is unsophisticated. England and the United States, between them, have succeeded in dumping their cast-off fashions there: jazz upholstery, orange taffeta, imitation Sheraton interspersed with chromium tubular experiments still dominate the average middle-class home. Farmers' daughters, with moony-milky faces of the 1840 album type, go to Mass or to town in crenellated veil-hung hats. Rich manufacturers copy the *Tatler* photographs, enlarging the check of the tweeds by half again. Not much wine is drunk – after the fall of France, when imports stopped, supplies lasted much longer in Ireland. Gala food is at the twelve-year-old level: much mayonnaise and cream.

The expenditure of the rich middle classes is, in short, childish, resulting in an effect of innocent vulgarity. There is one inhibition, a lurking fear of any ostentation that could be jumped upon. Why? Because in Ireland it is fatal, the beginning of the end, to expose oneself to ridicule. And nothing is found more ridiculous, nothing is visited more cruelly, than the attempt to hoist oneself out of one's own class.

This must be true of the bourgeoisie of any country still haunted by the romantic-reactionary idea. That idea makes for a far greater austerity than is now thought. It denies moral prestige to the possession of money. (Land is another thing.) Class, in itself, as a principle, is not attacked in Ireland: it is part of the *status quo* that the Church supports. The landed gentry and aristocracy were denounced in so far as they were British *protégés*, collaborators from the national point of view, and in possession of forcibly seized land: now the land has gone back to the people, they are innocuous. And more, they have gained a place, if a shadowy one, in the Irish moral-mystical plan. Their obligations have outlived their wealth: so long as they live up to their obligations they are welcome to stay. Those who were not wanted had their houses burned by the people between 1919 and 1922. Those who stayed farm the acres of their remaining land, and are linked with their employees and neighbours in the struggle for life. They are the Protestant minority, decimated by several wars; their sons always fight in the British army – though the attitude of the Irish gentry towards England is by now equivocal.

This is true of the Ireland of up to now. I should say, of up to 1939 – for the war's effect on neutral Ireland was that of cold storage. The isolation of Eire (after the suspension of travel in 1940) acted as a preservative: if anything, traits and habits became more set and more marked. At the same time, independent ideas of some value began to germinate. *Now*, those are being threatened – as everything else in Ireland is being threatened – from the outside: by the postwar invasion.

Now, not in spite of but because of being old-fashioned, Ireland has become very desirable. Not only her food but her mood is being suddenly bid for and bought up. The boom, the inrush shows a reaction against the fatigues and horrors of the mid-1940s. Normal travel facilities from England (though not yet *to* England) having been restored, summer holidaymakers came over in thousands to eat, rest and look at places which have not known war. Tourists are no part of the menace of which I speak; they were expected, and prepared for.

No; the menace (which we may exaggerate) is the exploitation of Eire as a residential playground for the non-indigenous rich. Just now, Irish country houses are fetching fabulous prices. In Eire, sport – hunting, shooting, fishing – remains unthreatened; comparatively speaking, their cost is low. The lower income tax is an inducement to naturalise. Drink and food plentiful; a pretty steady supply of domestic servants. Wages (as above stated) still, as compared to England, fantastically low. A climatic blend of ease and hilarity. In short, in fact, apparently, the good-timers' paradise.

And, of course, the multiplying and speeding up of air services is a great factor. Eire finds herself suddenly in the heart of the map. The Shannon Airport links her with America on the one hand, the European continent on the other. Collinstown Airport (Dublin) connects with London.

Eire doesn't want her rates of living sent up by people who can afford to pay any prices, and her morals sent down by sophisticates who imagine that in Ireland anything goes. The country, actually, *is* making its own slow but dogged way towards progress, to an enlightened concept of living. Her government has the problems of housing, town-planning, health, and education under closer consideration than might appear. Eire, at this juncture, vitally does not want her apparent backwardness patronised and exploited. Above all, she does not want 'passenger' residents, a new wave of settlers whose object is to bypass responsibility. The country has a strong, inbred sense of propriety – woe, in the long run, to those who offend. Six years of isolated neutrality, with its problems, have gone far to help Eire to grow up. She does not feel like a playground and does not want to be one. Against this new weapon, the cheque book, what defences is she going to put up?

Writings from Paris Peace Conference, 1946, *Cork Examiner*

It is hard to separate the Peace Conference, 1946, from its setting, Paris. For me it would be, even, hopeless to try. The power to purge facts from one's own impressions belongs to the seasoned journalist that I am not. I am here as a free-lance, an onlooker, granted the *entrée* to the Luxembourg by the goodwill of those who hold that novelists should be let picture history, in its actual making, though they may not record it. Showing my pass, I entered the Palace courtyard, on the day of the Opening, with a sensation of awe – and that has not worn off since. Many things that the diplomat or the journalist proper would take for granted were new to me: from that hour, I have remained absorbed and impressed. At the same time I cannot leave behind me, when I enter the Luxembourg, my continuous consciousness of Paris at its gates – a Paris I had not seen since spring 1939, and which therefore invaded me with a renewed magic and a renewed force.

Or, should I say a quarter of Paris? The city, after years in which so much has happened, is still too much for me to take in as a whole. Perhaps deliberately, though also because the Conference ties me here, I have kept – except for a few excursions across the river – to this uphill world of the Luxembourg (Gardens as well as Palace), the Odéon, the fringes of the Sorbonne. Up here, it is very quiet, almost provincial; and one may see – as perhaps in no other quarter of any other great city – the pattern of everyday life. The narrow streets run deep between high, old, mysterious, dust-pale houses. There are intermittent, small, brave, rather empty provision shops; modest restaurants; hand-laundries from which comes the warm smell of ironing. At the top are the railings of the Luxembourg Gardens, with, between the clipped chestnuts, enchanting glimpses of pools, statues, the purple and rose and crimson of flowerbeds. The Gardens drain into themselves all the child-life of the quarter – and, they surround the Conference on three sides. It is very quiet – at the height of the day you hear a canary singing, a child practising the piano, dishes being washed up after a meal. And, every quarter-hour, the soft, toneless striking of the Luxembourg clock. It is a neighbourhood of old people, their faces inscrutable with memories and thoughts, and of sleek cats.

Housewives come and go, with their high-spirited faces and flat-heeled walk. This is the quarter, the silence through which go roaring, a long urgent file, the Delegates' cars – on their way to the Conference, from the Right Bank. This is the plan of small lives – lives which have lost much, and have desperately much to hope for – which reaches up to the very walls of the Palace in which the world's future is being planned.

In my consciousness, I feel a connecting thread between the men, in there, sitting round the green tables, and the children, out there, playing among the green lawns.

Certainly, the Conference has not been set on a drab stage. About the Luxembourg Palace, for all its strength, there is something feminine: one does not forget that it was built by a Queen.[6] In the brilliant blue weather, heatwave, of early August, the Palace gave out all it had of dignified theatricality. For renascent Paris, as well as for the visiting delegates, the opening, July 29, was an emotional as well as a spectacular day. People pressed up to the barriers as the cars streamed under the beflagged archway. Followed, inevitably, an anticlimax: lessening interest outside, threatening boredom within – for, indeed, the initial Plenary Sessions, inescapable, time-losing tribute to formality and to the *amour propre* of the Delegations, not only did not cut very much ice but made one doubt whether ice ever could *be* cut. Resounding phrases, irreproachable testaments to ideals, rolled, one after another, up to the dome of baking, chocolate-and-gold Hemicycle, through afternoon after afternoon of the heatwave. Tier upon tier sat the impassive diplomats, the distinguished visitors, the saturated journalists at the top. Nothing, one learned, would begin; nothing that was anything could be expected to begin, till the Plenary Sessions had run their course. Gloves were due to come off; and gloves came off, pretty promptly, with the opening of the Debates on Procedure – which were to put Conference nerves to their first test by being held at night, and running on, at the worst, into the small hours of the morning.

For the present, the Hemicycle plays no more part. All matters the Conference has in hand are concentrated in the different Commission rooms, behind sound-proof, heavily moulded doors. From the courtyard, the original bustle has subsided – the hands of the clock above the archway move round; the gendarmes half in a dream maintain their official stance – occasionally, the mid-morning or mid-afternoon hush is broken by an amplified voice calling for the car of a Delegate who has decided to leave early. Yes, everything happens indoors: from ten in the morning on through to a late lunch-hour, from three or four in the afternoon till around eight o'clock, the interior Luxembourg, on three sides of the courtyard, hums with the muted steadiness of a dynamo. Through the downstairs hall and stone passages of the centre block reverberate, with oddly ghostly effect, amplified voices of speakers at the Commissions. From the Press Room, Reception Bureau, and honeycomb-like offices of the secretariat comes the rustling stutter of typewriters, small and great. Piercingly, and irregularly, an electric bell rings. The dim electricity of the passages lights announcement-boards to which stencils are being always repinned. Packages of documents, weighty, are unloaded from vans, carried up steps. The come-and-go of messengers, on the stairs, in the anterooms, through the long enfilades of gold-and-white doors, is by now methodical and unhurried. On the grand entrance staircase used by the Delegates, the cherry-pink carpet, since August, has worn perceptibly thinner.

The tempo, temperature, temper of the Peace Conference has, manifestly, varied from week to week. Press and radio have, in a broad way, registered its variations. Of course, as news must be news, there can but be a tendency to headline crises, or 'duels,' and to understress the no less trying effect of long dragging, nagging sessions which lead nowhere. Inside the Luxembourg, it is late August that remains on record as the worst bad patch, so far. Blotting-out rain, the strain of over-much work on small staffs, claustrophobia, and the rawness of feeling on subjects not to be got past set up a mood of discouragement, which, plus some verbal fireworks, could but have its effect on the outside world. On August 10 I had to go home to Ireland for three weeks: thus, I was to have for that period the singularly depressing long-distance view. 'What,' they said, 'you've been at the Peace Conference? Doesn't come to much, does it? There they sit and sit . . . How it drags on . . . Can't well get up from their tables till they've accomplished *something* . . . No doubt the Delegates are in no hurry to leave Paris? . . . One hears they go to parties the whole time?'

Cheerful falsehood embedded in a certain amount of melancholy truth makes one smile. There has been little of the Congress of Vienna about the Paris Conference, 1946. Receptions on the part of the Delegations have been reciprocal, functional and demure. No ladies, others than those in the secretariat, have accompanied any of the parties; and the Russians and some of the Central Europeans have not burdened their luggage with evening dress. Among those who prefer to make the concession, '*le smoking*' rather than the white tie is the rule. At the same time – and, surely, happily? – things cannot but be kept at a particular psychic-social pitch by this enveloping element of *la ville lumière* – the floodlit Place de la Concorde, in which cars move like dark fish in a sea of gold. Most telling of all, as host to the Conference, the French Government brings to its hospitality an inspired sense of the romantic, the nostalgic and the spectacular. Instance – among many – the gala night at the Opera (when the façade became, to the eye, a cut-out of crimson cellophane and staircase and foyer challenged a Lubitsch[7] *mise-en-scène)* and the Versailles sunset party – where, as the last reflections died in the *Galerie des Glaces*, bugles called from the terrace over the darkening trees and more and more lights blazed on the indoor flowers. Versailles was, for that evening, called from the past to play her part of glory. And, surely these voices France can call on speak? The undying Old World seems to salute the New.

My return to Paris early in September synchronised, by chance, with yet one more of those changes in the interior climate of the Luxembourg. (Outwardly, too, there was movement, acceleration – brighter, alternately clouding and sunny skies; the chestnut trees in the Gardens now crisp with autumn.) Some of the smaller Commissions had in sight, already, the accomplishment of their work; all had, in their different rooms of the Palace, moved clear of the fulvous zone. In an atmosphere of, if anything, colourless equability, business was moving forward, points were being decided – things (though the world might not know it) were getting done. In August, I had been content to hover about the Conference in general – aware of its currents, interested by its rumours. This time, in September, this new, stimulating concentration in the Conference air made me wish to attach myself to one Commission only, and to follow it steadily through its work. The Political and Territorial Commission, Italy, was – and remains – the core and nerve-centre of Luxembourg. At it, all Delegations are represented. Its extensive agenda holds two combustible items: the Italo-Yugoslav frontier, and Trieste.

The Italian Commission (to give it its brief name) sits in the *Grande Salle*, upstairs in the centre block. The *salle*, of immense length, is of an over-gilded, tasteless magnificence that comes, with time, to have a hypnotic charm. Six high windows open, north, on the courtyard; a vast chandelier, above the conference table, with bunches of crystal wall-lamps, light up on darker mornings. Smoking is permitted: a blue haze hangs in the air above the Delegates' heads. This Commission, surprising as it may seem, has, so far, set up a record of amiability: the good feeling has, by now, been going on long enough to become a matter of comment by the Chairman. Actually, the Chairman (the South African Mr Lief Egeland) is himself to be congratulated, and one may hope will be – he combines a close executive grip with a sort of smiling, social control; not unlike that of a host's over his table. There may also be the factor (Harold Nicolson suggests this elsewhere) that a number of men cannot sit around the same table, in the same places, day after day without striking up some sort of physical-neighbourly good accord. Here, in the *Grande Salle* of the Luxembourg, one is in the presence of men whose features, traits, intonations, gestures, and casts of mind have become, to each other, familiar; one might say, sympathetic. M. Vishinsky's[8] shovelling gestures and pachydermatous, seeking turns of the head; the ironical smile and quizzical, heavy-lidded sidelong glance of M. Bebler (on whom devolved the long exposition of the Yugoslav claims); the youthful, clear-cut frown of concentration on the brow of the South African Mr Jordaan; the doglike attentive attitude (hands, like paws, on the table) of Australia's Colonel Hodgson – these are looked for, in turn. No less does a rustle of expectation precede the rising of Senator Connall – to turn impressively, to make a pause no less so, to state, adjure, invoke. Only one personality, M. Molotov's, gives off, when present, an absolute and inhuman greyness. Speech, with him, seems a calculated emission: it comes out in an atmosphere that is cold, dead.

In spite – or is it because? – of the *Grande Salle's* calmness, widening divisions of purpose are to be strongly felt; and still more, in the case of the Russian *bloc*, the functioning of the iron directive. It could but be obvious to a child, to a savage, that Poles, Czechs, Ukrainians, Yugoslavs are attached to the USSR as are the fingers to the palm of a hand. Charges of pro-Italianism, of reactionary sympathies, against the other (or, 'Western') Delegations are not for long allowed to remain absent from the lips of any of that *bloc*. For the onlooker, there is the sinister fascination of watching Russia create, by her own suspicions, a psycho-political situation that, actually, not only has not existed so far but need not, in spite of Russia, ever exist at all.

* * *

General Smuts's tribute to French recovery has been well-timed. It had been felt to be owing. One honours the General for this *amende honorable*. But also, apart from the speaker's wish to withdraw former hurting remarks, he has given voice to a very general impression. Whatever the achievement of the Peace Conference, nobody who has attended it has anything but praise for its setting, and for the smoothness with which the machinery of the Luxembourg has run. Paris, indeed, has thrown herself heart and soul into her role as host of the delegations. Civility and consideration have appeared at all points; and, still better, there has been a heart-warming atmosphere of goodwill. For my own part, I remember, before the war, a certain crossness on the part of the French functionaries: one hesitated to address oneself to a gendarme or present oneself at an official desk. The Parisian temper once seemed, to the visitor, overbearing and often short.

This has corrected itself in a striking way. Not merely politeness but real good nature reigns in the Paris air – nor is it confined to the surround of the Luxembourg. This seems worth remarking because, surely, good temper is a sign of good morale. The Paris gendarmes of 1946 are young and keen; they enter with smiling zest into the extra duties imposed on them by the Conference. At the outset, until a routine had established itself, those duties were sufficiently arduous; nor, in the weeks since the Conference has had time to settle into its course, has there been any marked relaxation. The scrutiny of entrance cards to the Palace has, though conducted politely, remained inexorably close. Before a major session, the business of getting an apparently endless stream of official cars in under one narrow archway into the Palace courtyard, directing their movements in that constricted space, parking the more important cars round the walls and getting the others out again through another arch, is no small one. At the close of the session the same process must be gone through in reverse. Cars the courtyard cannot contain are parked in neighbouring streets; and are expected to present themselves within a few seconds of being summoned by the loud-speaker. Any delay in a delegate's car arriving could cause endless umbrage – for national vanity, it must be said, among the twenty-one nations lies pretty near the surface.

The days of the opening, July 29 and the days immediately after it, did, it is true, just verge on confusion. Paris, for that first fortnight or so, was in the grip of a radiant heatwave. Cloudless blue skies and brilliant sunshine – in which the flags of the nations gave out their full effect – could not but be seen as a good omen: none the less, the heat for many meant extra strain. The Peace Conference formally opened at three o'clock, but since early morning the Palace had been a Babel. The world's Press, presenting credentials and queuing up for their cards, were vociferous and not always easy-tempered: here, again, national *amour propre* came in. It transpired that while the issue of blue cards (admitting journalists to the Palace itself) could, with discretion, be fairly liberal, the supply of pink cards must be severely cut. Pink cards gave admission to the Hemicycle, where the inaugural Plenary Sessions were to be held. The Hemicycle is considerably less roomy than the Dáil in Dublin; and accommodation for the Press, in the top gallery, was found to be hopelessly insufficient. All and more of the tact of the French staff at the reception bureau was required. Disappointed news-hawks clamoured and milled around. Many, resigned, took up a more or less permanent position in the Press bar. The serving of refreshments was not the only function of the bar – a large, pleasant, white-and-gold room with French windows opening on to a garden. Adjoining the Press room – in which a table was allotted to the Press of each of the nations – the bar assumed the nature of a club. There was no better place for taking, from day-to-day, the temperature of the Conference. Soon, an amicable (if quite unofficial) system of lending out the pink tickets was arranged: there was no journalist who, as far as I know, did not at one time or another mount the stairs to the Hemicycle. Many, to be frank, were soon driven down again by the pompousness of some of the delegates' opening speeches and by the grilling heat. It was agreed that the Conference would not get down to brass tacks till it had entered upon the committee stage. There was an immediate rise of tension and interest once those early Plenary Sessions were declared over. 'Fireworks' began with the Debates on Procedure, which continued late into the hot nights. It was known, any gap or loophole left in rules for procedure might, sooner or later, cause a breakdown. It was during those Procedure debates that Russia first showed her determination to pull things her way.

Yes, it was then that raised, tense and suspicious voices first travelled over the amplifiers into the outlying rooms and stone passages of the Luxembourg. To myself, the effect of this amplification was uncanny. After the Plenary Sessions, one or another commission was 'laid on' (for the benefit of the Press and general personnel of the Conference) at all hours of the Luxembourg's working days – and nights.

About the character and position of the Luxembourg Palace there is something propitious to the idea of peace. The Luxembourg, as many will remember, stands uphill, on the left bank of the river. It is surrounded on three sides by public gardens as lovely as any in the world – where children play, fountains plash, flowerbeds send up their mosaic of colour, old people potter serenely along the shady alleys of clipped chestnuts, and statues, gleaming against the foliage, embody the happiest memories of France. In my own mind, as the Conference proceeded, I never ceased to feel a vital connection between the unconscious children playing around the green lawns, outdoors, and the intent men, indoors, seated around the green tables. A French mother, by whom I sat for a moment in the shade of a flowering oleander tree, raised her head from her sewing and gave a glance at the Palace. 'Peace for our children,' she said. 'That is what we are praying for; that is what we want.'

These, now as the Conference nears its close, are a few of my memories of its opening. I shall write, next, of my glimpses of it at work.

* * *

My time at the Peace Conference, in the capacity of freelance journalist, divided itself into two visits. I was in Paris and daily at the Luxembourg, from July 28 (the day before the opening) up to August 10; then, again, from September 3 to 25. In the interval I was at my house in Co. Cork. When I left Paris the first time, towards the middle of August, the Conference was just getting down to brass tacks – and some of these, as we know, were to prove uncomfortably sharp. While in Co. Cork I received – as we all did – the impression conveyed by Press and radio that things in the Luxembourg were going slowly, badly, in an atmosphere of acrimony and frustration. None of the friends with whom I talked here seemed to regard the future of the Conference with anything but pessimism. In a sense it was interesting to obtain, halfway through my time at the Luxembourg, this outside view. The Luxembourg, with its close concentration and esoteric talk, tends, inevitably, to become a world in itself: one loses the sense of what is going on outside. While in Ireland, I could endeavour to see things in perspective; also, to gather the repercussions of what was happening, from day-to-day in Paris, on the public – the ordinary man and woman. It might have been well had some of the delegates and their overworked staffs been able to take this kind of 'breather' too.

For, when I returned to Paris, early in September, I found that discouraging reports had not been exaggerated. The Conference *had* been going through a bad patch – though this bad patch, it turned out, was towards its end. There had been stormy weather outdoors and in. The narrow, monotonous, taxing life of the delegations had been beginning to tell on the nerves of many – and that, unexpectedly early on. The average day of a member of a delegation is spent either in the Right

Bank hotel which is his headquarters, or in a committee room of the Luxembourg. Transit between one and the other is hurriedly made in a glassed-in car. Evenings and the great parts of nights are spent either over papers or in informal but none the less exacting conference with members of other delegations. Official entertainments remain official, merely providing an ironically festive background for the further talking of Conference 'shop.' The delegation member seldom meets outside people – except sometimes on Sunday when he may take a short tour through the surrounding country, he has no opportunity to relax or let up. It is not to be wondered at that, in his tired mind, in which the affairs of his particular committee go round and round, irritations should tend to loom over-large and difficulties to take on a false proportion.

Such conditions are, I suppose, unavoidable. The delegations are in Paris to work; their work has been, from the earliest, planned to schedule; extreme concentration, at whatever cost, is necessary. But these men, who have undertaken the almost superhuman task of building up world peace, are, it must be remembered, only human. In this particular, the East would appear to have the advantage of the West; the Russians, with their adherents, the Slav *bloc*, would seem not to have a nerve in their stocky frames. Eating largely, presumably sleeping deep, the Slavs (at least, those in evidence at the Conference) seem rubber-tyred against fatigue. Their irritability arises from quite another source: their by now palpable persecution-mania – which, I was told, even takes the form of a touchy childishness on the subject of seating accommodation, etc. It cannot be doubted that, in the late August 'bad patch,' the Russians were calculating upon, and exploiting, the temporary nerviness of their Western colleagues (or, as they preferred to see them, antagonists). It was the ideal moment to adopt a policy of obstruction for obstruction's sake. The effect of a Russian voice going unintelligibly on and on in an already jaded committee room can be that, exactly, of an electric drill.

I speak of 'temporary' nerviness, because, with the start of September, the Conference entered upon a better phase. It might be described as getting its second wind. Conditions, as above described, did not change; but somehow the delegations surmounted them. Myself being back in Paris by this time, I no longer saw any home newspapers or heard broadcasts; therefore I do not know whether Press and radio registered, as they should have done, this indoor climatic improvement in the Luxembourg. There was nothing spectacular in this psychological change; possibly one could only feel it inside the palace. 'We are all now as amiable as lambs,' a friend said to me. 'You might almost think that nothing could be happening. But quite a lot is happening – we are, I believe, beginning to get things done.'

I noticed other changes, on my September return. For one thing, the Press Bar and Press Room were comparatively empty. The Conference, as a discouraging topic, had, on the whole, been faded out of the news; the news-hawks had taken wing to more likely fields. Then, in the chains of secretarial rooms, up and down the stairs and along the passages, the original hectic clatter of the opening fortnight had given place to a steady workmanlike hum, to an orderly and methodical come and go. Returning, I felt an unexpected confidence in the Luxembourg as a factory of peace. Outside in the gardens, autumn gave crispness to the rustle of the trees.

During my August visit I had been content – like many other journalists, free-lance and otherwise – to hover about the Conference in general – picking up rumours, observing types and personalities, making flying entrances to the Hemicycle on a borrowed pink ticket, listening to snatches of radio-transfusion. That first fortnight of the Conference – my first Peace Conference – had been a deep and exciting draught in itself. But this second time on my September return, the increasing purposefulness of the Luxembourg atmosphere infected me. I wished to attach myself strictly to one commission and, during my time in Paris, follow its work through. I was fortunate in being able to obtain a ticket for the proceedings which were my immediate aim – the Territorial and Political Commission, Italy. This, one did not need telling, was now the core of the Conference. It was large, being attended by at least two or three members of each of the delegations. It was work of vast, one might say dangerous, importance; it had to deal with the combustible question of Trieste and also of the Italo-Yugoslav frontier – the proposed 'French Line.' That Commission has now, as you know, concluded its work. It is of some impressions gleaned from my three weeks' attendance at it that I am proposing next time to write.

Introduction to the Cresset Press edition of *Uncle Silas*, by Sheridan Le Fanu, 1947

I

Uncle Silas is a romance of terror. Joseph Sheridan Le Fanu lets us know that he expanded it from a short story (length, about fifteen pages) which he wrote earlier in his literary life and published, anonymously, in a magazine – under the title of 'A Passage in the Secret History of an Irish Countess'. As he does not give the name of the magazine I have not, so far, been able to trace the story. I should make further efforts to do so could I feel that its interest was very great: its initial interest, that is to say, *qua* story. It holds, it is true, the germ of the later novel – or, at least, of its plot. But about that plot itself there is little new. The exterior plot of *Uncle Silas* is traditional, well worn by the time Le Fanu took up his pen. What have we? The Wicked Uncle and the Endangered Heir. I need not point out the precedents even in English history. Also, this is the Babes in the Wood theme – but in *Uncle Silas* we have only one babe – feminine, in her late adolescence, and, therefore, the no less perpetual Beauty in Distress. Maud Ruthyn has her heroine-prototype in a large body of fiction which ran to excess in the gothic romances but is not finished yet – the distraught young lady clasping her hands and casting her eyes skyward to Heaven: she has no other friend . . . No, it is hard to see that simply uncle and niece, her sufferings, his designs, compressed, as they were at first, into a number of pages so small as to limit 'treatment' (Le Fanu's *forte*) could have made up into anything much more than the conventional magazine story of the day.

What *is* interesting is that Le Fanu, having written the story, should have been unable, still, to discharge its theme from his mind. He must have continued, throughout the years, to be obsessed, if subconsciously, by the niece and uncle. More, these two and their relationship to each other became magnetic to everything strangest and most powerful in his own imagination and temperament. The resultant novel, our *Uncle Silas*, owes the pressure, volume and spiritual urgency which make it comparable to *Wuthering Heights* to just this phenomenon of accretion. Accretion is a major factor in art. Le Fanu could not be rid of the niece and uncle till he had built around them a comprehensive book.

Something else draws my interest to the original story: its heroine, by the showing of the title, was Irish, by marriage if not birth. Joseph Sheridan Le Fanu (1814–73, grand-nephew of Sheridan the dramatist) was Irish; or rather Anglo-Irish. And *Uncle Silas* has always struck me as being an Irish story transposed to an English setting. The hermetic solitude and the autocracy of the great country house, the demonic power of the family myth, fatalism, feudalism and the 'ascendency' outlook are accepted facts of life for the race of hybrids from which Le Fanu sprang. For the psychological background of *Uncle Silas* it was necessary for him to invent nothing. Rather, he was at once exploiting in art and exploring for its more terrible implications what would have been the norm of his own heredity. Having, for reasons which are inscrutable, pitched on England as the setting for *Uncle Silas*, he wisely chose the North, the wildness of Derbyshire. Up there, in the vast estates of the landed old stock, there appeared, in the years when Le Fanu wrote (and still more in the years of which he wrote: the early 1840's) a time lag – just such a time lag as, in a more marked form, separates Ireland from England more effectually than any sea.

Le Fanu was not, in his generation, alone in seeing the possibilities of the country house from the point of view of drama, tension and mystery. We may comment on 'atmosphere': almost all the Victorians who were novelists used it without fuss. Wilkie Collins, for instance, wrings the last drop of effect from the woodgirt Hampshire mansion in *The Woman in White*, with its muffling, oppressive silence and eerie lake. The castles, granges and lonely halls back through romantic fiction are innumerable. One might, even, say that Le Fanu showed himself as traditional, or unoriginal, in his choice of setting as in his choice of plot. Only, while his contemporaries, the by then urbanized Victorian English, viewed the ancestral scene from the outside, the Irishman wrote out of what was in his bones.

Uncle Silas is, as a novel, Irish in two other ways: it is sexless, and it shows a sublimated infantilism. It may, for all I know, bristle with symbolism; but I speak of the story, not of its implications – in the story, no force from anyone of the main characters runs into the channel of sexual feeling. The reactions of Maud, the narrator-heroine, throughout are those of a highly intelligent, still more highly sensitive, child of twelve. This may, to a degree, be accounted for by seclusion and a repressive father – but not, I think entirely: I should doubt whether Le Fanu himself realized Maud's abnormality as a heroine. She is an uncertain keyboard, on which some notes sound clearly, deeply and truly, others not at all. There is no question, here, of Victorian censorship, with its suggestive gaps: Maud, on the subject of anything she does feel, is uninhibited, sometimes disconcerting. And equally, in the feeling of people round her we are to take it that, child-like, she misses nothing. The distribution of power throughout the writing is equal, even: the briefest scene is accorded brimming sensuous content. We must in fact note how Maud's sensuousness (which is un-English) disperses, expends itself through the story in so much small change. She shows, at every turn, the carelessness, or acquiescence, of the predestined person: Maud is, by nature, a bride of Death. She delays, she equivocates, she looks wildly sideways; she delights in fire and candlelight, bedroom tea-drinking, cosy feminine company, but her bias is marked. The wind blowing her way from the family mausoleum troubles our heroine like a mating cry. Her survival after those frightful hours in the locked bedroom at Bartram-Haugh is, one can but feel, somewhat ghostly: she has cheated her Bridegroom only for the time being. Her human lover is colourless; her marriage – unexceptionable as to level and in felicity – is little more than the shell of a happy ending. From the parenthesis in her 'Conclusion' (Maud writes down her story after some years of marriage) we learn that her first child dies.

Is, then, *Uncle Silas* 'morbid'? I cannot say so. For one thing, morbidity seems to me little else than sentimentality of a peculiar tint, and nothing of that survives in the drastic air of the book. For another, Maud is counterpoised by two other characters, her unalike cousins Monica Knollys and Milly Ruthyn, who not only desire life but are its apostles. And, life itself is painted in brilliant colours – colours sometimes tantalizing, as though life were an alternative out of grasp; sometimes insidious, disturbing, as though life were a temptation. I know, as a matter of fact, of few Victorian novels in which cosiness, gaiety and the delights of friendship are so sweetly rendered or play such a telling part. Le Fanu's style, translucent, at once simple and subtle, is ideal for such transitions. He has a genius for the unexpected – in mood as well as event. One example – a knowing twist of his art – is that Maud, whose arrival at Bartram-Haugh has been fraught with sinister apprehension, should, for the first few months, delight in her uncle's house. After Knowl – overcast, repressive; stiff with proprieties – Bartram-Haugh seems to be Liberty Hall. She runs wild in the woods with her cousin Milly; for the first time, she has company of her own age. Really, it is the drama of Maud's feelings, the heightening of conflict in her between hopes and fears, rather than the melodrama of her approaching fate, which ties one to *Uncle Silas*, page after page, breathless, unwilling to miss a word.

II

Le Fanu either felt or claimed to feel uneasy as to the reception of *Uncle Silas*. He mentions the genesis of the novel, not for its interest as a creative fact, but in order to clear himself, in advance, of the charge of plagiarism: his long-ago short story had been anonymous. And, in the same 'Preliminary Word' he enters a plea that the novel be not dismissed as 'sensation' fiction. *Uncle Silas* was published in 1864: the plea would not be necessary to-day. Sensationalism, for its own sake, does, it is true, remain in poor repute; but sensation (of the kind which packs *Uncle Silas*) is not only not disdained, it is placed in art. The most irreproachable pens, the most poetic imaginations pursue and refine it. The status of the psychological thriller is, to-day, high. *Uncle Silas* was in advance of, not behind, its time: it is not the last, belated Gothic romance but the first (or among the first) of the psychological thrillers. And it has, as terror-writing, a voluptuousness not approached since. (It was of the voluptuousness in his own writing that Le Fanu may, really, have been afraid.) The novel, like others of its now honoured type, relies upon suspense and mystification: I should be doing wrong to it and the reader were I to outline the story or more than hint at its end. To say that a rich, lonely girl is placed, by her father's will, in charge of an uncle who, already suspected of one murder, would be the first to profit by her death is, I think, at once sufficient and fair. But, the real suspense of the story emanates from the characters; it is they who keep the tale charged with mystery. The people in *Uncle Silas* show an extraordinary power of doubling upon or of covering their tracks. Maud seldom knows where she stands with any of them; neither do we. They are all at one remove from us, seen through the eyes of Maud. The gain to a story of this nature of being told in the first person is obvious (but for the fact that the teller, for all her dangers, must, we take it, survive, in order to tell the tale). All the same, it is not to this device that Le Fanu owes the main part of his effects – you and I, as readers, constantly intercept glances or changes in tones of voice that Maud just notes but does not interpret aright. No, Maud has little advantage over you or me. Temperamentally, and because of her upbringing, she is someone who moves about in a world of strangers. She is alternately blind and unnecessarily suspicious. Her attitude towards every newcomer is one of fatalistic mistrust; and this attitude almost, but not quite (which is subtle) communicates itself to the reader. We do not, for instance, know, for an unreasonably but enjoyably long time, whether Milly, for all her rustic frankness, may not at heart be a Little Robber Girl, or Lady Knollys a schemer under her good nature.

> You perceive [says Maud] that I had more spirit than courage. I think I had the mental attributes of courage; but then I was but an hysterical girl, and in so far neither more nor less than a coward.
>
> No wonder I distrusted myself; no wonder my will stood out against my timidity. It was a struggle, then; a proud, wild struggle against constitutional cowardice.
>
> Those who have ever had cast upon them more than their

> strength seems framed to bear – the weak, the aspiring, the adventurous in will, and the faltering in nerve – will understand the kind of agony which I sometimes endured.

And later, on receiving comforting news:

> You will say then that my spirits and my serenity were quite restored. Not quite. How marvellously lie our anxieties, in filmy layers, one over the other! Take away that which has lain on the upper surface for so long – the care of cares – the only one, as it seemed to you, between your soul and the radiance of Heaven – and straight you find a new stratum there. As physical science tells us no fluid is without its skin, so does it seem with this fine medium of the soul, and those successive films of care that form upon its surface on mere contact with the upper air and light.

Who are the characters whom, in *Uncle Silas*, this at once nervous and spirited girl confronts? There is her father, Austin Ruthyn of Knowl, scion and reigning head of an ancient family, wealthy, recluse, widower, given up to Swedenborgian religion. There is Mr Ruthyn's spiritual director Dr Bryerly – 'bilious, bewigged, black-eyed' – whose nocturnal comings and goings seem to bode no good. There is Mr Ruthyn's first cousin Lady Knollys, woman of the world, who comes to stay at Knowl and interests herself in Maud. There is Maud's French governess Madame de la Rougierre, who, arriving early on in the story, gibbers in moonlight outside the drawing-room window.

Half-way through, story and heroine cross sixty miles of country. Austin Ruthyn is dead: his place in Maud's life is taken by his younger brother Silas, of Bartram-Haugh – reformed rake, widower and, again, religious recluse. Silas's marriage to a barmaid had dealt the first, though not yet the worst, blow to Ruthyn family pride. Children of the marriage are Milly ('a very rustic Miranda,' her father says) and Dudley, a sinister Tony Lumpkin. In the Bartram-Haugh woods dwell an ill-spoken miller and his passionate daughter . . . In both great houses there is the usual cast of servants – at Knowl, correct, many and reassuring; at Bartram-Haugh few and queer. On from this point, characterization, in any full sense, stops: we are left with 'types,' existing, solely and flatly, for the requirements of the plot. A fortune-hunting officer, three clergymen, two lawyers and a thoughtful peer, Maud's future husband, come under this heading.

That last group, uninspired and barely tinted in, represents Le Fanu's one economy. In the main, it could be a charge against him that too many of the characters in *Uncle Silas* are overcharged, and that they break their bounds. There is abnormal pressure, from every side; the psychic air is often overheated. And all the time, we must remember, this is a story intended to be dominated by the figure of one man: Uncle Silas. All through, Uncle Silas meets competition. He is, I think, most nearly played off the stage by Madame de la Rougierre. Apart from that he is (as central character) at a disadvantage: *is* he, constantly, big enough for his own build-up? Is there or is there not, in scenes in which he actually appears, a just perceptible drop into anti-climax? Le Fanu, in dealing with Uncle Silas, was up against a difficulty inherent in his kind of oblique, suggestive art. He has overdrawn on his Silas in advance. In the flesh, Uncle Silas enters the story late: by this time, his build-up has reached towering heights. It is true that most of the time at Bartram-Haugh he remains off stage, and that those intervals allow of batteries being recharged. At Knowl, still only a name, he was ever-present – in the tormented silences of his brother, the hinting uneasy chatter of Lady Knollys, and Maud's dreams.

> I don't [Lady Knollys admits, to Maud] understand metaphysics, my dear, nor witchcraft. I sometimes believe in the supernatural, and sometimes I don't. Silas Ruthyn is himself alone, and I can't define him because I don't understand him. Perhaps other souls than human are sometimes born into the world, and clothed in flesh. It is not only about that dreadful occurrence, but nearly always throughout his life; early and late he has puzzled me . . . At one time of his life I am sure he was awfully wicked – eccentric indeed in his wickedness – gay, frivolous, secret and dangerous. At one time I think he could have made poor Austin do almost anything; but his influence vanished with his marriage, never to return again. No; I don't understand him. He has always bewildered me, like a shifting face, sometimes smiling, but always sinister, in an unpleasant dream.

Here is Maud, on arrival at Bartram-Haugh, fresh from her first meeting with her uncle:

> When I lay down in my bed and reviewed the day, it seemed like a month of wonders. Uncle Silas was always before me; the voice so silvery for an old man – so preternaturally soft; the manner so sweet, so gentle; the aspect smiling, suffering, spectral. It was no longer a shadow; I had now seen him in the flesh. But, after all, was he more than a shadow to me? When I closed my eyes I saw him before me still, in necromantic black, ashy with a pallor on which I looked with

> fear and pain, a face so dazzlingly pale, and those hollow, fiery, awful eyes! It sometimes seemed to me as though the curtain had opened, and I had seen a ghost.

'What a sweet, gentle, insufferable voice he has!' exclaims, later, Lady Knollys, who, for Maud's sake, has tried to reopen relations with Bartram-Haugh. And, towards the end, we hear the beleaguered Maud: 'There were the sensualities of the gourmet for his body, and there ended his human nature, as it seemed to me. Through that semi-transparent structure I thought I could now and then discern the light or glare of his inner life . . . Was, then, all his kindness but a phosphoric radiance covering something colder and more awful than the grave?'

Of the French governess, what is one to say? She is Uncle Silas's rival or counterpart. She is physical as opposed to metaphysical evil. No question of 'semi-transparent structure' here – the Frenchwoman is of the rankest bodily coarseness: one can smell her breath, as it were, at every turn. In the *Uncle Silas* atmosphere, bleached of sex, she is no more woman than he is man; yet, somehow, her marelike coquetry – that prinking with finery and those tales of lovers – is the final, grotesque element of offence. As a woman, she can intrude on the girl at all points. She is obscene; and not least so in the alternate pinchings and pawings to which she subjects Maud. While the uncle gains in monstrousness by distance, the governess gains in monstrousness by closeness.

Madame de la Rougierre is unhandicapped by a preliminary build-up: she enters the story without warning and makes growth, page by page, as she goes along. Le Fanu, through the mouths of his characters, is a crack marksman in the matter of epithets: nothing said of the governess goes wide. He had, it is true, with this Frenchwoman a great vein to work on: with Wilkie Collins and Dickens he could exploit the British concept of the foreigner as sinister. Her broken English (with its peculiar rhythm, like no other known broken English, specially coined for her) further twists, in speech, the thoughts of her hideous mind. Like Uncle Silas, Madame de la Rougierre is, morally, of an unrelieved black: considering how much we are in her company it is wonderful that she does not become monotonous – the variations Le Fanu *has* contrived to give her are to be admired. 'When things went well,' we are told, 'her soul lighted up into sulphureous good-humour.' The stress is most often upon this woman's mouth – a 'large-featured, smirking phantom' is Maud's first view of her, through the drawing-room window. We have her 'wide, wet grin.' She would 'smile with her great carious teeth.'

This creature's background is never fully given. Indeed, her engagement, as his daughter's companion, by Mr Ruthyn of Knowl, is, with his obstinate tolerance of her presence, one of the first anomalies of the plot.

III

Uncle Silas, as a novel, derives its power from an inner momentum. In the exterior plot there are certain weaknesses, inconsistencies and loose ends. In this regard, the book has about it a sort of brilliant – nay, even inspired – amateurishness; a sort of negligent virtuosity in which Le Fanu shows his race. This may be the reason why *Uncle Silas* has never yet quite made the popular grade. It has not so far, that is to say, moved forward from being a favourite book of individual people into the rank of accepted Victorian classics.

It cannot, I think, be said that most Victorian novels are guiltless of loose ends. But, in their elaborate plots with their substructures, crowds of characters and varied, shifting scenes, there is usually more to distract the eye: reader as well as author may well overlook something. *Uncle Silas* is, in this matter, defenceless in its simplicity: it has no subplots and contains comparatively few people. The writing is no less simple: this, its beauty apart, is its great virtue. The effect of the simplicity is, that every sentence of Le Fanu's – or, at least, its content – incises itself deeply upon one's memory: one can forget not the slightest hint or statement or question. And, the excitingness of the story keeps one on the stretch, at once watchful and challenging, like a child listener. Like the child, one finds oneself breaking in, from time to time, with: 'But–? . . . But, I thought you *said*–?'

The omissions or inconsistencies of the plot are not psychological; they are practical or mechanical. They do not, to my mind, detract from or injure the real story, because they are not on its reallest plane. However, there they are. I do not feel it to be the function of this Introduction to point them out to the reader in advance – I intend, therefore, only to mention one, which could hardly escape the most careless eye. *Who* was the concealed witness who relayed to Maud the conversation between Madame de la Rougierre and Dudley Ruthyn at Church Scarsdale? A witness who must, by the way, have been no less observant and subtle than Maud herself, for no inflection, gesture or glance is lost. We are never told who it is. The most likely bid is Tom Brice, the girl Beauty's lover and, at one time, Dudley's hanger-on. Tom might have told Beauty, who might have told Maud. But the account does not sound as though it had come through the mouths of two peasants . . . Elsewhere, the fact that the degree and origin of the Frenchwoman's relationship with the Bartram-Haugh Ruthyns is never stated may worry some readers. We are left to infer that she was, already, their agent from before the time she arrived at Knowl.

The plot is obfuscated (sometimes, one may say, helpfully) by an extraordinary vagueness about time. This is a book in which it is impossible to keep a check on the passage of weeks, months, years. The novel is dominated by one single season in whose mood it is pitched: autumn. Practically no other season is implied or named. (Yes, we have a Christmas visit to Elvaston, and a mention, elsewhere, of January rain. And after Madame de la Rougierre's departure from Knowl Maud, in the joy of her release, is conscious of singing birds and blue skies – but those could be in September.) The whole orchestral range of the novel's weather is autumnal – tranced dripping melancholy, crystal morning zest, the radiance of the magnified harvest moon, or the howl and straining of gales through not yet quite leafless woods. The daylight part of Maud's drive to her uncle's house is through an amber landscape. The opening words of the novel are, it is true, 'It was winter . . .' But our heroine, contradictory with her first breath, then adds: 'the second week in November.' By this reckoning Maud, in telling Lady Knollys that Madame de la Rougierre had arrived at Knowl 'in February' is incorrect. The Frenchwoman, we had been clearly told, arrived 'about a fortnight' after the opening scene . . . No, there is nothing for it: one must submit oneself to Le Fanu's hypnotizing, perpetual autumn. One autumn merges into another: hopeless to ask how much has happened between! Yet always, against this nebulous flow of time stand out the moments – each unique, comprehensive, crystal, painfully sharp.

The inner, non-practical, psychological plot of *Uncle Silas* is, I suggest, faultless: it has no inconsistencies. The story springs from and is rooted in an obsession, and the obsession never looses its hold. Austin Ruthyn of Knowl, by an inexorable posthumous act, engages his daughter's safety in order to rescue his brother's honour. Or rather, less Silas's honour than the family name's. Silas Ruthyn is a man under a cloud: he has never yet been cleared of a charge against him. Austin's having committed Maud to his brother's keeping is to demonstrate, to the eyes of a hostile world, his absolute faith in his brother's innocence. By surviving years under his lonely roof, Maud, whose next heir he is, is to vindicate Silas. Maud has, during her father's lifetime, agreed in principle to the trust. (She has still, be it said, to hear the terms of the will, and to learn the full story of Silas from Lady Knollys.)

> I think [Austin says to his daughter] little Maud would like to contribute to the restitution of her family name . . . The character and influence of an ancient family is a peculiar heritage – sacred but destructible; and woe to him who either destroys or suffers it to perish.

Call this *folie de grandeur*, or a fanaticism of the Almanach de Gotha. It is the extreme of a point of view less foreign to Le Fanu than to his readers. It was a point of view that they, creatures of an industrialized English nineteenth century, were bound to challenge, and could deride. It could only hope to be made acceptable, as mainspring and premise of his story, by being challenged, criticized – even, by implication, derided – in advance, and on behalf of the reader, by a person located somewhere inside the story. The necessary mouthpiece is Dr Bryerly. Dr Bryerly's little speech to Maud is a piece of, as it were, insurance, on Le Fanu's part. 'There are people,' remarks Dr Bryerly, 'who think themselves just as great as the Ruthyns, or greater; and your poor father's idea of carrying it by a demonstration was simply the dream of a man who had forgotten the world, and learned to exaggerate himself by his long seclusion.' True – and how effective. The reader's misgivings, his fear of being implicated in something insanely disproportionate, have been set at rest. He is now prepared to lean back and accept, as Le Fanu wished, the idea on one – but that a great – merit purely: its validity for the purposes of the tale.

One more comment, before we leave the plot. In the disposition of characters (including what I have called functional types) about the field of the story, Le Fanu shows himself, as a novelist, admirably professional, in a sense that few of his contemporaries were. Not a single, even the slightest, character is superfluous; not one fails to play his or her part in the plot, or detains us for a second after that part is played. One or two (such as the house party guests at Elvaston) are merely called in to act on Maud's state of mind. But Maud's mind, we must remember, reflects, and colours according to its states; the action of the interior plot. No person is in the story simply to fill up space, to give the Victorian reader his money's worth, or to revive flagging interest – Le Fanu, rightly, did not expect interest to flag.

IV

The background, or atmosphere, needs little discussion: in the first few pages one recognizes the master-touch. The story of *Uncle Silas* is, as I have indicated, divided between two houses: Knowl and Bartram-Haugh. The contrast between the two houses contributes drama. Knowl, black and white, timbered, set in well-tended gardens, is a rich man's home. It is comfortable; fires roar in the grates; pictures and panelling gleam; the servants do all they should. As against this, Knowl [*sic*][9] is overcast, rigid, haunted: Mr Ruthyn is closeted with dark mysteries; there are two ghosts, and, nearby, the family mausoleum, in which Maud's young mother lies and to which her father is to be carried under the most charnel circumstances of death.

Maud, sitting with Lady Knollys after Austin's death, hears the wind come roaring her way through the woods from the mausoleum. The wind, Lady Knollys can but point out, comes, too, from the more threatening direction of Bartram-Haugh. Uncle Silas's house, already the scene of one violent death, is, beforehand, invested with every terror. Bartram-Haugh, as first seen, demands a John Piper drawing:

> I was almost breathless as I approached. The bright moon shining fully on the white front of the old house revealed not only its highly decorated style, its fluted pillars and doorway, rich and florid carving and balustraded summit, but also its stained and mossgrown front. Two giant trees, overthrown at last by the recent storm, lay with their upturned roots, and their yellow foliage still flickering on the sprays that were to bloom no more, where they had fallen, at the right side of the courtyard, which, like the avenue, was tufted with weeds and grass.

'The mind is,' as Maud elsewhere remarks, 'a different organ by night and by day.' Next morning's awakening is reassuring – a wakening to bright morning through bare windows, a cheerful breakfast, superb if neglected stretches of parkland, a blackberrying walk. Exploration, with Milly, of whole closed derelict floors and internal galleries brings only a fleeting memory of the ill-fated Charke. The psychological weather of those first Bartram-Haugh chapters is like the out-of-doors weather: gay and tingling. Till Milly is sent away, nothing goes wholly wrong.

From *that* point, the closing in is continuous. The ruined rooms, the discovery of the ogress-governess in hiding, introduce the beginning of the end. . . . All through Le Fanu's writing, there is an ecstatic sensitivity to light, and an abnormal recoil from its inverse, darkness. *Uncle Silas* is full of outdoor weather – we enjoy the rides and glades, cross the brooks and stiles, meet the cottagers and feel the enclosing walls of two kingdom-like great estates. Though static in ever-autumn, those scenes change: there is more than the rolling across them of clouds or sunshine. Indeed we are looking at their reflection in the lightening or darkening mirror of Maud's mind.

V

Uncle Silas is a romance of terror, written more than eighty years ago. Between then and now, human susceptibilities have altered – some may have atrophied, others developed further. The terror-formula of yesterday might not work to-day. Will *Uncle Silas* act on the modern reader?

I think so, and for several reasons. Le Fanu's strength, here, is not so much in his story as in the mode of its telling. *Uncle Silas*, as it is written, plays on one constant factor – our childish fears. These leave their work at the base of our natures, and are never to be rationalized away. Two things are terrible in childhood: helplessness (being in other people's power) and apprehension – the apprehension that something is being concealed from us because it is too bad to be told. Maud Ruthyn, vehicle of the story, is helpless apprehension itself, in person: this is what gets under our skin. Maud, simplified (in the chemical sense, reduced) for her creator's purpose, is, we may tell ourselves, an extreme case. She has a predisposition towards fear: we are to watch her – and be her – along her way towards the consummation of perfect terror – just as, were this a love story, we should be sharing her journey towards a consummation of a different kind. Proust has pointed out that the predisposition to love creates its own objects: is this not true of fear? At the start Maud, in her unconscious search, experiments with Dr Bryerly: she fears him. He acts as the forecast shadow of Uncle Silas – and, that he may play this rôle for the first act, he is given all the necessary trappings. Then, the Doctor discloses a character in point-blank reverse: he is levelheaded, a man of daylight, unfailing good counsellor, champion, friend. But by that time, what the Doctor is does not matter: using the love-fear analogy, he is an off-cast love. He has been superseded by Uncle Silas, past whom Maud has no further to look.

Maud had suspected in Dr Bryerly a supernatural element of evil: his influence on her father appeared malign. This brings us to another terror-ingredient: moral dread. Should one call this timeless, or is it modern? Let us say, it is timeless, but that its refinement in literature has been modern. (By modern I mean, modern at the best.) Henry

James inspired, and remains at the head of, a whole school of moral horror stories – I need not point out that it is the stench of evil, not the mere fact of the super-natural, which is the genuine horror of *The Turn of the Screw*. Our ancestors may have had an agreeable-dreadful reflex from the idea of the Devil or a skull-headed revenant popping in and out through a closed door: we need, to make us shiver, the effluence from a damned soul. In *Uncle Silas*, there is no supernatural element in the ordinary sense – the Knowl ghosts exist merely to key Maud up. The genuine horror is the non-natural. Lady Knollys, in her chatter, suggests that Silas may be a non-human soul clothed in a human body.

What Maud dreads, face-to-face with Silas, is not her own death.

Physically, Maud's nerve is extremely good. She stands up to Madame de la Rougierre, to whom her reactions are those of intense dislike, repugnance and disdain. She is frightened only of what she cannot measure, and she has got the governess taped. With the same blend of disdain and clear-sightedness, she stands up to Dudley. She shows, I think, remarkable nonchalance in re-exploring the top rooms alone, in the late dusk, after Milly's departure. As the plot thickens round her and door after door clangs to, she shows herself fanatically disposed, up to the very last minute, to give her uncle the benefit of the doubt. Were she, in fact, a goose or weakling, the story would lack the essential tension: *Uncle Silas* would fail. As it is, we have the impact of a crescendo of hints and happenings on taut, hyper-controlled and thus very modern nerves. Is there to be a breaking-point? If so, why, how, when? That, not the question of Maud's bodily fate, sets up the real excitement of *Uncle Silas*.

The let-up, the pause for recuperation, even the apparent solicitude: these are among the sciences of the torture chamber. 'The victim must regain his power to suffer fully. The let-ups in *Uncle Silas* – the fine days, the walks, the returned illusions of safety – are, for Maud and the reader, artfully timed. Nothing goes on for long enough either to dull you or to exhaust itself. And the light, the open air, the outdoor perspective enhance, by contrast, the last of the horror-constants – claustrophobia. On the keyboard of any normal reader *Uncle Silas* will not, I think, fail to strike one or another note: upon the claustrophobic it plays a fugue. The sense of the tightening circle, the shrinking and darkening room . . .

Just as the outer plot of *Uncle Silas* is traditional, or unoriginal, Le Fanu does draw also, for fear or horror, out of the traditional bag of tricks – the lonely ruinous house, the closed rooms, the burning eyes, the midnight voices, the hired assassins, and so on. Maud herself, exploring Bartram-Haugh in the dusk, has in mind the romances of Mrs Radcliffe. The induction of misery and despair preparatory to slaughter is Elizabethan . . . In so far as *Uncle Silas* uses physical horror, the use is extremely sophisticated: Maud's quick and almost voluptuous reactions to sound, sight, touch and smell make her the perfect reagent. The actual sound of a murder, a messy butchery, has probably never, in any gangster story, been registered as it is here.

The function of an Introduction is, I think, to indicate the nature of a book and to suggest some angles for judgment. That judgment the reader himself must form. *Uncle Silas* will, in this new edition, reach, among others, a generation of readers who have grown up since the novel was last in print. They may read into it more than I have found. That it will have meaning for them I do not doubt.

Chapter 4

A New Ireland
1950s

Christmas at Bowen's Court, December 1950, *Flair* 1.11, Essay

My home in County Cork is lonely, even as places in Ireland go. In midwinter, it stands in a tract of silence – the hum of summer, the furious gales of autumn have subsided; through the stripped woods may be seen the empty distances and the mountains. No other season, here, might ever have been. Around Christmas, the sun rises late behind a group of elms some way up the lawn in front of the house, casting the shadows of the tree trunks in spokes, fanwise, toward the door. Seldom does snow fall: everything is shining and moist and still – as day goes on, the grasslands grazed by sheep take on a blond colour. The darkness of the mornings is atoned for by those long whitish glimmering evenings of the West.

The bald square light grey house is backed by a semi-circle of shallow woods; behind rise the Ballyhoura Mountains. The outlook in front is clear, and on fine days sunny. The limestone of which the house is built was quarried nearby; high up under the roof is incised the date, 1775. Here, since then, my family in unbroken succession have celebrated their Christmases: settlers turned farming squires, they seldom went from home. They made life here, living what they had made. Now it comes to my own day, without anything having greatly changed – some trees have grown to majestic height, others have fallen; indoors the rooms have weathered under the force of daylight coming in for so many years through so many windows. This keeping of everything as it was is due neither to piety nor to taste: the Bowens have never been rich enough to be drastic: any new things brought in have so quickly faded as to be indistinguishable from what was there before.

It is at Christmas that the place looks oldest: its bony under-structure stands out. The accumulated character of the house seems as inevitable as the lie of the land. All who have ever lived here are to be felt.

It is not, however, in order to spend Christmas with my ancestors that

I return here each year from London. A journey through the cold winter skies needs a warmer motive: instinct, not sentiment, brings me home.

Bowen's Court is fifty-five miles from Shannon Airport. The first of Ireland on which I set foot, each time, is that glaring no-place of runways, hut buildings, transatlantic airliners refuelling – alongside those, our small Aer Lingus car taxis with confidence into place. All airports are so alike that, at the minute of landing, one might be anywhere – then, the eyes turn to the Clare hills in the distance; the lungs draw in the first soft breath of Irish winter air from the river flatlands. The track leading from Shannon into the country is a hard white ribbon, still too like a runway: my car races, as though to be clear of something. Not till one makes the junction with the ancient Limerick–Ennis road are the neutralising tensity of the journey, and, still more, the last of the nerve-gripping tentacles of London quite shaken off.

From now on reappear landmarks – the hogbacked bridge, the spectacular ruined castle, the crossroads with the lemon-coloured inn. Afternoon is mirrored in the glassy curves of the River Fergus; other glints of water thread through the landscape; blue-brown horizons melt off into the sky. Hedges, cutting all this from sight, rise: I wind down the window to smell the fern-rot. Skeleton leaves have gummed themselves to the tarmac; split beech-husks crackle under the tires. A sheepdog leaps over a gate, attempting to head the car. Yes, this is Ireland, though not yet County Cork.

My route home crosses Limerick city. Christmas, now close at hand, has intoxicated, congested the lengthy streets. Autos nose their way on a sustained note from the horn; carts abruptly back out of alleys; buses slither and grind. Country people for miles around have surged into town. The tallness of the shabby Georgian houses, which have known grand days, sets up premature dusk, into which blazes the incoherent splendour of shop displays. Few are Limerick shops which do not stock everything: at this season, all things burst into view, with an overlay of attractive 'novelties.'

Onward from Kilmallock, my road home runs through the Ballyhoura Mountains. Evening slips up their flanks as they unfold: a moon may be seen in the still translucent sky. A ridge of rock in the road announces, by an unavoidable bump, that one is crossing the boundary into County Cork. At the hour when I drive up to Bowen's Court, glimmers are still caught in the bare trees and reflected in the panes of the windows. A few rooks circle.

To speak of the house as awaiting one would be untrue – by coming back, one no more than rejoins oneself to an existence which is absolutely, tranquilly and timelessly independent of any one person. The effect of this is balm – the sense of fret, of crisis which one has come to associate with one's own identity slips away. In that moment, one becomes simply another wanderer back for Christmas. As for Christmas, it has already fully taken possession. To this, the Festival, the house does defer, as it does to no individual son or daughter. An august, additional presence is to be felt as I walk from one to another of the firelit rooms.

In London I look on Christmas as an ordeal. Some have called it a racket. In town we live on our nerves, dissect our feelings, know too much – and, at the same time, nothing. Here the mood waits, with its priority over all other feeling. Nor can it be called a mood, for it is outside oneself and thereby commands one. It has authority; it is racial, primal, mysterious and compelling. In so far as Bowen's Court like a vessel contains Christmas, it does so by virtue of being part of Ireland: the natural pulse of the country beats in its rooms, surrounding influences flow through it. One is aware, for one thing, of the ancient Christianity inherent in her very rocks and earth. Small ruined ivy-bound chapels alone in fields or on lake islands, destroyed but still sacred abbeys beside the rivers, continue to send out something.

From Bowen's Court, I hear the dogs in the distance barking. I hear the countryfolk who live 'out behind' making their late way home through my woods – and sometimes a plane above the clouds droning its way in or out of Shannon. But I am to hear this only when I open a window and lean out, alone for a moment, to breathe the night air. For by now my house is also crowded and full of voices.

My grandfather had ten children and kept much company. He read prayers, on Sundays and feasts of the Church, at the billiard table which was in his day the principal feature of the hall, with the portraits of his (and my) more rakish and scatty Georgian forebears looking down quizzically. He wore a fine Victorian beard and was so masterful in his carving of the turkey, or possibly pair of turkeys, that all around the rest of the Christmas table there was an awe-struck hush. The diningroom, deeply curtained, was massive with sideboards, dotted with decanters, ornate with silver. The table could be extended to any length and had an equipment of twenty-four chairs – few of which, at Christmas, my grandfather expected to see unoccupied. Subsidiary relatives were bidden; respectful neighbours also could claim a place. Before his time the Bowens were more carelessly arrogant and more nonchalant, certainly gayer, perhaps happier: he inherited from them many acres in the counties of Tipperary and Cork.

Shorn of aunts and uncles, myself childless, and with my few Bowen cousins living across the sea, I am happy in my inherited neighbours. These, in default of other ties, have become my family. We have the same traditions, come of the same stock. At Christmas, the sociable pattern of the countryside repeats itself in my intercourse with their houses. In the late afternoon, we keep up a to-and-fro along white high-hedged damply glimmering roads. At nights, my car's headlights rake the dark of their avenues, or their cars' headlights rake the dark of mine. Together we are not casual: Christmas stylises everything with a light, sure touch of the ceremonial. In Ireland, however, ceremony, together with the magic of an occasion, exalts good spirits rather than constrains them. We are by bread rhetorical. We drink to the season, each other and the regretted dead. We drink – in fire-tinged rooms, strewn with dogs and jammed with obsolete furniture – out of hilarity, not in pursuit of it: tongues are unleashed before the glass is set to the lips.

Christmas Eve also brings more quiet, preparatory ceremonies to Bowen's Court. Some are generic to all homes, some special to here. The decoration, with holly and other foliage, of the pale blue inside of our Protestant church occupies the morning, the parcelling and delivery of presents to children and very old friends the afternoon. Beggars, whose status with us is almost sacred, come one by one up the steps to stand at the door. Many but not all of them are women, stately, draped in their rusty black shawls they bless the house before and after receiving alms. The Holy Saints, we hope, do indeed not fail to look down. The crux, toward the close of the day, is the installation by me of the Christmas candle – of scarlet, jade green, yellow or pink wax. Designed to burn from tonight until the Feast of the Kings, the candle is some twenty-four inches high and moreover of a circumference which forbids it to fit into the socket of any candlestick. I can only wedge it upright into an alabaster vase brought back by my grandfather from his Italian honeymoon.

The candle, having been lit, burns in a book-darkened corner of the library, consecrating into a nameless altar the card table upon which it stands. Its fellows are in every home at my gate. Slowly, with the coming and passing of Christmas Day, it diminishes, shedding coloured grease over the whorls of the alabaster – sometimes its flame swerves, as though caught by a breath. This ever-burning, ever-sinking candle becomes a timepiece: the dear season is not after all what it seems to be, an eternity.

Outdoors, however, time seems to have come to a shining standstill. The moss on the trees brightens to emerald; no shadow lengthens. This is the noon of winter – the fields smile, the mountains are pink in the sun. The bell from the hill has ceased; for minutes together there is no sound, no sound. The postman comes slowly up the avenue.

Come to Ireland, *Ireland and the Irish*, by Charles Duff, 1952, Harry Ransom Center, unpublished review

Any book about Ireland almost always reflects, strongly, the temperament of its author – this may come from ours being a country about which it is hard to be impersonal. Or possibly, something in the climate tends to exaggerate feeling: at any rate, a completely detached, objective study of us, our way of life, our past and our institutions, is still lacking; and could be, at this stage, of some assistance to our development. Mr Charles Duff's *Ireland and the Irish* is, in the main, no exception to the above rule, but has one rare good quality – it is non-partisan. Mr Duff sees the most knotty of our internal problems from both sides: he is Irish, born north of the Border, but of parents who came from south of that fatal line. He enjoys the extra advantage of having been to school in Ulster and in what has since become the Republic, and of having rounded off his education in England. He has travelled the world; and to do that, as Chesterton pointed out, is the ideal way to arrive at 'seeing' one's first home. His distances and absences from Ireland have served to keep intact his illusions; his writing has at times this romantic glow most often imparted by nostalgia. He has been, however, far from always away; he does *know* the country – evidently he has kept contacts alive; he is abreast with changes, and offers information which (thanks in part, we are told, to help from the Irish Tourist Association) is up-to-date. Above all, he has steeped himself in Irish pre-history and history, Gaelic literature, myth and folklore. Generous, energetic and optimistic, brimful of gusto and possessor of a reliable memory, Mr Duff has succeeded in giving us a many-sided, respect-worthy book on Ireland. His flaw as a writer ishis extreme difficulty in for long keeping to any one point.

Ireland and the Irish does, therefore, although carefully planned, tend to overflow bounds and become somewhat inchoate. Mr Duff's idea, an excellent one, was to devote the first half of the book to the Irish – their evolution, background and temperament – and the second to Ireland – geographically and more or less from the traveller's point of view – but the distinction does not always prevail. Much of the way, he has had to battle with misconceptions, and this distracts him. He may or may not be right in feeling the Irish have been traduced; he is certainly right in pointing out that they have been liked, not to say patronised, for the wrong reasons, and that playboyism – often, in its manifestations, more tedious than Mr Duff in his kindness will allow – was in the first place a protest against inferiority, and persists because oppressions leave their after-effect. The desire to please, a likeable trait, is strong; for a long time the Irish, through weakness, have had to bid for attention and if possible favour by going through antics, or still worse, by exporting a comic myth. England called the tune, and the English view has to a point affected Ireland's view of herself. This Mr Duff reiterates, not perhaps too often: argument interests him, and it is hard to argue without generalizing. His generalizations, however, do not sweep too much, and the absence from them of heat and bitterness must, again, be praised.

That the principal tragedies of Ireland have been the reduction, through poverty, of the expressive, native life of the country and the break in the cultural continuity now seems clear. The former leaves its traces in low standards, slatternliness and fatalism; the latter, in the sad isolation of ancient literary wealth from the modern mind. Will 'The Cattle Drive of Cooley' (Irish *Iliad*, which Mr Duff's summary makes one wish to read) ever displace from its hold on our young readers the imported 'Western'? One hopes so, but fears not. The strength of English tradition resides not only in richness, genius and beauty but in its *continuous* hold on people; in Ireland, the equivalent vital link was broken. In the same way, the country's way of living – that is, above a certain level of wealth – has until lately been an imposed one. Ireland now must seek a style and idiom which shall be quite her own, and which shall have – as have, for instance, the idiom and style of France – the attractiveness of being unique to her. Towards this ideal, some of us feel, the movement should be more conscious, direct and active. So far, complacency is the foe: so well pleased are we at being on our own that most things seem good, whereas in fact few are. One misgiving inspired by Mr Duff's book is, that it may well encourage complacency. Nor is the book, this reviewer feels bound to say, as free from the more radical of conventions as the author seems to desire and to suppose.

Lack of originality does, for instance, show in the illustrations. The photographs, excellent *as* such, feature a devastating repetition of peasants, donkeys, cabins, ruins, mountains and lakes – in fact, again the time-honoured hand-out. We also have, it is true, aspects of Guinness's brewery, the Shannon hydro-electric scheme, Dublin streets, and non-detailed views of other towns and cities from nearby hill-tops. The photographs, we find with little surprise, were supplied by the Irish Tourist Association (Dublin) and the Ulster Tourist and Development Board (Belfast). Why did not Mr Duff, whose descriptive writing has much visual charm, not either take his own photographs or find a friend to do so? The endearing, haunting beauties of Ireland are intimate, subtle and unconventional – they most often lie round the corners of dusty towns (e.g. the river-front of Clonmel) or in regions off the tourist main track – willow-grey reaches of river, ridged limestone contours. The photographer for the Come-to-Ireland brochure almost unfailingly overlooks there; and with brochure-photography (though at its best, perhaps) Mr Duff has allowed himself to be fobbed off.

Mr Duff's debt to the ITA, and therefore loyalty to its precepts, results in some lack of frankness as to Irish amenities. Our hotels, with some fine exceptions, are at their present stage tolerable; few can be found enjoyable. Food (except in very small pubs, which keep the native smoky and racy flavour) is dim, and sometimes listlessly served; wine lists are likely to be discouraging. Scenery is the lure; but for days together this may be blotted out by rain. Should it not be the wish of an honest Ireland that the tourist should continue to seek our shores not in ignorance of our shortcomings, but in spite of them? Or even, we might arrive at improvement. Ireland *has* something to give – sweet air, deep sleep, magical break-through of colour and light, hearts whose warmth and manners, whose kindliness have not been exaggerated, and a soothing disregard of the stress of Time. There is also something beyond all this which the intelligent, sensitive and imaginative stranger will sense, seek and may be certain to find. Why should we not, on our side, court the ideal, which is to say the discriminating tourist? To such a one, I feel, does *Ireland and the Irish* aim to address itself. In that case, there should have been more warnings – as, for instance, against the touts and claustrophobia of over-commercialized Killarney. There remains only one more count to settle with Mr Duff: he misspells the names of two eminent Irish writers, Edith Somerville and Stephen Gwynn.[1] His book, with these few reservations, is to be recommended: travel advice is constructive; the earlier 'background' part holds enough enchantment to float one through wet evenings in our hotels.

The Anglo-Irish, by Brian Fitzgerald, 16 November 1952, *Observer*, Review

This book traces the rise to power of what has been called 'a race within a race'. Ascendancy, Mr Fitzgerald shows, cannot be merely inherited or arrived at; neither birth nor careerist achievement quite accounts for it; only by character is it to be maintained. Continuous action and demonstration, morale and energy are required. Those qualities are exemplified by the three persons here chosen as illustrating the central theme – Richard Boyle[2], first Earl of Cork; James Butler, twelfth Earl and later first Duke of Ormonde[3], and Dean Swift. In all other aspects no three could be more unlike. Each overlapping a little upon the other's time, the capitalist adventurer, the martial aristocrat and the intellectual succeeded to one another upon a stage left empty when, at the Battle of Kinsale, 1601, the Gaelic, feudal aristocracy of Ireland was swept away.

Anglo-Irish dominance lasted for three centuries – dawned with the seventeenth, entered upon its twilight with the close of the nineteenth. Of this period, Mr Fitzgerald's study covers exactly half: that is, from the start to the culmination. We open with Boyle's arrival in Ireland, close with Swift's death, and watch, through a hundred and fifty years, the first harsh, individual enterprise give place to Protestant nationalism. Grattan is next to come.

The contribution the Anglo-Irish have made to Ireland is now recognized: it is one sign of a happier epoch that the extent, nature and worth of the contribution should be, by general consent, examined. Mr Fitzgerald's relation of characters to history, his threading of continuity through three different lives, is therefore not only skilful but apposite. Boyle came to Ireland, frankly, to make his fortune, and, in consolidating himself and his family, founded something more than was swept away when the 1641 rising ravaged Munster. Antipathetic to many as he can but remain (in spite of Mr Fitzgerald's engaging portraiture), Boyle brought in with him the ideas of the then new world, and imposed one kind of mould on civilization – fruitful land, busy ports, thriving strong little cities, foundries, markets, bridges, and roads.

Boyle *became* Anglo-Irish: Ormonde was born as such. (Of the Butlers, Mr Fitzgerald says: 'Ireland might not be their nation, but it was very definitely their country.') For centuries his Norman-descended family had ruled from Kilkenny, strong and illustrious: it was for him to meet the crisis caused by revolution in England. 'Out of the feudal wreckage something indestructible survived, something that was vital to him: the habit of service.' From the impact on Ireland of Charles I's breach with his Parliament, total chaos nearly resulted: that it did not was due to Ormond's temperate leadership. He was to live to see re-emergence and, with it, some disillusion: pre-eminently, he justified his class at a time when its worth to Ireland was put to test, by transforming 'faith into honour, morals into manners'. Thanks to the Ormonde prototype, his kind were to befriend as well as to ornament their country for two centuries more.

With Swift comes the voice. The dooming, one might almost say, of the English Dean to become never quite an Irishman but an Irish patriot provides the third, most telling, part of this book, and gives context for a picture of miseries with which Anglo-Ireland failed, till too late, to grapple. Exploitation of land and labour, repetitive, crippling blows to trade and industries, from the English side, make the dire background of these hundred and fifty years. In the Anglo-Irish, those invaders and settlers who came to conquer, stayed to possess and love, national responsibility did come to be born, but social responsibility, alas, not. Where there was benevolence, there should have been reform.

Mr Fitzgerald, whose increasing importance as a historian and biographer is to be noted, gives us a book to be read on both sides of the Irish Sea. He writes disinterestedly, and his hope that this analysis of the past may throw light on some of Ireland's present-day problems should, the reader will feel, be realized. And *The Anglo-Irish* has a second possible theme: i.e. the effect of Ireland on English history.

Preface to the Second US edition of *The Last September*, 1952

This, my second novel, was published in 1929, having been written the year before. I was still young, or at least young as a writer, and, in spite of having accomplished *The Hotel*, still afraid of novels – that was, as an undertaking. Fewer alarms surrounded the short story. Now I have more experience it appears to me that problems, inherent in any writing, loom unduly large when one looks ahead. Though nothing is easy, little is quite impossible. It was a mistake to think of The Novel in the abstract, to be daunted by its 'musts' and its 'oughts', to imagine being constricted by its rules. At the outset, however, one cannot but shrink from anything one feels that one should attempt yet suspects oneself of feeling unequal to. Myself, I was most oppressed, in advance, by the difficulty of assembling a novel's cast – bringing the various characters to the same spot, keeping them there, accounting for their continued presence (in real life, people seemed to be constantly getting up and going away) and linking them close enough, and for long enough, to provide the interplay known as 'plot'. In the short story people intersected each other's lines of fate, but for moments only. So far the constituents of my fiction had been encounters, impressions, impacts, shocks. One can see that, generally, in the novel the characters are maintained in the same orbit by some situation which sets a trap for them – some magnetic interest, devilment, quest or passion. My solution was a more childish one: again in *The Last September*, as in *The Hotel*, I used the device of having my men and women actually under the same roof – to remain there, whether by choice or chance, for such time as the story should need to complete its course. To the Italian Riviera hotel of my first novel succeeded the large, lonely Irish house. I am, and am bound to be, a writer involved closely with place and time; for me these are more than elements, they are actors. The impending close of 'the season', everyone leaving, gives climax to the drama of *The Hotel*. *The Last September*, from first to last, takes its pitch from the month of the book's name.

Yet to suggest – if I have suggested? – that I came at *The Last September* as a solution of my major mechanical problem in novel writing would be gravely untrue. This, which of all my books is nearest my heart, had a deep, unclouded, spontaneous source. Though not poetic, it brims up with what could be the stuff of poetry, the sensations of youth. It is a work of instinct rather than knowledge – to a degree, a 'recall' book, but there had been no such recall before. In 'real' life, my girlhood summers in County Cork, in the house called Danielstown in the story, had been, though touched by romantic pleasure, mainly times of impatience, frivolity, or lassitude. I asked myself *what* I should be, and when? The young (ironically, so much envied) all face those patches of barren worry. In my personal memory, I do not idealize that September of 1920, the month in which this novel chose to be set. But the book, not 'true' (it deals with invented happenings, imagined persons) is at many, many removes from autobiography. Proust remarks that it is those very periods of existence which are lived through, by the writer or future writer, carelessly, unwillingly or in boredom that most often fructify into art.

The Last September is the only one of my novels to be set back deliberately, in a former time. In all others I wanted readers to contemplate what could appear to be the immediate moment – so much so, that to give the sense of the 'now' has been, for me, one imperative of writing.

For *The Last September*, that went into reverse – the 'then' (the past) as an element was demanded. The cast of my characters, and their doings, were to reflect the mood of a vanished time. 'All this,' I willed the reader to know, 'is done with and over.' From the start, the reader must look, be conscious of looking, backward – down a backward perspective of eight years. Fear that he might miss that viewpoint, that he might read so much as my first pages under misapprehension, haunted me. The ordinary narrative past tense, so much in usage, seemed unlikely to be forceful enough; so I opened my second paragraph with a pointer: 'In those days, girls wore crisp white skirts and transparent blouses clotted with white flowers; ribbons threaded through . . . appeared over the shoulders.' Lois's ribbons, already, were part of history.

When one is young, years count for more, seem longer: to have lived through a few, even, appears a conquest. And in most lives the years between twenty and twenty-eight *are* often important, packed with changes, decisive. When I sat in Old Headington, Oxford, writing *The Last September*, 1920 seemed a longtime ago. By now (the year of the writing: 1928) peace had settled on Ireland; trees were already branching inside the shells of large burned-out houses; lawns, once flitted over by pleasures, usefully merged into grazing land. I myself was no longer a tennis girl but a writer; aimlessness was gone, like a morning mist. Not an hour had not a meaning, and a centre. Also changes had altered my sense of space – Ireland seemed immensely distant from Oxford, more like another world than another land. Here I was, living a life dreamed of when, like Lois, I drove the pony trap along endless lanes. Civilization (a word constantly on my 1928 lips) was now around me. I was in company with the articulate and the learned. Yet, onward from the start of *The Last September*, it was that other era that took command – nor is it hard (now that 1928 seems as distant as 1920) to see why. The writer, like a swimmer caught by an undertow, is borne in an unexpected direction. He is carried to a subject which has awaited him – a subject sometimes no part of his conscious plan. Reality, the reality of sensation, has accumulated where it was least sought. To write is to be captured – captured by some experience to which one may have hardly given a thought.

The factual background of *The Last September* – state of affairs round Danielstown, outside happenings which impact on the story may, for non-Irish readers, need explanation. The action takes place during 'the Troubled Times' – i.e. the roving armed conflict between the Irish Republican Army and British forces still garrisoning Ireland. Ambushes, arrests, captures and burnings, reprisals and counter-reprisals kept the country and country people distraught and tense. The British patrolled and hunted; the Irish planned, lay in wait, and struck. The Army lorry heard in the breathless evening, the purposeful young man glimpsed in the Danielstown woods, the shot in the ruined mill, the barbed-wire fence round the dancers, and the ambush in which the subaltern Gerald, falls – these are fiction with the texture of history. In such an atmosphere, the carrying on of orthodox conventional social life (as they did at Danielstown) might seem either foolhardy or inhuman. One can only say, it appeared the best thing to do. The festivities I have pictured are authentic – they ceased, admittedly, in the more menacing 1921. Irish–British hostilities were brought to an end by the Treaty of 1922; though upon that followed the further chaos caused by the Irish Civil War.

During the Troubles, the position of such Anglo-Irish landowning families as the Naylors, of Danielstown, was not only ambiguous but was more nearly heart-breaking than they cared to show. Inherited loyalty (or at least, adherence) to Britain – where their sons were schooled, in whose wars their sons had for generations fought, and to which they owed their 'Ascendancy' lands and power – pulled them one way; their own temperamental Irishness the other. The Naylors and their kind entertained British officers because this was a hospitable tradition – see most Anglo-Irish memoirs or old-time novels. Though the custom now made for danger, or disrepute, the gentry welcomed the military, as before. But the Troubles troubled everything, even friendliness – see Sir Richard's sombre reaction to Gerald's company. Repugnant became the patrols and raids, the proclaimed intention of 'holding the country down'. If it seems that Sir Richard and Lady Naylor are snobs with regard to Lois's young officers, recall that the uncle's and aunt's ideas dated back to impeccable years before 1914. 'The Army's not what it was' – death had seen to that! Lois's war-damaged gallants of 1920 came of less favoured stock than had Lady Naylor's – nor could they endear themselves by enjoying Ireland: *was* this the time? Lady Naylor's ambivalent attitude to the English, in general, should however be noted; it is a marked Anglo-Irish trait. Why was Lois, at her romantic age, not more harrowed, or stirred, by the national struggle round her? In part, would not this be self-defence? This was a creature still half-awake, the soul not yet open, nor yet the eyes. And world war had shadowed her school-days: *that* was enough – now she wanted order. Trying enough it is to have to grow up, more so to grow up at a trying time. Her generation, mine, put out few rebels and fewer zealots. Like it or not, however, she acquiesced to strife, abnormalities and danger. Violence was contained in her sense of life, along with dance music, the sweet-pea in the garden, the inexorable raininess of days. Tragedy, she could only touch at the margin – not Gerald's death, but her failure to love. Was it sorrow to her, Danielstown's burning? She was niece always, never child, of that house.

I *was* the child of the house from which Danielstown derives. Bowen's Court survived – nevertheless, so often in my mind's eye did I see it burning that the terrible last event in *The Last September* is more real than anything I have lived through.

Ireland 1950, Harry Ransom Center, Essay

As a country, Ireland is at once old and young. She has a lengthy romantic past, a short modern practical history. Her smallness, her geographic position, outlying Europe on the extreme West, have presented her with peculiar problems, which in her new independence she must meet. The problems are social, cultural and, above all, economic – the Republic of Ireland, though now autonomous, remains linked to the British currency system. The country's principal assets are good agrarian lands, faith in herself and a beauty which draws the tourist.

Ireland, as she first meets the tourist's eye, might seem not only pleasing but wholly blessed. Here, there is an illusion of time having stood still; changes work benevolently and gently. The sleepy towns and tracts of unspoiled landscape make the traveller feel he has re-entered the past – there is something nostalgic about the smell of woodsmoke, the rattle of horse-drawn carts, the white-walled farms, the mansions sunk in trees. Here it seems possible to conduct life on the old pattern: tradition has not been broken, it underlies action, feeling and thought. The mould of existence is narrow, but still strong; the individual feels himself under less pressure. As a compensation – it might seem – for her long past of repression, rigour and deprivation, Ireland has been spared the catastrophes which, within recent decades, have unheaved Europe. Consequently, the country has for the visitor the charm of a sheltered slow-motion nonchalance – manners are friendly, good humour abounds. To the Britisher, willing to leave behind him strain, regimentation and anxieties, to the American coming from the competitive speed of his own land, Ireland appears an 'escape' country.

Everything heightens this illusion. The Atlantic climate, its curdling [*sic*] mists and sweeping rains, confers a brilliant richness of colouring: all tones of green compose the Emerald Isle. To alight from a plane is to feel at once, to arrive by ship up an estuary is to feel more slowly, a differentiation of atmosphere. The air breathed in is soporific; the distances hold other-worldly gleam. Winds, often languid but seldom still, draw a play of light over sheeny foliage, bend the blue smoke from chimneys, carry sea-freshness or pungent smells from bogs. The landscape is at few points not bright with water – hurrying tea-brown streams, mirroring rivers and tidal estuaries, bog pools, farm ponds, blandly romantic lakes. Ridgy mountain ranges, alternately frowning or diaphanous as the light shifts, give out a sense of sleeping Eternity. Ruins – and there are many – by now seem natural to the country, as do rocks cliffs and quarries: skeleton castles, crumbling towers, broken-arched abbeys, mounds where once houses stood are, for the traveller, nothing but picturesque. Nor have these monuments much to say to the modern, utilitarian, growing Ireland – yet, each stands for a scar on history, for a vestige never obliterated. In the climate, as in the temperament of the people (for all the smiles), there is a melancholy, an underlying sombreness.

Contradictions are many, and soon apparent. The Irish face expresses fatalism brightening to animation, eagerness shading into mistrust. Moods change as dramatically as does the light. Expansive, racy, quick, rhetorical talk gives frontage to wary reserve – a reserve actually deeper and more unyielding than that for which the British are famed. The Irishman, outwardly so forthcoming, is in fact not easy to know: his would-be friends, at the start confident, go through phases of discouragement, disillusionment. Dealing with the Irish, there is more to be overcome than the stranger knows – a race-history of resistance and insecurity. Not for centuries, it must be recalled, has this country been in anything but a weak position; not until very lately has she been quite her own. She has yet, therefore, to learn how to handle herself.

April 1948 saw the declaration of the Irish Republic: this, ending some eight hundred years of conquest, stood for the ultimate severance of the tie with Britain. The declaration savoured of a symbolic act; for, virtually, Ireland had been autonomous since the Treaty of 1922, with which went the setting up of the Free State. But the Irish Free State given Dominion status, remained within the British Commonwealth – that the Free State as a compromise, might not last was shown by political restlessness in the country. The movement for unqualified Irish freedom had behind it an accumulated, ancient, passionate force – challenging memories of the struggle were not, in the last issue, to be gainsaid. The 1916 Easter Rising (whose anniversary the declaration of the Republic commemorated) still lived in the memories of a generation. There must be no stop on the way to the final goal.

1916 linked backwards on to the former risings, each with its heroes, each charged with abortive hopes. Executions, reprisals, repressions were nothing new. Pearse and the others of 1916 joined Wolfe Tone, Edward Fitzgerald and Robert Emmett upon the national roll of glory. And alongside secret organization had been carried the battle for Home Rule, waged in the Westminster parliament, by the Irish leaders – O'Connell, Butt, Parnell. The constitutional struggle, in its own way heroic, was too slow for those at home in Ireland. Gladstone's failure, Asquith's vacillations, John Redmond's[4] heart-breaking defeat all strengthened the hand of the revolutionary. Talk, parley, had ended in what? – nothing. There must be action. Action involved the gun.

For a long time the shadow of the gunman lay over Ireland. Fighting against the British garrison troops, brought to a stop by the Treaty, gave place to the Civil War: dissentients to the Treaty (Republicans) took up arms against the pro-Treaty Free State government. Dublin echoed bombardments; the skies above it, quiet since 1916, were once more crimsoned by fires. The outlying country suffered no less – there were raids, burnings, sinister midnight movements, accesses of individual violence. Throughout, in the cities and in the country, thousands of Irish people remained passive, tongue-tied, a hypnotized prey to terror. The guerrilla campaigns, whether against the British or in the Civil War, left behind them a backwash of private outrage. There was an era of panic, intimidation – when men dared speak hardly above a whisper, when few slept quietly in their beds.

To understand Ireland one must realize how lately she has had to absorb this past. Her roads are dotted with wayside crosses, where ambushed men fell. Memories lie closely under the surface. The last of this, it is true, happened some thirty years ago: the generation which has grown up since shows a symptomatic revulsion against yesterday. The young would wish to step clear of the tragic story: all the same, the story is in the blood. And the inflammatory notion will never quite lie down while Partition lasts. Partition, the border agreed by the Treaty-makers, cuts off the six northern, Ulster counties of Ireland from the twenty-six which compose the Irish Republic. Northern Ireland, though having its own parliament, remains by wish and by fact, affiliated to Britain. It was the Ulstermen, through their mouthpiece Carson[5], who at the last successfully blocked up Home Rule. And with Irish fanaticism, Scottish tenacity, continues to cling to her strange position: come in to the Irish Republic she will not. If the ruling war-fear were to dissipate some end to partition *might* be in sight. But Ulster's usefulness as a base for the Allies during the Second World War reinforces her claim so long as a Third pends. As a whole, Ireland forms, willy nilly, a key point on Europe's Atlantic front: the ports, the accommodation for troops withheld by the (then) Irish Free State, were provided by Ulster. Alone among the Dominions (of which she was then one), the Irish Free State chose to remain neutral. Her neutrality was, throughout, respected – one has yet to compute at how great a cost.

That neutrality, also, has left its mark. On the positive side, it represented Ireland's first independent decision: at her own risk the country decided to stand alone. It comprehended readiness for the state of war: the coast were patrolled, the Free State army stood at alert. A German try at invasion, any British attempt to seize the Southern Irish ports, would have been, equally, withstood. With a certain grimness the Irish faced out their isolation. The isolation, however, was in itself impairing – it made for neutrality's negative, losing side. Travel between Ireland and England was suspended: contacts, communication suffered accordingly. Censorship, of a cautiously nulling kind, inhibited Irish newspapers. Postal censorship (which had to operate at the British as well as the Irish end) clamped down on personal stories of war experiences – Dublin, for instance knew of the London blitz only by bloated, uncertain and ghastly rumour. Gratitude for exemption from the horrors mingled, in certain Irish people, with a sensation of being sidetracked, of being out of step with their generation. The insufficiency of all news produced uneasiness: what might next be brewing? Worst, there was the taboo on judgement – for if one is neutral one must not take sides – fostered, it became first discouraging, later unnecessary, to think. This, at the stage of growth on which Ireland had entered by 1939, was a set-back: it became harder to be adult in Ireland. What was lost, then, still has to be caught up with.

The neutral, cautious years went against the grain, for Ireland traffics very much in opinion. Speech, and speech with a bias, is the nation's delight. Loud, lordly talkers cluster in pubs, congregate in the villages after Mass, mill through horses, pigs or cattle upon a fair day. There is a love of language, and endless enterprise in vocabulary. In no other English-speaking country with so much verve and volume, subtlety or force, Irish-English, as spoken, not only gains charm from the intonation, it has an integral rhythm of its own. Sentence-formations persist in it from the lost Irish; here and there Elizabethan archaisms remain. There is often a vivid fresh-coined imagery. It is true the older people speak better than the younger, and the very old people best of all. The present-day young in Ireland are either less fanciful or more taciturn: they are, also, charged with the burden of two languages.

For, that Ireland *should* still be an English-speaking country is a cause of offense. The dying-out, or say starving-out – of her own language ranks as damage done by her conquered years. It has meant broken cultural continuity, the loss of her ancient Celtic literary wealth. Heretofore, the reinstatement of Irish as *the* national language has come, for those who are moulding the new-born country, to be an aim of the first importance – it is viewed as one of the first means of restoring national identity, of advancing Ireland's self-realization. The trouble is, Irish cannot merely be fanned back into existence: at the moment, it has to be *imposed*, and, in Ireland nobody likes compulsion. Compulsory Irish has been, since the Treaty, welded into the State educational system: no school failing to teach it is officially recognised. To qualify for teaching or the Civil Service, or to become a holder of public office, one must have passed a fairly exacting language-test. In the schools, a number of subjects have to be taught *in* Irish – an extra tax on teacher and pupils. The child may tend to associate Irish only with the schoolroom. That the country's educational standard is less high than it was prior to 1922 has been asserted in some quarters, denied in others. A further objection is, that the modern Irish language is synthetic, bearing about as much relation to old Irish as modern Greek does to ancient. There has had to be a somewhat grotesque inclusion of adapted twentieth-century words.

Whether the aim is to supplant English, or to make the Irish bilingual (as the Welsh are) does not yet seem clear. What, in fact, are the present aims of Irish education? Are the young to be qualified to maintain their places in a competitive outside world; or, are they formed as the citizens of a future, more intensely Irish Ireland?

Traditionally, many of the Irish have gone abroad to work, and they still do. To the rebuilders of the country this is discouraging: there are attempts to halt the outgoing stream. Fewer now (since the quota) go to America, more to Britain. Britain, with her high pay and gigantic need, has for some time been steadily draining off not only the unskilled labour, the boys and girls, but also doctors, engineers, trained nurses, master craftsmen, and others whose skill is wanted at home. The impulse to go is not always mercenary; it may be ambitious – to do well in Ireland is to be reminded that, probably, one could do better elsewhere. The clever, effective or restless person is likely to find his own small island claustrophobic. At the same time, by the simpler country people England is viewed with some dismay – though no longer with animosity. America offered the lure of a fine future; England, in her present vicissitudes, does not. The impression that things are not going well in England is very strong. You make money there, but you may lose your soul. A spectral vision of English cities, irreligious, crime-ridden, immoral, demoralized hangs over anxious parents in homes from which young are gone. And forebodings gain strength from the attitude of the Catholic Church: the Church does not countenance the outgoings.

This is a Catholic country – having therefore, in aspect, something in common with Italy, France and Spain. A land of chapel and convent bells, of circumspect Mass-going Sunday mornings and dancing evenings, of crucifixes at crossroads, shrines, flower-decked altars in the streets, civic–religious processions of a Renaissance glory, young dazzling white muslin processions of first communicants. Catholicism tinges, and in its way enriches, the atmosphere of any Irish society – be it peasant, artisan, farmer or middle-class. Religion is Ireland's governing social force: nothing can have done more to stabilise Ireland during the uncertain years of her new growth. A country bound to a faith can never wholly fail to be integrated. The Church wields its temporal power wisely. Officially (though, be it said, officially) it remained disassociated from the national movement during the phase of violence, blood and struggle. Since then, it has given unstinted countenance to the new regime: in return, most evaluations remain religious – i.e. a man known to be 'a bad Catholic' does not get far in public life. And prestige, success in business or the professions rests, more than may be admitted, upon observances.

Catholicism has kept Ireland European: thanks to the Church there has never been, as there might, a descent to total insularity. Also the Church gives face to the country's innate conservatism – though in Ireland 'Reds' are hardly there to denounce. It must be recalled that this country has found herself by means of a national, not social, revolution: internal issues of 'left' and 'right' have not, so far, declared themselves. Strife, any question of a class struggle, formerly centred around land ownership: this the Land Act of 1923 at least in principal adjusted. By its critics, the Catholic Church in Ireland has been suspected of a reactionary attitude to progress, charged with a tendency to regard improved housing, extended social and health services, and so on, as 'materialistic'. There seems little concrete evidence that this is so: on the contrary the Church would appear concerned to keep all aspects of life within its domain. The parish priest and the village schoolmaster maintain a close working alliance; and the Church sponsors – is one to say, restricts? – not only the education but the recreations and pleasures of its children – village carnivals, concerts, matches and dancing are conducted under a watching eye. Catholic concern for family life is well known. At present, the young people are giving trouble; they begin to slip from under control. Till lately, this was a country of cool passions, lasting celibacies, dilatory courtships and late marriages. But sex, in spite of rigorous supervision of reading-matter and films, has lately inconveniently been discovered. Denunciations thunder from the altar.

Ireland's Protestant minority fares well. Numerically, it is said to be on the decline; socially it is stable and compact. Some anxiety as to the fate of Protestants was felt in 1922: the Catholics, then assuming control, had centuries of grievance behind them; they had been victimised by the Penal Laws. Revenges seemed likely enough: in fact, there was equable generosity. The Protestant Church of Ireland, till the British withdrew, had been the official church of the country: disestablishment, halfway through the nineteenth century, did not effectively mitigate its power. All of Ireland's surviving ancient cathedrals were annexed by the British-supported Protestants: not one of them, so far, has been reclaimed. In general, the ugliness of Ireland's ecclesiastical buildings, whether Catholic or Protestant, is to be deplored: the ancient ornate beautiful English village church, with its windows and monuments, is unknown here. Here, a Protestant church is to be distinguished from a Catholic by the fact that its tower or steeple does not carry a cross – a cross is felt to savour of Popery. Of the squat grey Protestant churches dotting the countryside, many now are derelict or in ruin – shrinkage of Protestant populations made a re-grouping of their parishes necessary: many worshippers travel distances to their Sunday services.

In fact, the religious irritant, like the class irritant, was removed by British withdrawal. Protestantism had been the religion of the 'Ascendancy'; i.e. of the wealthy landlords, kept in place by Britain. Generally, Protestants still are well-to-do – landowning gentry, business or professional people, shopkeepers, farmers (in the cities only are there Protestant poor). Their contribution to the community has been recognised: Protestants, some of whom descend from distinguished Huguenot banking families, enjoy the reputation of being energetic, dependable and honest. In the main, they confine themselves to their own affairs, though some are re-entering public life. Their education receives aid from the State; transport is provided for scattered Protestant children to village schools. Formerly Unionist in their politics, such Protestants as have remained in Ireland give wholehearted support to the new regime. Their number have lately been reinforced by immigrant English – a wealthy new wave of settlers in flight from British post-war taxation. This influx, which began with the 1945 victory of Labour, is known in Ireland as 'the retreat from Moscow'. 'Once,' said a Dublin wit of the incoming English, 'y conquered us by the sword; now they conquer us by the cheque-book.' On the whole, these refugee-settlers have acclimatised themselves – they have repaired mansions and put money into the cultivation of land. Their value to Ireland is not great.

Ireland's sole architectural beauties (apart from surviving cathedrals) are of Ascendancy date. The eighteenth century, carrier of classicism, has left here its august mark. The cities of Dublin and Limerick are Georgian, elegant squares, streets and individual façades of the same epoch beautify dusty, outlying country towns. And, small or large, Georgian country houses are many. This enduring, classic, aristocratic touch is often overlooked by the tourist in search of more haphazard romantic beauties. The visitor may see Ireland as a peasant country with a kindly, somewhat primitive bourgeois overlay: in fact, it is at present a bourgeois country in search of a missing aristocracy. Passion for grandeur, written in stone or brick, can but effect the mentality. 'The fall of the big house' is a popular myth in romantic Irish writing: that it *is*, all the same, a myth should be stressed. Many mansions were burned during the fighting, but those not ruined are now inhabited. Ensconced on their own land, concealed by trees, such homes are mostly out of view of the tourist. They do exist, however: the way of life they preserve is a factor in the complexity of Ireland.

This is a countryman's country. Dublin is not Ireland, in the sense that Paris is not France, and the urbanization of the provincial cities is only skin-deep. Thousands of Irish go no further than their local country town – and the town, with its low irregular painted streets is little more than an extended village. The population is not only small but scattered; it sifts away into creeks and pockets, leaving great tracts of emptiness. Ireland breeds lean men, weathered but handsome women, vividly-coloured and independent children. The hardiness that goes with the way of life was, till lately, lessened by under-nutrition, and the standard of living is still low. The staple diet – potatoes, bread, black tea and skimmed milk (the cream goes to the creameries) – may receive, now, more sustaining additions – fatty 'green' bacon, a knuckle-end, tinned foods. But agricultural wages, though jacked up, still do not keep pace with the cost of living; said to be generally higher than in Britain. The countryman's sense of hardship is mitigated by physical conservatism: traditionally, he has never expected much – at any rate, he is doing better than his forebears. His isolation has been reduced by the bus services – which, with the trains, form part of the State-owned transport system. He otherwise makes his journeys to Mass, fairs, funerals by bicycle, ass-cart or pony-trap; the farmers are acquiring small Ford cars. Distances, time and weather count for little – respect for occasion, sense of observance, love of festivity or the wish to meet make whole countrysides travel the roads on Sundays or holidays. On summer nights, villages hold their carnivals – fancy-dress processions, decorated hay-wains, swing-boats, flare-lights, gambling-wheels. Hurling teams (the game is pronounced 'hurley') confront one another on Sunday afternoons. There is coursing, and there are greyhound trials. Working days finish in sociability – in the dusk men gather at the crossroads or on the bridges; the girls make off in chattering troupes. Cottage doors stand open to calling neighbours.

Irish who move to cities or cross the sea feel the breaking-up of the small, familiar unity, parish or neighbourhood. Until this can be reproduced, in some manner, in the new surroundings there is loneliness, and a threat of disintegration. The race is group-minded, dependent on knowing and being known – hence, in cities, the close-corporation character of the street or tenement. Slow, and not always beneficial, is the adaptation to city life: urbanism is always against the grain. The Dubliner, even the Cork man, is in physique inferior to his country brothers – looks are less good, morale lower. With this in view, the recent shift of the population from the country into the cities is to be viewed seriously: it is the dangerous side of the de Valera Government's pro-industrial policy. Industries, fostered by a protective tariff, are on the increase. Ireland does not bid for an outside market, but the aim is that she should be self-sufficient. Textiles, boots and shoes, glass and china, confectionary, biscuits, cosmetics, tobacco, hardware, paint and wallpaper, and so on, are now being manufactured within the shores. Distilleries and breweries date from further back. British firms have set up and given their names to factories which employ local labour. Ireland has one coal mine, in Co. Kilkenny: coal almost all has to be imported – hence the importance of electrification. The Shannon hydro-electrification scheme, masterpiece of German engineering, came into action in 1927; it is soon to be supplemented by another in Co. Dublin – the exploitation of water-power has been one of Ireland's most epoch-making advances: within the next few years it is hoped that districts still without electricity will have been linked with the main grid.

Farming, especially dairy farming, is expected to profit by this aid, though outlying farmers are still shy of it. Agriculturally, Ireland *should* rank with Denmark: she is still, however, held up by divided policy – tillage or grazing? During the late war (known here as 'the Emergency'), the spectre of wheat-shortage brought in compulsory tillage: manures were short, and too many crops were taken off the land, which has not yet quite recovered from its impoverishment. Given the good grass, grazing, with the raising of a sufficient crop of roots to feed stock in winter, would appear to be a solution. There is also the matter of feed for pigs and poultry. Sugar-beet (a tricky crop to raise) supplies adequate sugar-factories; and Ireland produces enough wheat to keep her existent flour mills turning – but self-sufficiency as to wheat would, again, shear off land from dairy-farming. The Government co-operative system under which the numerous creameries are run is leaving its mark, on the whole a good one, on Irish small-town and country life. Egg-collection and grading are also organised. The trend to the cities, by draining off country labour, again tends to tip the balance in favour of grazing and dairy-farming: tillage requires more men. The Dublin Ministry of Agriculture, at this juncture, has in hand what are the country's most vital problems.

Ireland's progressive sacrifice of the picturesque to the utilitarian may be deprecated by the tourist, but is a healthy sign. The reafforestation scheme carries conifer-plantations, like black fur over former bogs and up the bases of mountains. Land-reclamation schemes are in progress – bogs are being drained, formerly-flooding rivers have reinforced banks. In the central rich Bog of Allen, peat-cutting goes on under Government aegis – the square black clefts and near dark stacks may be viewed, from above, on the air-line from Dublin to Shannon. Work on roads extends from the main highways to the coastal and minor cross-country routes: the native or touring motorist, the bus and the sight-seeing char-a-banc thereby profit. The primitive two-roomed cabin with its mud walls and thatched top, dear to the artist's eye, has received overdue condemnation from health authorities: working-class Ireland is being rehoused – red-roofed family houses, monotonous in their alikeness but sound in plan, dot the countrysides and, in blocks with gardens, form modern annexes to the older towns. Water-supply – a rural innovation – and drainage, follow the new developments. One by one, village schools conform with the approved pattern; the health-clinic and the inspecting medico are no longer strangers. Most important: Ireland is waging war against her deep-rotting enemy, tuberculosis. The endemic habits of over-crowding, hygienic carelessness and fatalism are, however, not easily met. Maternity-centres and child-welfare projects still confront a sort of mystical opposition – who dare touch the sanctity of the home?

Ireland may draw abreast with modernization; she neither will nor can compete with the modern world. Her traditional assets remain her strong ones – for instance, this is the country of the horse: horse-breeding, horse-coping, fairs, hunting and racing. Horses have an aristocratic timelessness. To fail to attend a horse fair or horse show, to fail to make one of the crowds at races, is to know only half the reality of the country. Sporting and gambling are, as you care to see them, either the national passion or the national vice. Dog-racing stadiums spring up almost as fast as cinemas; gambling-wheels whirl at Church-sponsored carnivals; cards flicker, dice rattle deep into the nights. Here is a bizarre inverse to the also-prevailing strictness, caution and, in some aspects, Puritanism of life . . . Smoky-toned Irish tweeds, smoky-flavoured Irish whisky, both reaching back in origin, are, again, the most picturesquely popular of her products. As to amenities, there is still a lag: the Irish Tourist Association, bidding for the most promising, possible source of income, has subsidised and attempts to reform hotels, supplies information-brochures and has been forward in pressing for improvement of roads. Chromium, strip-lighting and plumbing, however, still add little more than a flashy surface to ancient habit. And cooking, when it aims for the higher flights, is not yet to be ranked among the Irish gifts. Bacon-and-eggs, mutton chops, boiled potatoes are done sublimely: the sub-Continental cuisine of the more ambitious hotels should be fought shy of. As to food, Ireland is conservative and, beyond that, indifferent. Ireland's tourist hopes have been somewhat dangerously inflated by prevailing currency restrictions: since the war, she has received thousands barred from holidays to the Continent. Her meat and eggs (however rising their cost) continue to lure in the hungry British. *Should* conditions ever return to normal, a considerable and maybe disheartening revaluation of her attractions will be necessary.

The Irish Republic has five principal cities – Limerick, Waterford, Galway, Cork and Dublin: all are ports. Small picturesque port towns, with vivid if sleepy quaysides, are also niched in the estuaries: these maintain themselves by fishing and minor traffic. Sea-goers breed in such places, and on satellite islands: the British Royal and Merchant Navies receive, annually, Irish recruits. This, with the outgo of workers and influx of tourists, keeps open the relation with Britain. Mutual interdependence is recognised – the exchange basis makes for amicability. Anglophobia, which at the worst of times was more theoretical than personal, has run its course, or died out for lack of fuel. Equally, a sort of political languor has set in – Ireland, now that freedom has been achieved, lacks the once enflaming national motive: anticlimax hangs, faintly, over internal politics. Election excitement, whipped up by the press, has not lately been sufficient to feed the polling-booths. The two main parties, Fianna Fáil (Mr de Valera's) and Fine Gael (in which Mr Costello[6] succeeded to Mr Cosgrave's leadership of the once pro-Treaty, 1922 group) have run each other close at recent elections: each, successively, winning by a narrow majority. Proportional representation, whose merits remain under debate, fails to present the countryman with the old, clear alternative – the system is not easy to grasp; at the count, numbers of voting-papers are found spoiled. No apathy, no obscuration of motives have, however, for long displaced Mr de Valera. His lasting hold on the country is a personal one.

Intellectual, non-rhetorical and detached, his is not a figure which one would have expected to appeal. Yet Ireland, notably fickle to patriots, has stayed true to him. He has achieved the all but impossible task of carrying the past, with its heroisms, forward into the present, with its prosaic practicalities. Revolutionary memory still invests the figure of this adult statesman – few in Europe have so calmly made the transition from the one to the other. Mathematical professor who took up arms – de Valera was active in 1916, in the subsequent fighting against the British and as Republican leader during the 1922 Civil War – he now brings mathematical philosophy to the art of government. Stubborn and, it has been suggested, authoritarian, he commands respect – Ireland, quickly iconoclastic, has hailed few wholly respected men. There is a touch of the grandee, also perhaps something sacerdotal and medieval, about his tall, thin, Spanish-avised person, on which a raincoat hangs like a robe. This man represents something *to* Ireland,

and touches something *in* Ireland, which would at present be irreplaceable. He has dared to ride full-tilt against illusion, illusion on which this country has lived – his 'austerity budget' of spring 1952 shook Ireland from her prosperity dream. The expected fall of his government did not follow: in three succeeding by-elections Fianna Fáil not only held but gained seats. From this man, the country takes what she does not like. Yet ultimately, illusion remains the element. Shift though it may, like light from hill to hill, it is always somewhere – entrancing the visitor, maddening the realist, sweetening and varying life for the simple soul. Ireland has shown, and shows – in her literature, her festivities, her relationships – glints of genius. In whatever country, one must live how one can: it may be seen why Ireland lives as she does.

Ireland, June 1954, *House and Garden*, Essay

Ireland is a little country with a long legend: many associations go with her name. She has a subtle hold upon the imagination; she haunts the memory – never, perhaps, growing quite familiar even to those who know her all their lives; for she is perpetually showing some unexpected aspect of her face. Weather, notably capricious, makes for the variations in her mood, and her landscape dramatically changes; within less than an hour along the road one may have left a rocky gorge for the suavest pasture-land, a verdant and humid river valley for a stark upland, or a towering promontory of cliffs, wave-beaten, haunted by mewing gulls, for the most serene golden-sanded bay. To visit Ireland means to carry away a strange and sometimes disturbing blend of impressions; can so much, the visitor asks himself, really have been contained in so small a space?

To travel in Ireland, it has been said, is to travel some way back in time. The pressures of the modern world seem to lighten; tensions relax. A sense of the past pervades the visitor, stealing over his senses with the tang of turf-smoke, the half-awake look of low roofed grey or white houses, the sleepy hum of the wind through trees. Horse and ass carts still set the paces of the highways; ironshod wheels rattle along the lanes; the swish and glitter of automobiles still seem something of an anachronism. Farms and mansions, sheltered by belts of woodland, have the air of being remote from change; the tiny and undulating fields, crisscrossed by unmortared stone walls or bosky hedgerows, look like a patchwork counterpane in a nursery. Life goes on, but beneath the spell of monotony Ireland *does* progress; she is shaking off the reproach of being a 'backward' country. New schools and hospitals go up, creameries thrive, industries revivify small communities, high roads acquire surface, and housing projects extend villages and add new outer zones to cities and towns. It will be long, however, before this strikes the visitor's eye; predominatingly, Ireland looks as she always has: wayward, unregulated and picturesque. The factory flanks upon the ruin; dusky dark-windowed stucco or stone façades soar over the up-to-date little shop-fronts. Modernity still seems an uncertain overlay, an experiment which does not go far – whole stretches of Ireland remain untouched by it.

Tourist organisation does much for Ireland; sometimes I fear, however, that it may confine the visitor somewhat too rigidly to the beaten tracks. Those who can spare us not more than three or four days must make do (and will do far from badly) with the motor coach, the planned route, the prescribed hotel and the more famous highpoints of our scenery – seacoast, mountain and lake. Wholly to shun the tourist areas would be to miss what has made Ireland famous in song and story: the drip of the waterfall in the lush woods of embowered Killarney, water-threaded Kenmare, Glengariff's tree-reflecting tides, the purple of Connemara, the blue of Donegal, the song-haunted glens and sculptured coastline of Antrim. These are among Ireland's jewels, and she is proud of them. But we have more than these numbered beauty-spots. This is not simply a country to be viewed, it is a country to be explored and savoured. Something here, in the air, is the foe of hurry. Spirit, like beauty, is elusive; mystery is lying ever ahead, beyond those still further ranges of hills, round valley's corner and the turn of the river. Ireland calls for individual voyages of discovery.

Our official scenery is on the grandiose side; in some lights it has almost a painted look, and it has perhaps been pictured rather too often. But we have also countrysides in a subtler vein: small mountains swell gently out of the cornfields; white roads twist and wander to destinations whose names have seldom been heard. The southwest coast is fretted with estuaries, up whose wooded silence creep lonely entering tides. Rivers trace a course which is worth pursuing: castles, abbeys and small towns, each with its history, are strung along them; one watches the salmon leap and the heron skim. Spanned by many arched bridges, overhung by crags, mounting meadows or terraced gardens, the rivers of Ireland are not less noble than the rivers of France; known to the fisherman, they are not enough (*I* think) sought out for their own sakes, for their romance and beauty. One hears less (and I always wonder why) of the Irish rivers than of the Irish lakes. Out of the western midlands, the heart of Ireland, the great Shannon sweeps onward past Clonmacnoise (with its grouped Celtic churches, crosses and towers) through the panorama of Limerick and Clare, widening out into sheets of water dotted with islands, narrowing in again between folding hills, till its banks fade with distance: it has come to the sea. But I think, too, of our Blackwater of the south, welling up away in the mists of Kerry, curving west-to-east through the counties of Cork and Waterford, under the bridges of Mallow, Fermoy, Lismore, till at Cappoquin it takes a right-angle turn, proceeding southward to the Atlantic between ranks of Ireland's mightiest trees. Youghal, small fortress city with crumbling battlements, keeps watch at the Blackwater's mouth. In its final reach, between Cappoquin and Youghal, the river is navigable by motor launch; elsewhere, good roads follow its course.

Youghal is an example of something else I count among Ireland's charms: historic and beautiful little towns. It, like the not far distant Kinsale (which, still more unspoiled, is also in County Cork), is built on an estuary; both have been thriving ports and are the holders of ancient charters. Both have been battlegrounds; both are now images of tranquillity – fishing boats bob on the tide by the sleepy wharves. Towns such as these were built when culture still stamped prosperity. There are Venetian windows and fanlit doorways and after dusk, when the lamps are lit, one looks into high-ceilinged, moulded-and-marbled rooms. Here merchants dwelled, and sea-going captains knew the pleasures of home. Steep silent streets and still steeper footways mount between garden walls; archways give on courtyards. In Kinsale, you see women in hooded black cloaks, fashioned a hundred years ago. Ireland's seaports of the southwest and west, set back in their sheltering bays and estuaries, have about them a touch of Latin Europe: from here there was trade with France and Spain. And on them (with the exception, perhaps, of Galway) sophistication has not yet laid its hand: the visitor is welcome but not exploited. Youghal boasts a *plage*, but this extends at a distance from the narrow traditional main street.

Inland, there are towns of no less character, small enough to be sweet with country air, but none the less sedate with a civic dignity: court-houses, clock-towers, fine façades, tree-planted walks on the river frontages. Indeed, these are cities in miniature; they contain a flavour of living – for generations they have been centres, social no less than commercial, for the outlying regions in which they stand. Having been at their height in the eighteenth century (when bad ads and difficult transport sundered most Irish countryfolk from Dublin) these tiny cities are august-provincial capitals, each with ghost-grey spell. Clonmel, in County Tipperary – which owes its wealth of classical architecture to the richness of the surrounding country, some of Ireland's finest pastoral land – and Westport, in County Mayo – whose town-plan was the work, I have always heard, of a Frenchman – are fair examples. These, and others, are places to hasten through: at the first glance they are apt to reveal little, but it is repaying to linger and gaze in them.

Where to stay in Ireland is a matter, clearly, for individual taste, the factors of time and cost. Against the larger, 'recommended' hotels, absolutely nothing is to be said except that they essentially *are* for tourists and, consequently, are lacking in local character. Conveniently placed in the famous beauty-spots, they cater for sightseers in a hurry; their cuisine, like their décor, is international. Those wishing to savour Ireland at more leisure would do well to try the hotels in the smaller towns, many of which have been brought, if not up-to-date, at least within reach of that objective; quite a number are good in a simple way. Former coaching inns keep their big bedrooms, mysterious corridors and (if you care for it) local colour: in the bars and coffee-rooms you hear racy talk. If you prefer to shun towns, seek out the guest-houses into which many family mansions have been converted: here, at the end of your day, you may fall asleep near a whispering river, the sheen of a lake or the natural somnolence of trees.

Irish cooking has not a promising name: it is fair to say it *is* bad when it is pretentious. Keep, if you can, to the simpler 'food of the country' (yet another reason to seek out the smaller inns). It has been remarked that the best of our specialities, as a drink and food, are characterised by a slightly smoky flavour: certainly that holds good of Irish whisky, tea, ham and bacon, eggs fried over an open fire, soda-bread (baked atop of a pot lid and strewn with ashes) and grilled or fried lamb or mutton chops. And the fluffiness of the Irish boiled potato, often cooked in its jacket, has not been overpraised. The deep-yellow 'farmers' butter' is deliciously salty. As against that, we are bad at pastry, poor at sauces; and our coffee-making notably is abominable (travellers would do well to import with them some 'instant' brand of coffee, and make their own).

At no season, I am compelled to say, should one come to Ireland without at least *some* warm clothing. Prepare for the worst as to weather: if you have done so it is likely our contrary climate may shower upon you bland golden days. Your most memorable, your sublimest moments in Ireland may be when ethereal light and transparent colour break through, the minute the rain has stopped. Bring with you, however, provision for indoor days or otherwise undiverted hotel evenings: playing-cards, games, puzzles, mystery stories (those last, in the British 'Penguin' edition, you are likely also to pick up along your way). And above all, get the most from your Irish travel by providing yourself with maps and the better guidebooks. I would recommend, too, a selection of 'background reading,' i.e. books not in the guidebook class, such as Frank O'Connor's *Irish Miles*, Seán O'Faoláin's *Irish Journey*, Dr Praeger's *The Way That I Went*, and (if you care for the still fairly recent past) Dr Constantia Maxwell's *Country and Town in Ireland Under the Georges*. A beforehand reading of any or all of these should help you plan your individual route. And why not a pocket-size volume of Irish history? More than one of such is, admirably, now on sale.

James Joyce's Dublin, by Patricia Hutchins, 8 May 1957, *Tatler*, Review

People who know Dublin may be divided into those who can and who cannot remember seeing her for the first time. Into the latter class fall the Dublin-born, for whom the city slid gradually into being, loomed by degrees up out of the natal mists, as the infant senses began to register. The visitor, on the other hand receives a sharp, clear impact of first impressions, which he digests consciously: *his* Dublin remains objective, to be analysed, compared with other capitals and discussed. For the native, however far he may travel, Dublin remains the norm – her range of lights, sounds, smells, suddenly-open spaces, lengthy perspectives, high flat facades, archways, mews, alleys, monuments, quays and river-reflections, ever-visible mountains and inblown tang of the sea compose, together, the primal base of all and every other experience. For the place is his first conception of any scene.

Of any 'early surroundings', in their effect upon any person, this may be true: what was first beheld keeps a special, quasi-symbolic significance. But in particular Dublin, with her intensive character, seems to possess the power to stamp herself on the most ordinary of her sons and daughters. In the case of the artist, with his ultra-susceptibility, the effect is double – and more. James Joyce was a Dublin child.

James Joyce's Dublin is not simply a work on the Joyce topography – Miss Hutchins goes further, tracing the link between the creative imagination and the matter on which it fed. Joyce has, by now, brought many pilgrims to Dublin: in making the round of places mentioned in the books or associated with the early years of the life she has not been unique. What is unique, here, is her attempt to enter, and moreover to travel, step by step, the landscape of Joyce's personal memory – that memory which was not among the least of the phenomenal elements in his art. 'I don't think Jim ever forgot a thing – all his life,' someone who knew him said. As we know, Joyce's total vision of Dublin was retrospective: he wrote in exile. Distance lent, in his case, not enchantment but a sort of haunted intensity to the view. The city which, by re-creating for himself he created immortally for others had driven him from herself, finally, while he was still young. In return for a torment the man could not endure, the artist added to Dublin a fourth dimension.

'It is not,' says Miss Hutchins in her Foreword, 'until the emergence of people, cultures, ideas and psychological tendencies have been studied with the care and comparative research now given to factual history, that the issues inherent in James Joyce's work will be clearly defined.' This must be true – James Joyce, as his work progressed, forced intellect over the bounds of consciousness, seeking a path of language over tracts not till then touched by coherent thought. His books are documents for the future: we, still, lack the equipment to take their full measure. Behind him, some way behind him, the literature of experience advances. His apparent modernity is no more than his own version of what is primitive: his myths and symbols root in river and rocks; monoliths cast their sometimes unintelligible shadows across his prose; pre-historical racial currents flow through it. Stephen Dedalus, beset by so-called reality, the so-called reality of Dublin, is a man of all time. Stephen's was the Dublin of an immediate yesterday: we confront him, are confronted by him, at every turn of Dublin today.

Bernard Shaw, having read several fragments of *Ulysses* in serial form, wrote: 'It is a revolting record of a disgusting phase of civilisation: but it is a truthful one.' (He himself had left Dublin when he was twenty.) The embryonic *Stephen Hero*, and *Portrait of the Artist*, could, with the culminating *Ulysses*, be called more fairly records *of* a revolt. The 'truthfulness' Mr Shaw concedes was as intrinsic as it was unavoidable – the novels bring transmuted autobiography. Joyce lived twice over – once in early 'real' life, again in re-creation – the moments and hours he set down: burned forever into him was the actuality of the Dublin scene from which those moments and hours were inseperable.

Miss Hutchins' writing about Dublin and its marine and inland environment is better than descriptive; it is evocative. Her sensitivity to places is unforced; so also is her aliveness to the many aspects of this one city – by turns sedate, melancholic, shabbily cosy, sordid, pungent, showy, jarring or lyrical. She captures the roar of a traffic nexus, the breezy openness of the sea wall, the faded backwater quietness of suburban roads in which she traced the succession of Joyce dwellings. Mr Joyce senior, forever flamboyant and insolvent, also from time to time housed his family in the more overcast portions of North Dublin. The Joyce who was Stephen Dedalus – intolerant, to some intolerable – remains perpetuated in many quarters: his character has been made to emerge with extraordinary freshness from these accounts of his contacts with streets and persons. Not in vain has she followed him through the Dublin years, visited Belvedere College and University College, studied old student magazines, entered the Martello tower, paced the strand, mounted the steps he mounted, opened the doors he opened, stopped and stared where he stopped and stared. That what gave off so much *to* him should not give off something *of* him is not, surely, fanciful to suppose?

The excellence, the intelligent continuity of the actual writing of *James Joyce's Dublin* should be stressed, at a first glance, the book might be outweighed by its illustrations. It might seem an album, a visual record purely – whereas Miss Hutchins does supply, in word-pictures, much that has not been covered by the camera. The photographs are eloquent and delightful: they comprehend several little-known portraits (a particular star should go to the one on page 18), and, apart from those, may be grouped as 'period' pieces of the Dublin of Joyce's day, and contemporary pictures of city detail. The former in their selection show taste and humour; the latter, a dramatic feeling for subject – exemplified by the sand-ripples and the foreshortened iron bridge. Miss Hutchins either took or was present at the taking of these present-day photographs, which are well in character with her prose.

Bowen's Court, 1958, *Holiday*, Essay

The house stands in lonely country. From its windows nothing but trees, grassland and, at the back, mountains are to be seen – no road, no other habitation. It is square, high and set in a shallow hollow, screened by plantations from the winds blowing over heather and bog behind it. Fair for tillage, better for grazing, the acres are watered by springs and streams, and here and there gashed by limestone cuttings – the stone the house is built of was quarried locally. White-grey, the classic façade stares out from its leafy background – still somewhat a foreigner to the landscape. Such is the home envisaged and brought to being in County Cork, some two miles from the Limerick border, by my ancestor Henry Bowen III, who in the year 1775 saw the roof on and moved in with his family. His descendants have lived here ever since.

The house faces south, on to a vast open field known as the lawn. Woods reach out and partly enclose the sides; at the back are the stables and stable yard; with, beyond them, the farm enclosures and buildings, and the walled three-acre vegetable garden. Everything functional is hidden: the Bowen's Court frontage is social. The main door gives on a terrace, from which steps descend to a gravel sweep – destined for the turning and drawing up of carriages yesterday, motorcars today. Henry Bowen III, high-spirited Georgian, could not have conceived of life without hospitality: the arrival of visitors from a distance continues to feature in our days and nights. So great is the silence around the place that one can hear anything coming miles away. The horse age lasted a long time in County Cork: clearly do I remember the spanking trotting, sound of whirling wheels, creak of leather and shafts. Motors turn in more stealthily at the far-off gateways, yet never take me totally by surprise.

Ireland, small as it is, can give the effect of being a stretching continent. Tract after tract of emptiness seems unbounded. Our distances reckoned in terms of miles work out to be tiny, all but laughable – but what counts here is distance as a *sensation*. Bowen's Court, today, is in fact, by no means out of the current world, yet its first isolation forever stamps it. The green illusion remains unbroken. But what I do not see is, all the same, there. Sunk between stone walls and belts of woodland, a main road runs glossily past my gates – the Dublin–Killarney through route. The diesels of the Cork–Dublin railway stop at Mallow, within half an hour's reach. Shannon Airport is fifty-two miles from me – in some weathers a big plane, off its course, thrums its way over Bowen's Court roof and treetops, far up over the cloud ceiling. The beat of the engines sounds lost, labourious, anxious – anachronistic. Not more so than the hum of the tractor in the next valley or, at harvest, the shuttling roar of the combine. Mechanisation no more than scratches the surface of that timeless enormous hush which is our norm.

The disturbers are what they have been always; wind, rain, thunder. The elements play cat-and-mouse with my innovations – I listen to radio, the reception crackles; I have a telephone, but the service is subject to inexhaustible 'acts of God.' All dwellers far out in the country,

I know, are hit by crises and dislocations. What is peculiar to Bowen's Court seems to be that it takes practically nothing to make one feel that the twentieth century is, after all, a fiction.

Henry Bowen III, in choosing his site, was not aiming at loneliness for its own sake. He built where seemed to him best, within limits set by the boundaries of his bare inherited land – hollow for shelter, aspect for sunshine. Nevertheless, his ambitious mansion islanded itself in a wide sea of country. He was neighbour to none.

In his correspondence, during the building years, I find no mention of any architect: I am told it is possible he did not employ one, but, instead, had Bowen's Court copied from a plate in one of those albums of classical architectural engravings much in circulation, then, among country gentry. It says much for Henry and his contemporaries that they let their fancies be fired in such a way. Crude as may have been their personal habits, brutish the noisier of their pleasures, they at least respected a culture they could not claim. The same spark appeared in Henry when he stocked his library with many noble classics, Latin, French, English. He had each binding stamped in gold with his wife's initials.

Alas, the Bowen's Court bookshelves suffered a furious later purge at the hands of a Mrs Eliza Bowen, wife of Henry III's second son Robert I. This took place *circa* 1820. Eliza, a vigorous Plymouth Sister, threw out all novels and many dramatic works, including the greater part of Shakespeare – how she overlooked Dryden I never know. She also banished card tables – slender circular models, folding into half moons, with which all livingrooms were provided.

(The delinquents, no worse for eighty years of disuse, were retrieved by my mother from a Bowen's Court cellar – their tops still caked with tallow from the candles of all-night players.)

Poor Robert I was a victim, and not the last, of the depletion of the family coffers caused by the over-expenditure on Bowen's Court. Henry III had called a halt, though not soon enough, when he had furnished and decorated the main rooms – contenting himself, when it came to the outdoor scene, with planting trees (now grown to great size) and throwing out one long avenue to the west. Thus the surround of Bowen's Court remained in more or less its untamed romantic state. My Victorian grandfather Robert II laid down a second long avenue, to the east, and levelled a croquet lawn under the drawing-room windows, ornamenting the slope above with exotic shrubs. Two water closets, encased in a sort of tower, were gummed by him on to the back of the house; he also added offices and a butler's pantry.

Henry VI, my father, kept Bowen's Court much as his father left it. As my father left it, it came to me.

From outside, the house looks larger than it is. Many are the windows: on front and flanks there is a polished expanse of glass. Inside, the rooms are spacious, elatingly high, surprisingly few. Bowen's Court is three floors high – four if you count the basement. The ground floor proper contains four livingrooms, all of the same size, and the capacious shaft of the main staircase. The entrance hall (to be numbered among the livingrooms), has on one side, the library, on the other, the drawing-room, behind which the diningroom is set.

Between room and room there are high mahogany doors; another, at the end of the hall, leads to the foot of the staircase. Two wide flights, massive with carved banisters, terminate in a gallery: the second floor. Opposite the head of the stairway opens 'the lobby,' an upper hall having on either side a square corner bedroom with narrow dressing room – a third, similar bedroom is approached from the gallery.

The *grand escalier* goes no further: due to economy it has shot its bolt! So to the third (and top) floor you must ascend by the 'back' stairs, more humbly zigzagging up from the service quarters. By this means you are landed into Bowen's Court's one startling feature: the Long Room. Long indeed, intended to be a ballroom, this runs right through the heart of the house, front to back, south-north. Each end holds three crouching windows – and each end seems unbelievably distant from the other. Along each side, spaced far apart, are doors: in all, six bedrooms give on to the Long Room. Above this? Nothing. Bat-haunted rafters, the Alpine slated formation of the roof. That is all. Our living space is contained in this one upright block: nothing straggles beyond it.

My purpose in keeping Bowen's Court going differs from that of my forebears, and more widely than difference in generation can account for. It is more specific. They were landowning gentry who administered property, farmed some hundreds of acres, drew rents from the rest. I am a writer, living by my pen. The house today is maintained as a place to write in: as such it happily is ideal – were it not, I could and would not maintain it.

Everything during the working day subordinates itself to the study table. As though on another planet the wind hums, a garden cart creaks, dishes clink on a tray. At all other times insistent, Bowen's Court *has* the power to disconnect itself from my consciousness. Yet not quite: something filters in from the green environment, feeding imagination, generating thought. Out of the timeless atmosphere comes, like a bright new moment, an idea. Yes, the place *is* crowded, not by phantoms but by images; other-than-physical inhabitants it has – the urgent characters in my growing stories. And this I find: at Bowen's Court, unlike elsewhere, there is no sharp break or disharmony between writing and life. To live is to be in company, to share. Of the friends who join me, many are writers.

The big livingrooms, asking for sociability, never are disappointed for long. Writers on the rebound from their exacting solitude are the gayest mortals: toward evening there is a banging-open of doors, a haste to look for each other, talk, exclamations, laughter. Bowen's Court then becomes what artists must have, an extensive playroom, and what friends like best, a non-desert island. It can be gone away from, then come back to – in the car we slip through a landscape liquid with sunset; or we walk in file through the woods in sight of the mountains, beating back brambles, talking over our shoulders. For a pause it is also a great thing to be sitting in twos or threes on the terrace steps, gazing at the lawn in front of the house as though it were the sea, we birds on a rock. Indoors we fool with invented games by the phantasmagoric light of a wood fire, or play cards at the original tables. Meals, now, we eat in the entrance hall (the former diningroom, at the back, having been abandoned: it was too cavernous).

The last act of any Bowen's Court day plays itself out in the library or drawing-room . . . Pink curtains drawn, lamp-lit, with a fire in a wreathed Victorian grate, my grandmother's drawing-room has the effect of keying us up to its mild grandeur. It was decorated, and has not been changed since, when that Elizabeth came here as a bride: 1859. She loved its grey-and-gold scrolled wallpaper, and plaster frieze swagged with roses – and I don't wonder. I and my friends crowd stylishly, if not formally, on the central outsize vermilion sofa. In here, the only cerebral touch is the ebony bookcase she gave her eldest son, my father, for his mounting number of school-prize volumes. The shelves were gentle to them, being velvet lined.

The library, family livingroom (for we *are* a family) looks slap-dash, weathered and workaday by day: book-lined walls, book-loaded tables, capacious shabby honey-corduroy chairs. But it takes on a majesty with nightfall. Deep in their ranks sunk between the windows, books seem, while receding into the dark, to exhale their being into our talk; their intellectual wealth mellows the air into curls of our cigarette smoke. In here, conversation sweeps, swoops, takes an unforeseeable course – by now the ribbed velvet arms of the chairs are rubbed to a gloss by the hands of excited talkers. ('Your intellectual friends,' said one of my aunts, 'seem to be exceedingly hard on furniture!') Book-housing space has become a problem: by now my own bright-jacketed newcomers are wedged alongside calf-bound classics of the age of the house, or crushed between stout Victorians in maroon or olive. Each season's hatch out, from New York or London, must find for itself a footing, where it can – and each year, some author bids for permanent place. Do we need a second Eliza, a thrower-out?

It is in the library that I remember Eudora Welty in the first hour of her first visit, turning her head, remarking, 'I've just realised, I don't think I've ever been so far north before.' (We checked on an atlas later: she was right.) Eudora, gracing the drawing-room both in her own way and as a Southerner can, played the plaintive, long-neglected piano; one June midnight, too, she emerged from the kitchen having conjured into existence an onion pie. In the library I recollect Evelyn Waugh, scooping desultorily, a little crossly, at a bat which had shattered the evening for me by flying in – I cannot stay in a room with a bat: I cannot endure them! David Cecil, having retired for the night, was heard by his floor neighbours in a spooky monologue. It transpired next morning that a white owl had stood unblinking at the end of his bed; in vain had he reasoned with the intruder. Nor are bats and owls the only nocturnals. Oxford talkers take little count of the clock: David, again, and his colleague Isaiah Berlin are known to have started a conversation at the foot of the stairs, around midnight, and to have finished it close on two hours later, not more than six steps up.

Cyril Connolly's visit, one sunny April, coincided with that of Virginia Woolf. By mischance nothing was recorded, for Cyril's diary, otherwise ever ready, was of the kind which has a lock: at Bowen's Court locked it had to remain, for no sooner had he arrived than he lost the key. Cyril, a themic creative talker, developed at least one theory in this house: he traced the low ebb of Irish romantic passion to the anaphrodisiac effects of the constant potato. Virginia, serenely standing out on the steps, watched her spaniel racing over the grass in front. Dynamic, speedy and graceful country walker, she outdistanced the rest of us on our pilgrimage across the fields to the Bowen's Court wishing well. (Few leave this house without having 'had a wish.') What she wished, as she cupped the spring water in her hands, I shall never know . . . When Virginia'd gone, I told my matriarch cook, 'That was the greatest living woman writer.' Old Sarah, who disliked any connection between ink and the should-be elegant sex, sniffed, 'I'd have known she was a *lady* by the stately go of her!'

Seán O'Faoláin, helping me lock up – a nightly ritual involving heaving an iron bar into place, then fastening the hall door on the inside with massive chains – remarked that *here* was a Big House ready for a siege! Complex race memories, conflicts, the raids and burning of the Troubles of his young days and mine simultaneously stirred in us two Irish – I whose first Irish ancestor had come from Wales, he descended from the ancient inhabitants of the land.

Frank O'Connor, chanting in the library, dropping his head back as did Yeats, recalled the magnificence of the Midnight Court, poetry and bawdry of an Ireland before the potato had struck root. New Ireland tore to my doors in the form of my cousin Dudley Colley, a racing ace: his glorious Frazer-Nash enraptured Carson McCullers. In a flash, long-legged Carson was in the driver's seat. 'I'm off,' she cried. So strong is visionary force, the stationary car seemed to roar and devour space: Carson's face grew tense with the thought of speed, veritably her hair streamed back from her forehead.

Bernard Shaw has denounced one fatal cleft in society: Heart-break House on one side, Horseback Hall on the other. Yet by happy accident, Bowen's Court is a merger. Yes, I live right in horse country: fox hunting, racing and stud farming occupy the majority of my neighbours. Of these neighbours many are, also, my friends – there is a to and fro, when the day's work's over, between their and my far-apart houses. In the main my neighbours still live much as my forebears used to: farming, thinking concretely, cultivating their gardens (in a manner for which the reward is lovely). Do I feel a dissonance, or a dislocation, when they and writers meet round my dinner table? None being there to *be* felt, I do not. On the one hand, Cork native sociability is omnivorous, unsuspicious, eager, quick to be charmed and won. On the other, nothing is like the life from creative people at play: poets, novelists, philosophers, even critics effervesce like uncorked champagne. There is laughter sparked by new contacts; there is the spell of the card game. Wildly assorted Bowen's Court parties may be – country folk, visiting aunts and cousins, house guests literary or academic, plus transients on the road for business or pleasure. However, people take to each other. 'How does it feel,' I find myself asked, 'living with ancestors right on top of you?' Or more simply: 'Don't you ever feel crowded?' At a glance, the question is sound enough: it could be oppressive, were this place no more than a pocket of ancient sentiment.

But you cannot discount the force with which life renews itself: what chance has the past against the vividness of the living moment? Family continuity has the interest of *any* continuity: just that – it in no way acts as a spell. My predecessors in Bowen's Court were my kin: this makes for my knowing more about them than I should had they been of some other stock. Letters, personal papers and legal documents, birth, marriage and death dates entered in the family Bible give me the objective facts with regard to them; the factual outline is coloured in by intuition, hearsay, maybe legend. Moreover I can see what most of them looked like – many of the Bowens and their spouses had their portraits painted; the pictures in tarnished gilded frames hang in a crowd round the hall walls; elsewhere, cabinet drawers are stuffed with daguerreotypes and photographs. All this serves to fix my ancestors for me as four-square persons who, though unknown to history, become in their way historic through having lived. While I in my turn live, they are not forgotten. But on top of me? No.

Traces of themselves they have left behind them are concrete–broken musical instruments, signatures diamond-scratched on window panes, curios brought home from foreign travel, a silent gold heavy half-hunter watch, a riding crop with the thong gone, a compass with needle forever still. A big shell from Naples cameo-carved, a bracket on the wings of a tiny eagle. Such trifles are eloquent; they speak of foibles, tastes or tenderness.

There are, in addition, relics of broken-off activities: grandfather Robert II's close-kept estate ledgers, now musty, or a milking stool half-painted with water lilies. And between those who were here and me there is a physical link, forged of touch and sight – a matter of handling the same door knobs, mounting the same stairs, looking out at the same scene through the same windows. But most of all they and I are akin in one thing: the business of keeping going.

The keeping going of Bowen's Court has from the first preoccupied its owners. Good years, bad years have but slightly varied the weight of the undertaking. To an extent I profit by my ancestors' forethought, to an extent I am hampered by their misjudgements. The place is rich in outdated innovations. *I* face a paradox: by today's notions Bowen's Court is an anachronism; none the less, by the light of today I can solve some of yesterday's problems. Once this house was operated by hosts of servants: wages were low, labour never scarce – chains of hands slung the dishes, piping hot, from dusky kitchen to shining diningroom table. Rainwater, steaming in monster jugs, was levitated upstairs to many bathtubs. Now electrification and plumbing do most of that, plus the ingenuity of my cook and maid, a modicum of my energies, aid from guests.

One thing makes the house contemporary: its straightforward plan – no passages, whimsical complications or murky corners. (The Georgian living pattern fits today's better than the Victorian.) I use just over half the number of rooms, on each floor the sunniest; those withdrawn from, are kept sweet by the air coming in at their large windows; there is something placid and seemly about their emptiness. Bowen's Court has lent itself to this compromise – had it not, indeed, it could not survive: a saving pact has been reached between past and present. My standards of comfort, habitability, are far from those of my ancestors, which is well. I suspect sometimes that I am better off, thanks to concentration of heat, lighting, colour into a smaller living space, here, now, in my own way, than they in theirs. Yet I don't doubt they had their own satisfactions: this is a house constructed to be enjoyed, by whatever stratagems, in what-ever manner.

At the outset I spoke of this house as social, with hospitality as its inbuilt ideal. Now I think again, there is something more to it. This house was built for a family – so it makes one.

Bowen's Court seems to me like a ship that has steadily, forwardly voyaged through time. Almost two hundred years, today, since the launching. From having forged through storms, sheered its way past reefs and pulled clear of whirlpools, it has accumulated organic confidence. Yet also it *is* a house, founded very deep. From its daylit big rooms and green surrounding lands a succession of sorrows, deaths, trials, debts, disappointments have somehow evaporated like mists in sunshine. Hopeful as to its being, in spite of all, it begets hope; serenity is the constant.

Like Bowens before me, when grey rain sheets County Cork and gales rattle windows and buffet the house corners, I take exercise indoors – I walk the Long Room. This has been play deck since it first began: violent tennis and hockey and roller skating have taken place here; and generations of children have pounded or slid, yelling, from end to end. Circuses have been staged, melodramas improvised; talent ran, also, to whistle concerts and shadow shows.

Only one thing has this commodious ballroom never once been the scene of – dancing. Any ball is held, by tradition, down in the drawing-room. Why? *The Long Room floor will not stand up to vibration.* So I was told by my father, he by his, his by his father, whom his father had told. No one of us, in consequence, ever tried. This anomaly, typical of my family, strikes my closing note. Acceptances, do they not make up life? I wonder, looking out of the Long Room windows at the mountains behind, at the lawns in front and the lights through the veil of rain sifting softly, slowly over the lonely country.

Chapter 5

A Clean End
1960s

Bowen's Court: An Afterword, 1963

So, Henry VI died, and I as his only child inherited Bowen's Court. I was the first woman heir; already I had changed my father's name for my husband's. We had no children.

We continued, onward from 1930, to live for the greater part of the time in England, where Alan Cameron worked and we had a home – first at the edge of Oxford and then in London. Not until 1952 was there any question (that was to say, any possibility) of our taking up a continuous life at Bowen's Court. Nonetheless, since the place had become mine it became familiar to me at every time of year: hitherto, I had known it in summer only. Till 1939, when the war came, I was in the way of crossing the sea to Bowen's Court, known to be waiting there. When Alan could he came with me; sometimes I went alone. Existence there, though in fact it was discontinuous, did not seem so: each time one came back, it was as though one had not been away. I was surprised, I remember, when one of our visitors from England spoke of Bowen's Court (commendingly) as 'a holiday house.' It was never that. It was, however, designed for people, and there were many there.

World War II, while it lasted, put a stop to our coming and going. After 1945, that began again. Friends from England and America, as well as from other parts of Ireland, came to stay with us. And, as a family house, Bowen's Court was made happy by the presence of our relations, members of Alan's family and of mine. It became part of the memories of many children. August and September were the most sociable months, but in spring and early summer, and sometimes also around Christmas, there were people in most of the rooms too.

In anything like summer, we used to sit out on the steps in the sun, walk in the demesne or the country round, drive to Bridgetown to swim in the Blackwater or to Youghal to swim in the sea. In wet weather we played deck tennis or French cricket up in the Long Room. In the evenings we played *vingt-et-un* at Henry IV's card tables in the library, or paper games in the half-ring of chairs round the fire. Superficially, my way of living at Bowen's Court, either alone or in company, could not have been more unlike, in idea and manner, that of my grandfather Robert. It was less reflective and diligent than Henry V's, less racy than Henry IV's, less ample than Henry III's. But the house stamped its character on all ways of living: the same fundamental ran through them all.

One year I stayed on at Bowen's Court through the late autumn: for the first time I saw the last of the leaves hang glistening, here and there, in the transparent woods or flittering on the slopes of the avenues. The rooks subsided after their harvest flights; in the gale season one or two gulls, blown inland, circled over the lawns. I heard the woods roaring, and, like pistol shots, the cracking of boughs. For years the house had been empty at this season.

At Christmas itself – and there were many Christmases – I remember no storms. All winds dropped then: a miraculous quiet rose from the land. When we came back from walking, at an hour when it would have been dark in England, the white mid-winter twilight was still reflected in the many windows. We had a cycle of mild Christmases – the moss up the trees was emerald, the hollies and laurels sticky with light; lambs had been born already; sun-pink mountains glowed behind the demesne. On one such Christmas morning we were able to sit on the steps, waiting for aunts and uncles, remaining children of Robert, to come to dinner. Only for Christmas dinner, eaten at midday, did I re-open my grandfather's dining-room.

Christmases, later, became colder: for one we had a thin fall of snow. Or, the lawns were tufted and crisp with hoar-frost; the sun rose tawny, the moon curdled through low lying, frosty mists. That change of temperature was no more than a return to the rule of the past – when, I am told, Bowen's Court Christmases always were very cold. It had been a mistake to think that my own rule was to see in a new era of weather.

At that season, the family house felt the authority of its long tradition. It also embraced those of the country round. Every Christmas Eve I lit the Christmas candle, gift of a neighbour in Farahy. Very tall and thick, of green, pink or yellow wax, the candle was planned to burn until Twelfth Night. Wreathed at its base with holly, on to whose berries the wax dropped, it stood on a folded card-table at the north end of the library – here was once Eliza Wade's room. In the cottages of Farahy and Kildorrery the fellows of that candle were alight. Here, the room was so high that any light faded before it reached the ceiling. In the silence you heard the sound of the fire; the underneath of Robert's white marble mantelpiece and its two supporting pillars were flushed. When the library shutters had been shut for the night and the dark heavy curtains drawn over them, mist, starlight or a cloud-thickened darkness lay forgotten outside the chilling panes. In the shadow cast up by the mantelpiece stood vases of holly, and Christmas cards. Footsteps of people taking the shortcut through the demesne were heard, now and then, under the windows.

Outside that room, the house. Darkness succeeded daylight in the naked windows of the staircase and lobby: we burned no lights here. The shaft of the staircase was faintly warmed by vibrations up from the hall stove. Under the portrait of Henry IV the stove sent out through its mica a square dull glow – thanks to its presence, the hall portraits were now no longer filmed over by winter damp; they were now only dimmed by their own age. In the deserted drawing-room, which in my grandmother's day used to be the focus of Christmas, the black iron bars across the shutters revealed themselves to any momentary light: that same light travelled into the deep of mirrors framing perspectives of empty room. Yes, life had shifted – but not lost intensity.

The empty parts of the house, piled up in the winter darkness, palpably and powerfully existed. I was not conscious of the lives of the dead there. It may be that, like so many writers, I have not much imagination to spare. But the unconsciousness – the unknowingness, the passivity – in which so much of those finished lives had been passed did somehow reach and enter my own. What runs on most through a family living in one place is a continuous, semi-physical dream. Above this dream-level successive lives show their tips, their little conscious formations of will and thought. With the end of each generation, the lives that submerged here were absorbed again. With each death, the air of the place had thickened: it had been added to. The dead do not need to visit Bowen's Court rooms – as I said, we had no ghosts in that house – because they already permeated them. Their extinct senses were present in lights and forms. The land outside Bowen's Court windows left prints on my ancestors' eyes that looked out: perhaps their eyes left, also, prints on the scene? If so, those prints were part of the scene to me.

I accepted the ignorance, set up by time and death, that divided my ancestors' conscious lives from mine. In the writing of this book, sheer information would not have taken me very much of the way – only a little displaced by my researches, the greater part of that ignorance still remains: it is natural. So, I have made the frame of this family history from hearsay and some certain retrieved facts. Inside this frame, I have written about the Bowens out of what I do know but do not know why I know. Intuitions that I cannot challenge have moved me to colour their outlines in.

Though I have stressed, in writing about the Bowens, the recurrent factor of the family will, it is the involuntary, or spontaneous, aspect of their behaviour that interests me most. Having looked back at them steadily, I begin to notice, if I cannot define, the pattern they unconsciously went to make. And I can see that that pattern has its relation to the outside more definite pattern of history.

The Bowens' relation to history was an unconscious one. I can only suggest a compulsion they did not know of by a series of breaks, contrasts and juxtapositions – in short, by interleaving the family story with passages from the history of Ireland. My family, though notably 'unhistoric,' had their part in a drama outside themselves. Their assertions, their compliances, their refusals as men and women went, year by year, generation by generation, to give history direction, as well as colour and stuff. Each of the family, in their different manners, were more than their time's products; they were its agents.

I may seem to have made use of history to illustrate the Bowens rather than the Bowens to illustrate history. Inevitably, I have stressed such outside events as may make the Bowen story, since the coming to Ireland, more comprehensible and significant. But I have tried not to wrest from their larger contexts events relevant to the moral plan of this book.

In my re-writing of history, a considerable naivety may appear. In the course of my reading for *Bowen's Court*, I have learnt a good deal that I did not know. I am, evidently, not a historian, and it seemed to me more honest to leave my reactions to history their first freshness, rather than to attempt to evaluate. Conclusions have been suggested rather than drawn. I cannot tell to how many of my readers the past – this particular past of Anglo-Ireland – will be as new as much of it was to me, or to how many it is familiar already. My transcripts of history have, at least, been drawn from sources beyond reproach: I have relied upon no authority who did not place fact above passion or interest. The stretches of the past I have had to cover have been, on the whole, painful: my family got their position and drew their power from a situation that shows an inherent wrong. In the grip of that situation, England and Ireland each turned to the other a closed, harsh, distorted face – a face that, in each case, their lovers would hardly know. With the Treaty, with which I virtually close my book, a new hopeful phase started: I believe in its promise. But we cannot afford to have ghosts on this clearing scene. I wish not to drag up the past but to help lay it. A past that Ireland still too much dwells on is still by England not enough recognized. But also, acts of good will, and good intentions that did or did not miscarry, have not been allowed by Ireland to stand to the English score . . . For my part, it has been necessary for me to embed my family story in at least some account of the growth of 'the Protestant nation,' and of the events that marked stages or declines in this growth. I have done my best to make the account fair.

I began to write *Bowen's Court* in the early summer of 1939. The first two chapters were, thus, completed before the outbreak of World War II. When, for instance, I wrote about ruins in County Cork there were as yet few ruins in England other than those preserved in fences and lawns. I do not know how much, after that September of 1939, the colour of my narration may have altered. The values with which I set out – my own values – did, at least to my own feeling, remain constant: they were accentuated rather than changed by war. The war-time urgency of the present, its relentless daily challenge, seemed to communicate itself to one's view of the past, until, to the most private act or decision, there attached one's sense of its part in some campaign. Those days, either everything mattered or nothing mattered. The past – private just as much as historic – seemed to me, therefore, to matter more than ever: it acquired meaning; it lost false mystery. In the savage and austere light of a burning world, details leaped out with significance. Nothing that ever happened, nothing that was ever even willed, planned or envisaged, could seem irrelevant. War is not an accident: it is an outcome. One cannot look back too far to ask, of what?

Inevitably, the ideas and emotions that were present in my initial plan of this book were challenged and sharpened by the succeeding war years in which the writing went on. I was writing (as though it were everlasting) about a home during a time when all homes were threatened and hundreds of thousands of them were being wiped out. I was taking the attachment of people to places as being generic to human life, at a time when the attachment was to be dreaded as a possible source of too much pain. During a time when individual destinies, the hopes and fears of the living, had to count for so little, I pursued through what might seem their tenuousness and their futility the hopes and fears of the long-ago dead. I was writing about self-centred people while all faces looked outward upon the world. But all that – that disparity or contrast between the time I was writing in and my subject – only so acted upon my subject as to make it, for me, the more important. I tried to make it *my* means to approach truth.

Possibly, the judgements of war-time affected my view of my family? These unhistoric figures are made historic by the fact that, as I show, they once lived. So, I examine them as we now re-examine historic figures. I have stressed as dominant in the Bowens factors I saw as dominant in the world I wrote in – for instance, subjection to fantasy and infatuation with the idea of power. While I was studying fantasy in the Bowens, we saw how it had impassioned race after race. Fantasy is toxic: the private cruelty and the world war both have their start in the heated brain. Showing fantasy, in one form or another, do its unhappy work in the lives of my ancestors, I was conscious at almost every moment of nightmarish big analogies everywhere. Also, the idea of power governed my analysis of the Bowens and of the means *they* took – these being, in some cases, emotional – to enforce themselves on their world. I showed, if only in the family sphere, people's conflicting wishes for domination. That few Bowens looked beyond Bowen's Court makes the place a fair microcosm, a representative if miniature theatre. Sketching in the society of which the Bowens were part, and the operations behind that society, I extended the conflict by one ring more: again, its isolation, what might be called its outlandishness, makes Anglo-Irish society microcosmic. For these people – my family and their associates – the idea of power was mostly vested in property (property having been acquired by use or misuse of power in the first place). One may say that while property lasted the dangerous power-idea stayed, like a sword in its scabbard, fairly safely at rest. At least, property gave my people and people like them the means to exercise power in a direct, concrete and therefore limited way. I have shown how their natures shifted direction – or the nature of the *débordement* that occurred – when property could no longer be guaranteed. Without putting up any plea for property unnecessary, for it is unlikely to be abolished – I submit that the power-loving temperament is more dangerous when it either prefers or is forced to operate in what is materially a void. We have everything to dread from the dispossessed. In the area of ideas we see more menacing dominations than the landlord exercised over land. The outsize will is not necessarily an evil: it is a phenomenon. It must have its outsize outlet, its big task. If the right scope is not offered it, it must seize the wrong. We should be able to harness this driving force. Not the will itself but its wastefulness is the dangerous thing.

Yes, the preoccupations of war-time may have caused me to see Bowens in a peculiar or too much intensified light. Some of their characteristics, here, may be overdrawn. They were in most ways, I take it, fairly ordinary Anglo-Irish country gentry. I have done my best to come at, then to transmit to paper, a detached picture of them. In the main, I do not feel that they require defence – you, on the other hand, may consider them indefensible. Having obtained their position through an injustice, they enjoyed that position through privilege. But, while they wasted no breath in deprecating an injustice it would not have been to their interest to set right, they did not abuse their privilege – on the whole. They honoured, if they did not justify, their own class, its traditions, its rule of life. If they formed a too-grand idea of themselves, they did at least exert themselves to live up to this: even vanity involves one kind of discipline. If their difficulties were of their own making, they combatted these with an energy I must praise. They found no facile solutions; they were not guilty of cant. Isolation, egotism and, on the whole, lack of culture made in them for an independence one has to notice because it becomes, in these days, rare. Independence was the first quality of a class now, I am told, becoming extinct. I recognize that a class, like a breed of animals, *is* due to lapse or become extinct should it fail to adapt itself to changing conditions – climate alters, the feeding-grounds disappear.

The gentry, as a class, may or may not prove able to make adaptations; that is one of the many things we must wait to see. To my mind, they are tougher than they appear. To live as though living gave them no trouble has been the first imperative of their make-up: to do this has taken a virtuosity into which courage enters more than has been allowed. In the last issue, they have lived at their own expense.

Bowen's Court, in that December of 1941 in which this book was finished, still stood in its particular island of quietness, in the south of an island country not at war. Only the wireless in the library conducted the world's urgency to the place. Wave after wave of war news broke upon the quiet air of the room and, in the daytime when the windows were open, passed out on to the sunny or overcast lawns. Here was a negative calm – or at least, the absence of any immediate physical threat. Yet, at the body of this house threats did strike – and in a sense they were never gone from the air. The air here had absorbed, in its very stillness, apprehensions general to mankind. It was always with some qualification – most often with that of an almost undue joy – that one beheld, at Bowen's Court, the picture of peace. Looking, for instance, across the country from the steps in the evening, one thought: '*Can* pain and danger exist?' But one did think that. Why? The scene was a crystal in which, while one was looking, a shadow formed.

Yes, there was the picture of peace in the house, in the country round. Like all pictures, it did not quite correspond with any reality. Or, you might have called the country a magic mirror, reflecting something that could not really exist. That illusion – peace at its most ecstatic – I held to, to sustain me throughout war. I suppose that everyone, fighting or just enduring, carried within him one private image, one peaceful scene. Mine was Bowen's Court. War made me that image out of a house built of anxious history.

And so great and calming was the authority of the light and quiet round Bowen's Court that it survived war-time. And it did more than that, it survived the house. It remains with me now that the house has gone.

The house, having played its part, has come to an end. It will not, after all, celebrate its two hundredth birthday – of that, it has fallen short by some thirteen years. The shallow hollow of land, under the mountains, on which Bowen's Court stood is again empty. Not one hewn stone left on another on the fresh-growing grass. Green covers all traces of the foundations. Today, so far as the eye can see, there might never have been a house there.

One cannot say that the space is empty. More, it is as it was – with no house there. How did this come to be?

It was not foreseen. Early in 1952, upon my husband's retirement from work, he and I left London, to live at Bowen's Court. This was the life we had always promised ourselves. We brought back with us furniture which, originally Bowen's Court's, had been absent long – first in Dublin, afterwards in England: travelled tables and chairs were reunited with those which had never known anything but County Cork. The house, after its many stretches of patient emptiness, of returns only to be followed by departures, looked like, now, entering upon a new phase of habitation – full and continuous habitation, such as it had been built for. It made us welcome. This homecoming was like no holiday visit. In spite of the cold of a bitter January, all promised well. We had the spring of that year, and the early summer. But then one night, that August, Alan Cameron died in his sleep.

I, remaining at Bowen's Court, tried to carry on the place, and the life which went with it there, alone. Already I could envisage no other home. I should, I thought, be able to maintain the place somehow. Had not others done so before me? But I was unable to.

For seven years I tried to do what was impossible. I was loth to realise how impossible it was. Costs rose: I had not enough money, and I had to face the fact that there never would be enough. Anxiety, the more deep for being repressed, increasingly slowed down my power to write, and it was upon my earnings, and those only, that Bowen's Court had by now come to depend. (Does not the economic back-history of the Bowens, as shown in this book, the quarrels, the lost law-suits, the father-and-son conflicts, the spasms of *folie de grandeur*, account for that?) Matters reached a crisis. By 1959 it had become inevitable that I should sell Bowen's Court.

The buyer was a County Cork man, a neighbour. He already was farming tracts of land, and had the means wherewith to develop mine, and horses to put in the stables. It cheered me also to think that his handsome children would soon be running about the rooms – for it was, I believe, his honest intention, when first he bought the place from me, to inhabit the house. But in the end he did not find that practicable, and who is to blame him? He thought at one time, I understand, of compromising by taking off the top storey (I am glad he did not). Finally, he decided that there was nothing for it but to demolish the house entirely. So that was done.

It was a clean end. Bowen's Court never lived to be a ruin.

Loss has not been entire. When I think of Bowen's Court, there it is. And when others who knew it think of it, there it is, also. You will understand that I am more than ever glad that I wrote this book, and that I am grateful to Alfred and Blanche Knopf, who, having inspired the book in the first place, now are bringing it back into print again. Knowing, as you now do, that the house is no longer there, you may wonder why I have left my opening chapter, the room-to-room description of Bowen's Court, in the present tense. I can only say that *I* saw no reason to transpose it into the past. There is a sort of perpetuity about livingness, and it is part of the character of Bowen's Court to be, in sometimes its silent way, very much alive.

Kinsale, Son et Lumiere[1], 22 May 1966, Harry Ranson Center, drama (script)

I

Prologue

Here, we are on a rock
An ordained fortress –

Its base forever washed by the tides of History.
This is the outmost guardian
Of Kinsale estuary.
From this outpost, sentinel after sentinel
Has kept watch,
Scanning the open skyline of the Atlantic –
– *Who* will be coming – next?
Past the flank of our rock, the estuary cuts inland,
To go – between hills and farmlands
And stony steeps crowned by the ruins of castles –
Turning and shining,
Deep into the green of Munster,
Salt sea water meeting and swelling the peaty water of the River Bandon,
Coming from the mountains.
Our estuary opens into a wide bay.
To the west of that, the Old Head of Kinsale thrusts out, out,
So far into the ocean, that,
From *here*, it looks like another country –
A long, savage, irregular bastion, its cliffs
Rising out of the spray of the broken waves –
Broken on the teeth of the cruel rocks.
There are sea-washed caverns.
Fortified by Nature, the Old Head
Has again and again been fortified by man.
This place, with the built-up battlements, where *we* are,
Was Rincurran Castle . . .
Now, we know it as Charles Fort.
It has a brother-fortress across the estuary –
James Fort.
James Fort commands the narrowing, deepening channel
Further inland,
Nearer Kinsale town.
Kinsale harbour, one of the keys to Ireland – contested Ireland! –
Needed to be defended.
It was defended.
Kinsale *port* liked to be open –
Lively, wealthy, well-famed,
Embraced by hills,
Beautified by churches and civic buildings and comely houses,
Kinsale throve.

Trade hummed round her many jetties.
Ireland's most southern port . . .
Kinsale – before Cork was heard of – was a rival to Galway,
Could bid against Waterford.
One of the great main links, she was,
Between Ireland and the Continent – Europe.
And not only commerce made her important . . .
On the maps of the strategist, she was pin-pointed.
Kinsale – century after century –
Was involved in the power-game
Of embattled Europe.
She was a key, to be turned,
A prize, to be siezed.
She was an objective.

II

The Danes

History has no beginning . . .
Who was first invaded, who first defended, and when, and how,
And *what* – each time – was the outcome,
Is for speculation, theory and legend.
Assaults and battles of which there are no records
Become mythical.
We begin – tonight – inside the framework of knowledge,
Eight centuries after the birth of Christ.
The first marauders *known* to harass this coastline were Norsemen – Danes –
Daring, rapacious, merciless.
In the year 824,
Such a party swept up this estuary (*then*, unguarded),
Terror going ahead of their fierce, swift ships
Through the helpless land.
Imagine! – the people of *these* hills, hills of Rincurran,
Crouching,
Fascinatedly watching the Danes go by
On their dreadful errand.
From valley to valley ran
Unavailing warnings
[*Sound-effects*: Terrified
Murmurings, like en-

larged whispers – some
near, some further away.
Kinsale – happily for Kinsale! –
Then had hardly come into being.
No town, yet. Nothing more than a settlement,
Low-built, humble,
Along the edge of the water.
It promised few spoils.
The Danes despised it – which was to say, spared it.
On past Kinsale they swept, up the Bandon River
To Innishannon,
Devastating the country as they went.
Terrible was the fate of Innishannon,
Fair Innishannon, deep in its lush green valley,
Civilised in the manner of its day,
[*Sound-effects*:
Sounds of raid, in the distance:
Shrieks, shoutings, wailings of
children, clang of metal on
stone, rumble and crash of
falling buildings.]
Innocent, busy,
Doing no ill to any man,
And expecting none.
[Short silence.
Bellowing of stampeded
Cattle. Neighing of
Terrified horses.
[*Light-effects*:
A scarlet glare,
Palpitating as do flames,
To be turned on Charles
Fort from the direction
of Innishannon.]
Now – the raiders fell upon Inishannon,
Ravishing, seizing, looting, slaughtering, burning,
They demolished it.
The river ran red with blood.
Some of the mutilated dead – who knows? –
Floated downstream, into the gaze

Of dismayed Kinsale.
The intervening hills, through those awesome nights,
Stood out against a sky scarlet with flames.
But – the chronicler tells – there *was* retribution . . .
The Irish, the people of this region,
Rallying,
Made great by anguish and anger,
Took up arms
And went out against the raiders, as one man.
On the 'Slope of the Fountain'
The Danes were caught,
Cut off from their ships.
They got no mercy.
The 'Slope of the Fountain' was –
By every account –
Our Compass Hill:
Compass Hill, with its brambles and bracken and twisted pathways,
Familiarly rising
Above Kinsale.
There, one hundred-and-seventy Danes were put to the sword.
Innishannon was avenged.

III

The Normans

And next, the Normans.
The Normans were *not* raiders,
Striking, then flying away:
No. The Normans came not to despoil but to possess,
To enjoy their possessions,
And to defend them,
To rule, to exercise power
And create order.
Where they came, they remained.
[*Sound-effects*:
Sound of marching of
foot-soldiers, on and
on. Sound of companies
of horsemen, on and on.
Jingle and rattle of
accoutrements.

Sound of words of
command being shouted
[words unintelligible]
They made England Norman.
A *Norman*-implanted King of England it was
Who sent Strongbow[2] to Ireland,
At the head of a force.
Let us not forget, the doors was open to them [*sic*]
By our faction-fighting. They were invited in.
Thereafter,
The Normans streamed through our Four Kingdoms,
Taking over,
Commanding,
Fortifying,
As they went.
Fortresses, watch-towers sprang into being
Around our coasts;
Castles and towers guarded our loughs and rivers,
And kept watch over the passes
Through our mountains,
And dominated the calm
Of our green plains.
[*Sound effects*:
Distant and wistful,
singing of snatches
of the sing 'Let Erin
Remember.']
Also the Normans built cities, and set strong walls around them.
– Such a wall girt Kinsale.
Under the Norman yoke,
Ireland lay safe,
In return for her freedom
She gained safety –
For a term of time . . .
The Norman invader
Saw to it that no one *else* should invade!
Knowing the treacherous history of this coastline
and its toll of terror,
They took measures – making a strong place
Out of the Old Head.

At the narrow neck of the promontory – midway along it –
Upon more ancient foundations, they set two fortresses,
Gating the way across.
The landward end of the Old Head was – thus – defended
Against attack from the mainland.
From the *sea* this far-out end of the headland
Was, as ever, impregnable,
Thanks to the dropping cliffs,
And the lashing waves, and the hungry reefs . . .
Therefore,
Into this place cattle was to be driven,
Provender carried, and treasures brought
For safe keeping,
Should trouble come.
And for people this could be
A place of refuge.
Ireland, as time went on,
Drew the Normans into herself,
Wooing their military gauntress (gauntness?)
With her soft air,
Sending them minstrels,
Showing them visions.
Where they had come to sieze,
They came to belong.
Their stock mingled with ours:
They founded families – long lines,
Barrys, Burkes, Roches, Fitzgeralds,
Names to be counted, and honoured, among the Irish.
Over their tombs rose beautiful abbeys.
Their children's children
– Generations to come –
Were one with us in the fight for the Catholic faith,
And for freedom.
This region's Normans, Kinsale's overlords,
Were the De Courcy's
Their castle, Kilgobbin, towered over a reach
Of the Bandon river,
Benevolently.
Calm ran the glassy water.
Ireland beheld that peace

As she might a mirage:
There was a flaw in it,
A misgiving,
The shadow of a betrayal:
It could not last.

IV

Siege of Rincurran   Siege of Kinsale   Battle of Kinsale

As, one by one
The Plantagenet kings of England
Widened over the country their feudal network,
Ireland knew herself to be held in thrall.
The knowledge was bitter.
The 'emerald gem' was indeed, now,
'Set in the crown of a stranger.'
The Gaelic soul stirred.
Murmurings ran through the cheated people;
The very land seemed to be crying out:
'Stolen! Stolen – I have been stolen!'
One by one, the unsubdued Gaelic chieftains,
The Earls of Ireland,
Took down their spears from the walls,
And recollected a vanished glory,
And mused, and looked out of their windows, and thought of war.
Deep words, then, mantled great tracts of Ireland:
Man was hidden from man:
Untraversible boglands,
Treacherous river-marches, made for loneliness
Across which voices could not be heard.
Who could muster, who could gather together
A people so scattered
And isolated?
Therefore, though sense of oppression grew,
And anger smouldered,
There was for a long time no danger-signal but silence,
Tension, the stillness of a gathering storm.
The Tudor monarchy, with its graspingness,
And the Reformation,
Brought the thing to a head.
Protestantism was militant: it sought enemies.

Rumours of 'turbulence', apprehended 'conspiracies'
In Catholic Ireland,
Set going a savage repressive policy,
A trend, on the English side, towards persecution,
Which had in it the seeds of religious war.
To stamp the Faith out, and the country down,
Became the ambition.
That shame – the shame of hate and misgovernment –
Blots the fair name, and darkened the brave reign,
Of Elizabeth I –
– The 'Gloriana' of Spenser, her exiled poet,
Eating his heart out in north County Cork,
Under the Ballyhoura Mountains.
The tension snapped.
The year 1579 saw the Desmond Rebellion.
Gerald, 16th Earl of Desmond,
Norman-descended, head of the Munster Fitzgeralds,
Took up arms, and rose, and all Munster with him.
Down came Elizabeth's army.
For four years, this Munster country was racked by fighting,
Scorched, laid in ruins,
Desmond – frail in body, desperately strong in spirit –
Never gave in.
His end – and *the* end – came
When he was hacked to death in the wet woods
of Kerry.
Yet, inexorable Ireland was, too, the grave
Of many of Queen Elizabeth's trusted men,
Her once lusty compaigners,
Her courtier-generals.
Some lost their lives, some only their reputations:
Essex was to forfeit his handsome head.
Commander succeeded commander, each one to fail,
Until at last came Mountjoy[3] –
– Who did not.
It was Mountjoy who brought Kinsale
Into tragic history.
Here – on *these* hills –
Mountjoy defeated the two chieftains
To whom all Ireland had looked

Since the crushing of Desmond –
– The Great O'Neill (Hugh, 2nd Earl of Tyrone)
And Red Hugh O'Donnell,[4]
Tyrone's ally.
How did it come about that those two Hughs,
Being men of Ulster,
Gave battle so far off their own ground,
Here, in the South
– As far south as *can* be?
Up in the North, the two had bided their time,
Not betraying their purpose by so much as a flicker.
Young Red Hugh was the impatient one,
But O'Neill, the wily, had him on the leash.
O'Neill – philandering with the English
And double-crossing them,
Watching them build him in with a string of forts
– He, a man so big that he reigned like a king!
He, meanwhile, was deep in intrigues with Spain.
Spain . . .
The great Catholic power,
The Catholic ally,
The foe of England, the hope of Ireland . . .
On a Spanish landing in Ireland,
All plans hinged.
The landing was promised.
Through the summer of 1601, O'Neill and O'Donnell waited,
Each with his army,
In secret, at the alert.
The two earls' strategy
Was based on a clear – it *seemed* a clear – understanding
That the Spanish landing was to take place
Nearby Sligo. Near enough to the North.
With a lightening movement,
The earls and their allies
Would then join forces.
. . . God help the English!
But –
– What got into the Spanish? –
They chose Kinsale!
That was dreadful news to O'Neill;

It all but foundered him, and it well-nigh frenzied him.
Now, to contact the Spanish
He and Red Hugh must post the length of the country,
Leaving O'Neill's lands, his treasure, his house, his dear ones,
Unguarded, defenceless against his enemies
(Who were many)
For *anybody* to sieze . . . Indecision rent him.
He lost time, looking this way, that way.
He started late.
However, purpose burned in him.
Down Ireland, by different routes,
Dodging the English,
Wearing their men to bits with the forced marches,
Through the floods and gale-driven rains of a wicked autumn,
Came the earls from the North.
Mountjoy, entrenched near Kinsale,
Had been some time waiting . . .
Kinsale had had a great time
When the Spanish landed.
It was September 21st of that year, 1601,
When their ships were sighted,
Coming over the horizon of the Atlantic.
The ships swept in, up our estuary,
Where, in their lordly manner, they waited two days –
Admired by all.
Then the general, Don Juan del Aquila[5], stepped ashore,
On to the Little Quay,
With his captains after him.
Out came the Kinsale dignitaries, and the townspeople.
Salutes were exchanged.
In its tower, the old town bell rang wildly
– In joy, or in trepidation?
Troops streamed ashore; arms were grounded.
The dark-faced, eagle-sharp men
Swarmed through the town, and into the taverns . . .
Kinsale was well used to strangers
– A trading port.
But the Spanish were different: an army.
They brought in Faith with them.
Kinsale was – still – mediaeval.

Pointed-roof houses, crowded,
Drank up each others' light. There were squinting windows,
Twisted archaic stone staircases, vaulted cellars,
Deep-sunken courtyards, networks of alleys
– And much dusk.
The hills above and about her were densely wooded,
Darkening, by their reflections, the harbour water . . .
The three thousand, eight hundred and fourteen Spaniards
Now took up their quarters in this town,
Round which ran the zigzag wall of the Norman times.
For the young people, this coming of the Spaniards
Was a high excitement,
A kind of carnival.
But among their elders were many trembling hearts,
Forebodings. Some fled Kinsale – while they could:
They took to the woods, or fields,
Or sought shelter in ruins, or roofless cabins.

* * *

Those were the wise ones.

* * *

Mountjoy – it was known – was in Cork by the end of September.
What next? . . .
Mountjoy had affairs to see to:
Not till October 17th did he move south,
With his mounting thousands of men and his ominous guns.
He took up his position, then, on the hill
Overlooking Kinsale from the north-east.
Below lay the tortuous pattern of land and water,
The stout well encircling the town, and the gateways in it,
And those two forts,
Guardians of the harbour.
Mountjoy took in the pattern,
And drew up his plan of campaign accordingly.
First, he invested Kinsale, making dispositions
For what might, is necessary,
Be a lengthy siege.
Next – to open the harbour to his own ships,
And close it against Spanish reinforcements –
He would have to put out of action those two forts.

He began with Rincurran.
Rincurran.
Yes. *This* – here – where we are!
Look round you . . .
Strip away, in your *mind's* eye,
These hefty fortifications and massive battlements.
None of those were here *then.* Get them out of your heads!
Rincurran, before it became Charles Fort,
Was a naturally-placed, respectably strong stronghold
– At the latest, Norman. Adequate. More than able
To stand against the assaults of its own day,
The battering-ram, the scaling ladder,
The chance, fatal arrow quivering through the slit.
Rincurran was obsolete against modern warfare.
Mountjoy's was modern.
Rincurran, however, was –
– When Mountjoy attacked – manned by intrepid defenders:
A company of Spaniards, and a handful of Irish
Who had thrown in their lot with them:
Several women, some children, some men come in from the fields
– And an Irish swordsman, of some fame,
Dermot MacCarthy.
Bombardment began from the water – down *there*! –
From English ships coming round out of Oysterhaven.
But *those* guns were too small – Rincurran was merely chipped.
Heavier, deadlier cannon called Culverins were,
Therefore, rushed up on the land side. These opened fire.
Then, Rincurran *did* rock and shiver.
(Did the children bury their faces in the grass?)
The Culverins, choked by their own fury,
After some time shot themselves out of order.
Then some of the Spaniards sortied, breaking through the besiegers,
At the foot of the fort, and fought on like devils,
Downhill, towards Kinsale,
Through what is now Summercove.
The Culverins, repaired, blazed back into action,
And kept on at it.
There *could* – now – be only one end:
The Spanish garrision, encumbered
By the innocents who were with it,

Capitulated.
They were sent as prisoners to Cork. MacCarthy was hanged.
Of the fate of the mourning others
There is no record.
November 14th an English fleet
Came jostling into the mouth of the estuary.
It brought Mountjoy victuals, gunpowder,
Still bigger and better cannon,
Three thousand more men.
On the strength of this, Mountjoy tackled the second fort
– *Then* known as Castle Park. (Now, James Fort.)
Most of the Castle Park Spaniards escaped his clutches.
Having reduced this Fort, by his former method,
He emplaced, on the Castle headland,
Cannon. These stood trained, at short range, on Kinsale town.
Before fire was opened, the Spanish asked
For passes-out for Kinsale's women and children:
That having been granted, the full bombardment
Began on November 25th.
Simultaneously, there were cannon thundering also
Downward, from the north-eastern hill.
Down on to the roofs of Kinsale came a double barrage,
Which was continuous,
This being total war.
Why – in this year of commemoration –
Does Kinsale not deck her streets with laurel-wreaths,
To recall,
And to honour,
As great a stand
As was ever made by a little town?
Throughout the siege of Kinsale, the Spanish made sorties,
Falling on Mountjoy's troops with 'exceeding fury',
Driving them back, uphill.
With December, a whisper ran through the English ranks:
The Earls of the North *were* coming
– Might burst out of any wood, over any skyline –
O'Neill, O'Donnell:
Gigantic sky-riders, enlarged by terror and myth.
How great were the forces they headed? – and how savage?
Where would they strike?

The stoical Spanish – left here high-and-dry for two months –
Took further heart.
In the English entrenchments,
Where the rain-sodden men were hungry, sick and defaulting,
Morale was low.
O'Neill had the game in his hands.
Yet he let it go.
The epic Battle of Kinsale
Was tragic most of all in its tragic irony.
This – it seems – was a battle that need *not* have been fought!
Mountjoy himself never sought it;
O'Neill went into it with divided heart,
Prematurely – *some* say, even, by accident.
In this affray – which was, for hundreds of years
To dispirit Ireland, and blight her history –
One sees the work of some blind fatality.
A Shakespearean tempest, like a warning, ripped the skies open
Three nights before the battle.
The mystery is, what became of the Spanish?
Communications with them *had* been established, by O'Neill,
And he had not a doubt that they knew his timing,
On which everything hung.
But something went wrong.
Had a message been intercepted, and failed to reach them?
O'Neill hurled himself on the English in the expectation that,
Simultaneously, the Spanish, full force,
Would hurtle out of Kinsale
And throw themselves upon the enemy flank.
They did not. Not a stir or a sign came from them.
Though at the alert, and – one cannot but imagine –
Spoiling for action, after having been pent up for so long,
They continued to wait, down there in the town.
They never came.
The terrible Battle of Kinsale
Was fought in the dull dawn light of a Christmas morning,
In strangling mist.
Over its violence hangs confusion,
Its shape remains obscured, to this very day.
What we know is the outcome –
How the Irish were broken,

And so utterly
That the earls could do nothing but turn
And flee,
To be met by the bitter mockery of the people,
As their sad forces straggled through Innishannon.
But nothing is in vain,
Remember,
Nothing is in vain.
Would that the defeated could be consoled
– As we are –
By knowing that a heroic story has no end;
And that, though the sun sets,
It again rises.
The earls took ship,
Into exile,
Never to come back,
Taking with them
– For a long time, though not for always –
The hopes of Ireland.

V

Sir Walter Raleigh

We have seen
The Elizabethans who came to Ireland at their worst,
So far –
– Hostile, ruthless and overweening.
The face they turned to *us* – many of them –
Was inhuman.
Yet, their curious natures had an inverse,
In many cases.
Mountjoy himself was a man of intellect, a book-lover,
A person of fine feeling (when not in Ireland.)
Others of these men of action, also,
Were creatures of subtlety and taste,
Delighters in what was beautiful,
Tender, idealistic and lyrical when they fell in love.
There was a purity in their courage,
Which could be great.
Sir Walter Raleigh, the Queen's admiral,
Was an example of this duality

– A poet.
To the poet Ireland spoke – as she ever has.
He loved Ireland – and well that he did, for
In his days of prosperity, fortune and high favour,
He had possessed himself of great tracts of her
– Lands in Cork and Waterford,
Between the Knockmealdown Mountains and the sea coast,
Watered by the tributaries of the Blackwater,
And that river itself.
He had been Lord of Lismore.
But what was most dear to him was a garden he had in Youghal,
With a small manor-house.
This sweet and unworldly garden
– Far from the rivalries of the Court
And the tumultuousness of the high seas –
Contented him. There, smoking his long pipe, he dreamed
– No doubt reflecting, also, on the converse he had had
With his fellow-poet, Spenser
– By the Aubeg River, under the silver willows,
At Doneraile – and would have again.
In that garden he also – less romantically –
Planted our first potato.
(Or so legend says.)
Kinsale knew Raleigh late in his days.
In the world's eyes, he was already a fallen man,
Granted one last chance – and that one only.
Queen Elizabeth was dead; the Gloriana radiance was all over.
James I, her successor, had vented on Raleigh,
The former favourite,
The furious animosity of a warped nature.
Accusations heaped up against the admiral;
Charges brought, on the evidence of his enemies,
Were being built up into the charge of treason.
He had been imprisoned in the Tower of London
– Where he whiled the days away writing poetry –
To await trial.
Then came King James' offer.
The King was greedy; tales of the gold of Guinea
– An El Dorado – whetted and tantalised his imagination.
For an expedition there, Raleigh would be the man!

Should the venture prosper, and be rewarding,
Very great spoils brought home,
The King would pardon him.
Should it fail, Raleigh would pay for that on the scaffold.
King James made that plain,
The terms were clear.
Everything, therefore,
Was staked on this last throw.
Raleigh, and his son with him, set sail from Plymouth,
In the June of the year 1617,
With seven warships, three pinnaces, and three other ships.
Summer should have been favourable – but no:
Merciless, storm after storm battered them.
He lost one pinnace. Not till early August was Raleigh into Kinsale
– Where, in the landlocked quiet, two weeks were spent
Re-fitting and repairing the ships.
Kinsale – though still, surely, showing scars and gashes
Of the Mountjoy bombardment of sixteen years ago? –
Was again in good fettle. To Raleigh's eye,
Hallowed by many sorrows,
The smiling water-front must have been dear and cheering.
He may, too, have looked with a sigh at the Irish hills.
The once great owner now was a landless man
– All he'd possessed in Ireland sold to Boyles.
Lord Cork, the head of that family, reigned at Lismore,
Where – while the work on the ships went on –
Raleigh for some days visited him. In his former castle,
He was received with honour – Lord Cork[6], in token of sympathy,
Donating thirty-two gallons of whisky,
And other provisions, to Raleigh's fleet.
At the end of that August, Raleigh again set sail
– 'God Speed!' being – surely? – waved to him
From the town, and he steeps each side of the widening estuary.
Out on the open ocean, the seven warships,
The pinnaces, and the three others, dwindled,
Vanished – into the mementous future . . .
Raleigh aboard his flagship, the *Destiny*.
The venture failed.
Its terrible ins-and-outs are chronicled elsewhere.
Disaster, at every turn. Many ships were lost,

Many men killed, in the battles that beset the fleet,
Many more died of the sickness that followed them.
And . . . Raleigh's son was killed.
No gold was obtained for the King.
The last shot had been fired.
The last try
Had been made. That was that.
Raleigh's head was now forfeit.
On his way home, he came back into Kinsale,
With the shot-to-pieces, ragged, now barely sea-worthy
Remnants of his fleet, and his spent men,
Sick in body,
Sicker at heart.
This was spring – May, 1618.
He had been gone nine months.
May . . . the woods golden-green; the bracken uncurling.
Curlews dipping and calling;
On the headlands, gorse blazing.
The sweetness of life
Exhaling from everywhere.
The Kinsale people,
Knowing what waited in England,
Besought Raleigh and his company to remain with them.
Their hearts welled up with love for the unfortunate,
Honouring them the more for their misfortunes.
'Stay! Stay! Stay!' cried Ireland's siren voice,
As it has to many.
This was the last cry of love Raleigh was to hear,
The last loving-kindness he was to know.
The lonely man
May have looked, for a minute, into the fastnesses
Of the enfolding hills, or let his eye dwell
On the roofs of homes,
Of which one might, still, have been his.
But there was a debt to be honoured;
A bargain to be kept to,
Having been made.
Raleigh left his fleet
And sailed out of Kinsale, alone, on his flagship *Destiny*,
Back to England, to meet the disgrace and jeers,

And keep his appointment
With his death on the block.
Who knows what last of Ireland he carried with him
– The white flash of gull over the gorse?
The sunny sliding of waves
Over the rocks?
The ships and the men
Acceded to Kinsale's wishes: they stayed where they were,
And – so far as we know – never knew a regret.
Two of the captains, rather than go back to England,
Took to piracy, to make a living;
And, let us hope, did well.

VI

The Black Ships

The house of Stuart, with its ancient lineage,
Its tradition of kingship, its Catholic sympathies,
And its Scottishness – as opposed to the Tudor English –
Found favour with Ireland on the whole.
If there must *be* monarchs, extending their rule to Ireland,
These did as well as any,
Better than most. From all accounts, they were cut to the royal pattern,
And, though expecting money,
And using it as fast as they got their hands on it,
Made a good showing, and comported themselves with some grace.
There was this also; they were connected by marriage
With most of the Catholic royalties of Europe,
Which gave them status.
The trouble they were to make for Ireland was not,
At the outset,
To be foreseen.
At the shocking execution of Charles I
Most of our country held up its hands in horror.
You could hardly believe this, even of the English.
News of the fell deed, which had taken place
On January 30, 1649,
Would have reached County Cork, one imagines,
Some days later.
Not so long after that,
Kinsale was singled out for a great sensation

– A spectactular pageant of royal mourning,
A close-up of princely grief.
In this manner . . .
Prince Rupert, the late king's nephew,
Came sailing into Kinsale with three black-draped ships,
Silent as shadows,
Sombre as widows, sorrowful rippling the winter water –
– This apparition filling Kinsale with awe.
Prince Rupert of Bavaria's nobility,
His wonderful generalship in the King's army,
Against the Cromwellians,
And his devotion to his uncle,
Were by now known of all over the Three Kingdoms.
Kinsale,
Now honoured by this black drama,
No doubt darkened its doors and windows,
To show, by every sign, how it grieved with him
In this terrible loss he had sustained.
The hush lasted
– Till it was broken, suddenly.
Off came the black from the ships,
Many pennants flew.
Trumpets sounded.
Out rang the proclamation:
'*The King is dead,*
Long live the King!'
Prince Rupert proclaimed the accession of Charles II,
As King of England.
Kinsale harkened.
This new King had no kingdom:
He was in exile
– Did that endear him?
For Ireland, were not the good and great
Anways the children of banishment?
Had not the earls gone off
Into exile, too?

VII

Charles Fort

When Cromwell was scourging Ireland,
Reducing cities,
Destroying abbeys, visiting fierce retribution
On those who withstood him,
Kinsale kept out of it – by a miracle?
By a little tact, perhaps?
That terrible pounding she'd had from Mountjoy was still in memory.
Who wants to be heroic twice over,
In one and the same century?
Also, no Kinsale people had any liking
For the notion of being shipped off to the West Indies,
Which Cromwell dangled, it seems,
As one of the threats,
Should Kinsale show itself disobliging.
Kinsale, therefore, lay low and said nothing.
Kinsale, thus,
Had no further wounds to lick. She was doing well
– Indeed, enjoying a boom –
When King Charles II came home again,
And his glorious reign began.
Trade poured in, the Guilds and the Corporations
Were protected by a munificient Royal Charter.
The town and its outskirts bristled with handsome houses,
Which wine made merry.
Through her narrow streets – infernally noisy
From iron-shod traffic rattling over their cobbles –
Flitted colourful characters. Gay plumage,
High spirits, and general confidence
Distinguished the wealthier citizens of the town.
Kinsale's strategic importance was not lost sight of.
In 1666, the two guardian forts were inspected,
And reported upon, by the Earl of Orrery[7]. James Fort, he said,
Deserved to have money spent on it.
A year later, the scare of a French invasion
Brought Rincurran into the limelight. *This*, too,
Became a priority.
Then – therefore – began the conversion of the old 'castle'

Into the tremendous fortress
Now looming round us. Lord Orrery laid the first stone.
The work being undertaken was a triumph of military engineering.
The place accommodated two hundred cannon. It cost £80,000
– The equivalent, in our day, to £800,000.
It continued to be known as 'Rincurran Fort' until, 1681,
The Duke of Ormond[8] – pleased by the salvo of guns
That replied to his toasting of Charles II –
Re-named it.
Charles Fort it has remained.

VIII

Siege of Charles Fort

Charles Fort needed all its strength,
And all of its guns.
Once again,
Fate gave a twist to history.
Charles II, dying in 1685,
Had, as successor, his less popular brother – James II.
As Duke of York, James had been a successful admiral:
Alas, he fared less well as a king.
The rashness, the faulty judgement, the obstinacy
Of his father, the first Charles, came out again in James
– Who was willing to learn no lesson
From his father's downfall.
As a Catholic, he was held suspect by most of England.
His two daughters joined in the league against him.
1688 – three years after his accession –
James was deposed by a strong faction; and his son-in-law,
William of Orange – who had been long scheming –
Was enthroned in his place.
James fled to France.
Ireland, however, stayed faithful to this Stuart,
Whom – having not a King of her own left –
She saw as *her* King – and was willing to die for.
On Ireland centred James's unbroken hopes.
With support from France, he, accordingly, sailed from Brest
– Bringing with him one hundred French officers,
1,200 Irish refugees,
And ammunition and arms for 10,000 men –

And landed here, at Kinsale, on the 12 March 1669.
He slept one night in our town, then marched on to Cork,
Up hill, down dale – his men encumbered, on top of everything else,
By the many, weighty, jingling bags of French money –
Then on to Dublin.
All along his way, the returning Stuart was greeted
With cheers and fervour – a welcome outdoing dreams.
Cork opened its arms to him. In Dublin, bells rang.
Followers flocked to him.
James was a King again,
Till,
The hallucination ended.
Over came King Billy, the usurper,
With his iron army from England, and many mercenaries . . .
Up went James to the North
– He, and his Irish, and French officers
With great numbers joining them as they marched.
They all but had the enemy trapped in Derry.
They put the fear of death
In to the land-grabbing colonists there in Ulster
– Where O'Neill had reigned.
But disaster fell upon James' army at Newton Butler;
And then –
Came the unforgettable Battle of the Boyne . . .
The defeat of the Irish Jacobites was total.
Many, many, many of their dead, littering the field,
Lay looking up at the sky with unseeing eyes,
As had the dead, after
The Battle of Kinsale. Among those lying there,
Conquered by death only,
Would be descendents of those who had fought
For the earls.
James, his hopes all in ruins,
Turned, and went south down Ireland, back again to the port where he had landed
– The port, surely, unbearably haunted for him
By dreams, and schemes, and vision of victory? –
Kinsale.
From Kinsale he took ship and returned to France,
Leaving his cause kingless.

Nevertheless –
Those who had fought, fought on. – They fought, *now*, for Ireland.
These fighters still held the ports of Cork, Kinsale, Limerick and
Galway. They held on to them with fanatic determination – for why?
In expectation of a French landing. That had been promised.
Louis XIV's troops would be needing bases, supplies,
A secure foothold.
Should the incoming French fleet, unable to harbour,
Fall into English hands,
The game would be up for the Irish in Munster and Connaught.
King William,
Having failed to take Limerick at the first siege.
It was now 1690.
William's general, John Churchill,
1st Duke of Marlborough,
Perceiving Kinsale and Cork to be, no less, key-points,
Proposed sailing round to attack them. The king bade him to.
Marlborough's fleet – 80 ships – came into Cork waters:
The general invested Cork city on October 4,
And obtained its surrender four days later. He forthwith
Sent on a force ahead of him to Kinsale –
– 300 horses, 100 Dragoons, under command of a German colonel –
There had been Jacobite orders to burn the town down,
Sooner than let it be taken. These were not acted on.
Kinsale found herself occupied . . .
Meanwhile,
Her two forts, dauntless,
Jacobite-manned,
Made ready against the coming Marlborough.
The general, with his well-ordered army,
His cannon – more powerful than Mountjoy's
By all ninety years can do for heavy artillery –
Came over the hills from Cork on October 13.
He lost no time in investing Charles Fort.
He demanded that it surrender. The same demand
Went to James Fort. Both commanders refused.
The garrisons, with a sort of mocking hilarity, fired guns off,
And hung bloody flags out, in defiance.
Marlborough, while making his preparations for a long-term siege
And all-out bombardment of Charles Fort

– Which would be the harder nut to crack –
Had 800 men ferried across the water, to attack James Fort.
Inside James Fort, a powder-barrel blew up,
Killing fifty of the defenders. In the dismay and confusion,
Marlborough's men swarmed in and took the place –
– Swift work, to give them their due.
Charles Fort stood alone now.
Aid from the sea, from the French, was out of the question
(Where *were* the French?)
Aid from land, none.
Under a later Churchill, in 1940,
Awhole country stood alone, and at bay – but of good heart.
The hearts of this handful of Irish
– Crazy, were they, or inspired? –
Fighting for the past, hearing long-ago voices
Urging them on, out of the distances of their torn country –
But fighting also, you may be certain, for the future,
Hidden though it was –
The hearts of these Irish were good, too.
Yes, even – or perhaps ever the more so –
For having an indomitable Churchill arrayed against them?
(Look round you, you people! Look round you,
And take your hats off!
And breathe the air of Charles Fort in!
Bravery rises – as does the small of the grass which has grown since –
Out of this earth, here. Take thought of it!
Carry spirit away with you!)
The siege, accompanied by bombardment,
Dragged on through October. Fire was concentrated
Upon a bastion which was the inner strong-point,
The effective core, of the fort.
Huge walls also were breached, and battlements crumbled.
Marlborough – beset as Mountjoy had been
By pestiferous Irish rain, with its train of sicknesses –
Was impatient to end the thing.
The Governor of the almost demolished fort
Asked for a parley. Honourable terms were offered.
Further negotiations did not drag on too long. The decision
Had reached itself.
The terms of surrender were signed one midnight.

The garrison of Charles Fort – as had been accorded –
Marched out, bag and baggage, with full honours of war
And were conducted to Limerick, where they joined their comrades
– Limerick having capitulated also.
French ships *did* come into Limerick,
Later.
Too late . . . too late.
Nothing goes for nothing,
Remember!
But this was a hard relinquishment.
Nothing ahead, now, but a foreign shore,
Service with any army
That wanted you – over there –
And thoughts of an Ireland
You would not see again.

IX

The Wild Geese

The Wild Geese – as these Irish remnants came to be called –
Slipped out of Irish ports,
On foreign-bound ships,
On out-going tides,
In the dark.
They went from Limerick, Cork, Waterford,
And from Kinsale.
No one, it seems, hindered them. If there was a crying after them,
It was blown away in the wind,
Or drowned by the waves, as the ships they were on
Forged out into the open sea.
These Wild Geese, in their flight,
Were amount the many
– Generation after generation –
Of Ireland's sons whom she let go,
Having nothing to offer them, any more, now
– It seemed –
So long as they lived.
So, what of Ireland?
Listen!
Listen to Ireland . . .
She said, 'They gave me of their best

They lived, they gave their lives for me;
I tossed them to the howling waste,
And flung them to the foaming sea.'
She said, 'I never gave them aught,
Not mine the power, if mine the will;
I let them starve, I let them bleed, –
They bled and starved, and loved me still.'
She said, 'Ten times they fought for me,
Ten times they strove with might and main,
Ten times I saw them beaten down,
Ten times they rose, and fought again.'
She said, 'I stayed alone at home,
A dreary woman, grey and cold;
I never asked them how they fared,
Yet still they loved me as of old.'
She said, 'I never called them sons,
I almost ceased to breathe their name,
Then caught it echoing down the wind,
Blown backwards by the lips of Fame,'
She said, 'Not mine, not mine that fame;
Far over sea, far over land,
Cast off like rubbish from my shores,
They won it yonder, sword in hand.'
She said, 'God knows they owe me naught,
I tossed them to the foaming sea,
I tossed them to the howling waste,
YET STILL THEIR LOVE COMES BACK TO ME!'

Introduction to *The House by the Church-yard*, by Sheridan Le Fanu, 1968

The House by the Church-yard was first published in 1863, one year before Joseph Sheridan Le Fanu's other great novel, *Uncle Silas*. Of the two, *Uncle Silas*, with its small cast and highly concentrated psychological interest, may accommodate itself better to readers today: it being just over a century since both books were written, *Uncle Silas* may seem the more 'modern.' Those whose addiction to Le Fanu derived from the fascinations of *Uncle Silas* may (I do not say must) experience a set-back when first they embark on *The House by the Church-yard* – less taut, less apparently sure in 'tone,' disconcerting in its oscillations between sinister grimness and full-blooded jocosity and, here and there, threatened by diffuseness. Such, frankly, was, at the outset, the reaction of the writer of this introduction. It took time for the excellences, chief among which are the almost uncanny force and total originality of *The House by the Church-yard*, to seep through. That having happened, the novel obtained a grip nothing can dislodge.

Le Fanu, one may take it to be known, was an Irishman. When I had the privilege of writing an introduction to *Uncle Silas*, I spoke of its being an essentially Irish novel in an English setting. Something profoundly, temperamentally, differentiates it from the English–Victorian novel of mystery and suspense – such as Wilkie Collins' *The Woman in White*. The oblique and more than semi-mistrustful view of character (or characters), the unopposed great part played by obsession, the acceptance of more or less permanent insecurity as a basis for life, all belong to, all emanate from, the further side of the Irish sea. Le Fanu's Irishness, it could be argued, stood out the more strongly when, for the purposes of a story, he set himself to treating with English characters in England. *The House by the Church-yard*, I have now to admit, contradicts that. That the *mise-en-scène* is, and the entire cast, with one exception, are Irish doubles the author's own native characteristics. Le Fanu, here, is steeping his story in what was to him a prenatal atmosphere, an atmosphere so normal, so natural to him that he can – one might feel – for at any rate the duration of the story, conceive of no other as being possible. The point of view, the evaluations, the mood, the dilemmas are all Hibernian – what one does wonder is, how far they were comprehensible to his English readers? For Le Fanu's Ireland is far from being 'stage-Ireland'; it is Ireland as he knew her to be, for better or worse.

The happenings in the action of *The House by the Church-yard* pre-date by just less than a hundred years the time of the telling of the tale: 1767 is the date specified. The narrator is an anonymous old man, whose curiosity as to a bygone drama was, he explains to us, originally stirred, during his boyhood, by the coming to light in a village church-yard of a skull with two deep clefts, plus a round hole in the back of it. This old man (or rather, the Le Fanu behind him) cheats liberally – albeit with an effectiveness by which the cheating is twenty times justified – in the matter of what goes into his narrative: no amount of burning into the letters and diaries to which he purports to have had access could account for the authenticity, the sometimes fearful vividness, down to the last detail, he gives to what took place before he was born – or indeed, thought of – or for his omniscience as to not only the doings but feelings and thoughts of people on whom he had not, and never could have, set eyes. Not one scene in the book seems at one remove; on the contrary, the action of *The House by the Church-yard* unfolds itself directly, immediately, close-up to you and me. This good old man, with his singsong expressions of nostalgia for an epoch he fancies – perhaps rightly? – to have been more *simpatico,* more agreeable, than his own, early on is faded out of *The House by the Church-yard.* This I feel entitled to promise you – lest he put you off. (Why, incidentally, *did* Victorian writers burden themselves and their novels with 'intermediaries'? Why does Emily Brontë use them in *Wuthering Heights*?)

The House by the Church-yard is set in what since has come to be known to James Joyce devotees as the *Anna Livia* country: Chapelizod, in the Liffey Valley. Few making a Joyce tour, as now organised, will omit Chapelizod from their itinerary. Its name is now the poor place's remaining glory; apart from that it has come to be little more than a lustreless over-run from Dublin. Even by the 1860s it had, according to our narrator, lapsed, being dominated if not by Satanic Mills by frowsty, smoke-engendering factories. Bearable in his boyhood, it had been at its heyday in the 1760s: that is, when the events related in *The House by the Church-yard* were taking place. 'In those days, Chapelizod was about the gayest and prettiest of the outpost villages in which old Dublin took a complacent pride. The poplars which stood, in military rows, here and there, just showed a glimpse of formality among the orchards and old timber that lined the banks of the river and the valley with a lively sort of richness. The broad old streets looked hospitable and merry, with steep roofs and many coloured hall-doors . . . Then there was the village church, with its tower dark and rustling, from base to summit, with thick piled, bowering ivy.' Equivalents of the vanished prettiness and propriety of Chapelizod still are to be found – long may this be so! – in up-river Lucan and, still more, in the more-intact, further up-river Leixlip (Co. Kildare).

Poplars were not the only military feature: the Chapelizod of the time of *The House by the Church-yard* had the prestige and enjoyed the panache of being the headquarters of the Royal Irish Artillery, or RIA – not, pray, to be confused by English readers with the IRA! The barracks, the parade ground with its great gate, were along the riverside. The officers lodged on the drawing-room floors of sedate little houses on the aforesaid streets. The commander, 'fat, short, radiant General Chattesworth,' abode, with his lively spinster sister and pretty young daughter, in a nearby mansion, Belmont, over-looking the river from the heights – many such are, I am glad to say, still to be found in this neighbourhood. General Chattesworth is, we find, overshadowed socially only by the local peer, Lord Castlemallard, a dreamy bore.

The cast of *The House by the Church-yard*, in the main male, is largely though not wholly military. Civilians are represented by Dr. Walsingham, the Protestant rector, his genial Catholic opposite number Father Roach, the physician Toole (whose relations with Sturk, the army surgeon attached to the RIA are not so ideal as they should be), Irons, the lantern-jawed parish clerk, and, not by any means least, the dark-avised Nutter, Miller, whose chief income is derived from his agency of the surrounding Castlemallard properties. To these are added two men of mystery: haunted young Mr Mervyn, who arrives with a coffin and stays on, in a perpetual brooding frenzy which leads ladies to think he may be an *âme damnée*, and suave, sophisticated, middle-aged Mr Dangerfield, Englishman, who moves in for no declared purpose, renting a riverside villa delightfully known as The Brass Castle. Dangerfield is Lord Castlemallard's agent in England, where – Irish peers enjoyed the best of both worlds! – properties are yet more extensive, and more valuable. A second putative *âme damnée* is handsome Captain Devereux, of the RIA. The RIA contribute to our story also, most notably, corsetted, on-the-make Captain Cluffe; Lieutenant Fireworker O'Flaherty (one of the 'ferocious O'Flaherty's' from Galway) and dear, ingenuous, generous, fat little First Lieutenant Puddock . . . In spite of this bevy of males, if one may so call it, *The House by the Church-yard* could have been subtitled, 'a novel without a hero.' There is, actually, no one central character of either sex. As 'heroines,' Lilias Walsingham and Gertrude Chattesworth amicably divide the honours; yet, neither girl plays a major part in the plot – one of them is to be made momentous, and deeply moving, by her illness and death. Gertrude's Aunt Rebecca is more in the forefront – handsome, something of a volcano. Miss Magnolia Macnamara and her mother are comics (something in the splenetic Thackeray manner). It is two at the first glance inconspicuous matrons, Mrs Nutter and Mrs Sturk, who are to become most drastically involved, in whirlpools of menace, terror, piteous anxiety, darkling mystery. And there is an evil-precipitating adventuress out from Dublin, Mary Matchwell.

With near-genius, with which goes a friendly equalitarianism in regard to them, Le Fanu keeps this host of characters in play. Never for long does anyone of them leave the story. His hero-less plot is kept spinning by a diversity of crisscrossing passions. He *does*, one has to admit, introduce a villain, though so subtly, and with so many light and deluding touches, that this creature's enormities hardly are to be suspected until the end. Rivalries and antagonism are at work, pressures exerted. A criminal drama, set in another land, proves unfinished; it continues to operate in and round Chapelizod . . . All this sounds like, and indeed is, the stock material of one kind of fiction. What, then, causes *The House by the Church-yard* to soar above endless other novels of what might otherwise be its kind?

I would suggest, Le Fanu's curious, near-visionary manner of seeing and way of writing; his what one might call depth-charge perceptions into feeling and motive; his sympathy with the off-beat, with deviation; his none the less uncompromising sense of what *is* ethical; and, most of all, the acute, sometimes almost unbearable emotion, always too astringent to be emotionality or sentiment, with which he suffuses his key scenes. He is aware of the monstrous, and makes a not wholly ironical bow to it: his Black Dillon, that perverse young surgeon of genius cynically weltering in the stews of Dublin, plays but a brief part but is unforgettable.

This novel has rare, few, lovely and on the whole heartbreaking lyrical episodes. It is also roared through by an intense sociability. Bravura rates high, and 'gaieties' – in the full and enthusiastic connotation those have in Ireland – are dear to his pen. We have the shooting match, with its merry onlooking troops of ladies, the fair at Palmerstown, the military ball, the *al fresco* entertainment given by the RIA to the neighbourhood, fifes, bugles and other supporting instruments joyously loudening the air of the lady-adorned, tree-shaded riverside. The dinner party at Belmont, at which interesting Mr Dangerfield first appears, is rendered with every shade of social precision.

Note three particularly Irish attributes of Le Fanu's, all of them to the fore in this novel. (1) His feeling for, acceptance of, and matter-of-fact though none the less terrifying treatment of the supernatural, as exemplified by the hauntings of The Tiled House, young Mr Mervyn's dwelling. (2) His depiction of servants, together with more irregular hirelings who surround households, such as 'the Widow Macann . . . who carried the ten pailfuls of water up from the river to fill the butt in the backyard every Tuesday and Friday for a shilling a week and "a cup o' tay with the girls in the kitchen".' The intimacy, the complicity, the often-shared desperations of the employer–employed relationship, as it is in Ireland, can seldom have been, and may never be, better drawn. (3) His sense of the illimitable majesty of death, and its train of incurable desolations. We see a young student, agonised by sympathy, trying to tender comfort to an old clergyman bereft of his dear daughter:

'Oh, Dan – Dan – she's gone – little Lily.'

'You'll see her again, sir – oh, you'll see her again.'

'Oh, Dan! Dan! Till the heavens be no more they shall not awake, nor be raised out of their sleep. Oh, Dan, a day's so long – how am I to get over the time?'

In *The House by the Church-yard*, some enchanting lyrics, such as the one beginning:

The river ran between them,
And she looked upon the stream,
And the soldier looked upon her,
As a dreamer on a dream.

– are sung or recalled. And a long moralistic ballad is intoned in a pub, taking off thus:

There was a man near Ballymooney,
Was guilty of a deed o' blood,
For thravellin' alongside wiv ould Tim Rooney,
He kilt him in a lonesome wood.

Where did Le Fanu get these from, I wonder – did he write them? They stand, in their ways, for what might be called the opposite poles of the book – whose first event is a torchlit midnight burial, surrounded by secrecy, odour of disgrace and unspoken horror, and whose last is a sunlit, splendid young-aristocratic wedding. A damaged skull, we recall, set the story going. By the end, we have learned whose the skull was – yes, we *have* learned, but without greatly caring. That this should be so is, I feel, a tribute to and not a reflection upon *The House by the Church-yard*. So much has been stirred up, such an orchestrated variety of sensations has been lived through, so much that was unexpected has teased our nerves and so much that is tender and beautiful touched our senses and delighted our spirits, since the story began, that the original mystery has been swept away – on the much water that has, by now, flowed under the bridges.

The Irish Cousins, by Violet Powell, 31 January 1970, *The Spectator*, Review

The book jacket of Violet Powell's *The Irish Cousins* is adorned by a family group: a framed photograph. This perfectly sets the tone of what is within. Kinship, or a close degree of affinity, characterizes the features and general attitude of boater-hatted young women in starched white ankle-length skirts and moustached young men, one in a blazer, at rest at the edge of a tennis court, between games. Backdrop, a twinkling shrubbery. There is, to the Anglo-Irish eye, a palpable give-off of Anglo-Ireland; and in its heyday. conversation, suspended by the camera, leaves heads turned this way or that, alert and waiting. The *personae* are the interknit Somerville-Coghill tribes, soon to be further linked by another marriage. On the periphery may be taken to be either accepted neighbours or summer guests. The locale is Castletownshend, West County Cork, the time circa 1886.

In the forefront, vigorously seated, is Edith Œnone Somerville, 'Top Dog', by virtue of seniority, and more than that, of a generation consisting largely of brothers. Next to her, beautiful in profile, holding her racquet to her chin as one might a fan, is Edith's second cousin, Violet Martin – the 'Ross' of the collaboration to be. *The Irish Cousins* (which takes its title, only a plural added, from the firstfruit novel of that collaboration: *An Irish Cousin, 1889)* introduces itself as a study: 'The Books and Background of Somerville and Ross.' How inseparable the books and the background are, Lady Violet, Anglo-Irish herself, perceives, and goes on to illustrate.

Greater interest must concentrate on what was phenomenal: the collaboration. Interlocking minds, known more to criminal than aesthetic history? No, not that only: this was a rarer case – interlocking creative imaginations. Considering how savagely individual, how overweeningly solitary, as an activity, is inventive writing, how could two practitioners unify into one story? – *and* carry this off not once but again and again? The cousins, we learn, were plagued by what seemed to them fatuous questions on that subject: 'Who holds the pen – or pencil, and so on?' Oneself, one retains some sympathy with the questioners. Leave it, that this was a literary miracle, plus something other. Result, a superb degree of accomplishment, a tremendous range.

Lady Violet, too wise to analyse, contents herself with comments, – on the joint vision, its extra-powerful focus; on the stylishness of the joint style achieved, likened by her, in its variations, to shot silk. It may be supposed that Somerville, painter already, charged herself with that memorable verbal scene-painting, together with *outer* accounts of action (equine or human), weather, sailing adventures, meets, funerals, fairs, leaving to Ross, more fine-strung, 'aware' and tense, the control of dialogue and, where necessary, penetration into events or persons. Ross's death, in 1915, leaves, in the many succeeding novels and stories, a lacuna difficult to locate, bravely though 'communication' was carried on, defiantly though the works were, still, double-signed.

The answer may be that when the cousins met – which oddly, given the smallness of Ireland and the high value placed on getting together, failed to happen till both were in their late twenties – there occurred one of those fusions of personality which in one way or another can make history. Their, from then on, total attachment incurred no censure, and – still stranger, given the habitual jocularity of their relatives – seems to have drawn down no family mirth. Nor was its nature – as it might be in these days – speculated upon, Absolutely, the upper class, Anglo-Irish were (then) non-physical, far from keen participants, even, from what one hears of them, in the joys of marriage.

Edith and Violet loved to travel together, but desired no permanent break-away from parental homes. The Llangollen Ladies[9], whose Plas Newydd they viewed on a Welsh tour, seemed to them – it is recorded – extremely silly. This couple of gentlewomen from Ireland were encased, armoured, in the invincible heartiness of their extroverted tribe and specialized class. Round and upon them blew the prevailing gales of clean fun, anaphrodisiac laughter. Anything 'extreme' was comic: that went for passion, that went for art. Dogs, jokes, were the accepted currency. Their initial literary endeavours, daylong disappearances, together, to the neglect of tennis, side-split brothers and sisters, uncles and aunts. Only when books 'appeared' did menace begin. The two now ceased to be amateurs: things looked serious. The actual crux, or crunch, was *The Real Charlotte*.

It is owing to *The Real Charlotte* that all this matters: otherwise, who might care? Here, in their third novel, they cut the cable. They made their own a terrain of outrageousness, obliquity, unsavoury tragedy, sexual no less than ambitious passion. *What* fired them into full-stature artists? It is on this masterpiece (which long awaited full recognition) that, as almost unwilling, almost unwitting artists, they do in today's eyes take their stand . . . Secondary in literary glory, toweringly 'the thing' in terms of success, the *Irish RM* stories are less cut-to-pattern in comicality, turn less undeviatingly on blood sports, than anti-blood-sport generations have preferred to suppose. In these tales are no meaningless antic caperings: on the contrary, outsize characters, clashes, crises, realistic in their very delirium. These not only *were* Ireland – they still are Ireland, under the skin.

One would like to know more than there seems to be to be known about Violet Martin: 'Ross,' with her indomitable fragility, her dilated great beautiful hare's eyes – whose near-sightedness had to be aided by *pince-nez.* The Norman-descended Martins of Ross, County Galway, had it less good than the later coming, Scottish descended Somervilles, County Cork. Their fortunes foundered, under a succession of blows – those intricate troubles known to landowners. Ghosts were the least of the tribulations of the dying house.

Half-way through Violet's childhood, Ross, the mansion, had to be abandoned: her brother went off to seek a living in England; mother and a bevy of spinster girls (Violet the youngest) for some years camped, on the cheap, in Dublin (from whence sprang the rattling good Dublin passages in *The Real Charlotte*). After that, the heroic return to Galway; the struggle, headed by Violet, to rekindle life – such as it had been, never could be again – in the shell of the house. The whole of the wisdom of sorrow was this young woman's; she was early acquainted with wailings, dementia, speechless despairs. She is remembered for her delightful gaiety. Yet can one doubt, it was she who introduced into the Somerville and Ross combination that dark streak – which, at the same time, gave it validity?

Lady Violet is to be thanked for *The Irish Cousins.* Her sense of what *is* relevant to her subject, and her use of that, would seem to me faultless. Moreover, she has read, and assimilated, the Somerville-Ross writings in their entirety: no small task. She summarizes each of the many books, in some detail but without an instant of boringness. The effect is to whet a renewed appetite. How many of the lesser-known works are still in print, available, one would like to know? Could not publishing enterprise strike while the iron is hot? There may not yet be a boom; there *is* a 'revival' . . . Did these authors impact on their compatriot, James Joyce? Lady Violet holds that they did, and produces evidence – which is daring and interesting. Their place in the Irish literary Valhalla is accorded, their links with the great native tradition traced. I regret only, in this book, a lack of mention of Joseph Sheridan Le Fanu, with whose novels several outlined here would seem to have a marked, if unconscious, affinity.

Notes and References

INTRODUCTORY ESSAY. 'THE INDEFINITE GHOSTS OF THE PAST

1 Included in Chapter Two.
2 Terence Dooley, *The Decline of the Big House in Ireland* (Dublin: Wolfhound, 2001), p. 272.
3 Allan Hepburn, ed., *People, Places, Things* (Edinburgh: Edinburgh University Press, 2008), p. 2
4 See Hepburn, ed., *People, Places, Things* and *Listening In* (Edinburgh: Edinburgh University Press, 2010), and Hermione Lee, *The Mulberry Tree* (London: Virago Press 1986).
5 Maud Ellmann, *Elizabeth Bowen: The Shadow Across the Page* (Edinburgh: Edinburgh University Press, 2003), p. 9.
6 Ellmann, p. 10.
7 See the excellent collection *Elizabeth Bowen's Irish Stories*, introduction by Victoria Glendinning (Dublin: Poolbeg, 1978).
8 See W.J. McCormack's *Sheridan Le Fanu and Victorian Ireland* (Dublin: Lilliput Press, 1991).
9 Andrew Bennett and Nicholas Royle, *Elizabeth Bowen and the Dissolution of the Novel* (Hampshire: Macmillan 1995), p. 19.
10 See R.F. Foster, *Paddy and Mr Punch: Connections in Irish and English History* (London: Penguin, 1993), Heather Bryant Jordan, *How Will the Heart Endure? Elizabeth Bowen and the Landscape of War* (Ann Arbor: University of Michigan Press, 1992) and Clair Wills, *That Neutral Island* (London: Faber and Faber, 2007).
11 Phyllis Lassner, *Elizabeth Bowen* (Basingstoke: MacMillan, 1990), p. 2.
12 Sinéad Mooney, 'Bowen and the Modern Ghost' in *Elizabeth Bowen: Visions and Revisions*, ed., Éibhear Walshe (London: Irish Academic Press, 2008) p. 86.
13 Elizabeth Bowen. Introduction to the second US edition, 1952.
14 Sean O'Faolain to Elizabeth Bowen, 22 April 1937, Elizabeth Bowen Collection, Harry Ransom Center.
15 Sean O'Faolain, *Vive Moi* (London: Sinclair Stevenson, 1993), p. xi.
16 Sean O'Faolain to Elizabeth Bowen, 22 April 1937, Elizabeth Bowen Collection, Harry Ransom Center.
17 The first issue of *The Bell* in 1940 carried her essay 'The Big House' and she went on to write on Joyce for the March 1941 issue, as well as reviewing a novel called *The Talented Children* by Domhnaill O'Connail in April 1941. She also allowed O'Faolain to use two of her story stories, 'Sunday Afternoon' (October 1942) and 'Dancing in Daylight' (November 1942), for *The Bell* and she published her tribute essay on Mainie Jellett in the December 1944 issue.
18 I am grateful of Kalene Kennifick for this information on Bowen and *The Bell*.

19 *New Statesman and Nation*, 1943.
20 April 1945, vol x, 111.
21 *The Bell*, September 1942, p. 421.
22 Ibid., p. 420.
23 Ibid., p. 425.
24 Ibid., p. 425.
25 Sean O'Faolain, 'A Reading and Remembrance of Elizabeth Bowen', *London Review of Books* (4–17 March, 1982), pp. 15–16.
26 *Irish Independent*, 8 June 1939, p. 10.
27 Victoria Glendinning, *Elizabeth Bowen: Portrait of a Writer* (London: Weidenfeld and Nicolson, 1977), p. 127.
28 Elizabeth Bowen, preface to *The Demon Lover and Other Stories* (London: Cape 1945).
29 Elizabeth Bowen, *Seven Winters: Memories of a Dublin Childhood* (London: Longmans, 1943), p. 7.
30 Eunan O'Halpin, *Spying on Ireland* (Oxford: Oxford University Press, 2008), p. 139.
31 Clair Wills, *This Neutral Island*, p. 117.
32 Robert Fisk, *In Time of War* (Dublin: Gill and MacMillan, 1996), p. 584.
33 *Paddy and Mr Punch*, p. 118.
34 Fisk, p. 423n.
35 Heather Bryant Jordan, p. 100.
36 *The Irish Times*, 21 November 1942.
37 Ibid., p. 9.
38 Clair Wills, p. 176.
39 *The Irish Times*, 5 January 1946.
40 *The Spectator*, 3 July 1942.
41 *Sunday Independent,* 5 July 1942, p. 3.
42 *Irish Independent*, 15 July 1942, p. 2.
43 *The Irish Times* 4 July 1942.
44 Corcoran, *Elizabeth Bowen: The Enforced Return* (Oxford: Oxford UP, 2004), p. 168.
45 *The Heat of the Day* (London: Jonathan Cape, 1948), p. 166.
46 *The Irish Times*, 22 December 1951, p. 9.
47 *Irish Independent*, 22 December 1951.
48 Victoria Glendinning and Judith Robertson, eds, *Love's Civil War* (London: Simon and Schuster, 2009), p. 350.
49 Kilmallock is near Bowen's Cork in North Cork.
50 *Irish Writing*, 27 June 1954.
51 *Tatler and Bystander,* 30 June 1954.
52 *Observer*, 4 May 1952.
53 *The Anglo-Irish* by Brian Fitzgerald, *Observer*, 16 November 1952.
54 *The Irish Times*, 31 July 1954.
55 O'Hanaran to Kleinerman, 11 July 1960, National Archives, Dublin, s16882.
56 Kleinerman, ibid., 12 August 1960.
57 See Robert Savage in 'Constructing/Deconstructing the Image of Sean Lemass' Ireland: The Tear and the Smile', in *Nationalism: Visions and Revisions*, ed. Luke Dodd (Dublin: Film Institute of Ireland, 1999), p. 12.
58 Curtis Brown to Elizabeth Bowen HCR, 19 September 1960.
59 6 February 1961, s16882b/61.
60 Savage, 'Constructing/Deconstructing the Image of Sean Lemass' Ireland: The Tear and the Smile', p. 12

61 *Love's Civil War*, p. 363.
62 Ibid., p. 308. *A Time in Rome* was reviewed positively in the *Irish Independent* on 20 August 1960.
63 Jordan, p. 180.
64 *Love's Civil War*, p. 340.
65 Ibid., p. 341.
66 *Bowen's Court*, p. 559.
67 *Irish Independent*, 24 April 1965.
68 I am grateful to Allan Hepburn for sending me a copy of this broadcast which appears in his book *Listening In*.
69 *Paddy and Mr Punch*, p. 122.
70 Jordan, p. 9.

1. *OBLIQUE, FRAYED ISLAND* 1929–1940

1 Henry Grattan (1746–1820), patriot and politician.
2 Rt. Hon. Richard Brinsley Sheridan (1751–1816), Irish-born dramatist and poet and long-term owner of the London Theatre Royal, Drury Lane.
3 Lord Edward Fitzgerald (1763–1798), Irish aristocrat and revolutionary.
4 Disillusioned
5 Later King John
6 Thomas Cromwell, 1st Earl of Essex, K(c. 1485–28 July 1540), known as 1st Baron Cromwell of Wimbledon between 1536 and 1540, was an English statesman who served as chief minister of King Henry VIII of England from 1532 to 1540
7 Philosopher and patriot.
8 Wolfe Tone (1763–98), leader of the United Irishmen.
9 Robert Emmet (1778–1803), revolutionary leader, executed at twenty-five.
10 Daniel O'Connell (1775–1847), the Great Liberator, leader for Catholic Emancipation.
11 Charles Stewart Parnell (1845–91), MP and Protestant leader for Home Rule.
12 Jimmy O'Dea (1899–1965), Irish comic actor.
13 Coming and goings.
14 Hugh Lane (1875–1915), collector and art dealer.
15 Suspicion, unease.
16 Charlotte Brooke (*c.*1740–1793), writer and collector of Gaelic poetry.
17 Philip Barron (1802–c.1859), Waterford-born Irish language scholar
18 James Mangan (1803–1849), Irish poet.
19 John O'Donovan (1806–1861), Gaelic scholar.
20 Douglas Hyde (1860–1949), Gaelic scholar, first President of Ireland
21 Richard Butler, Dean of Clonmacnoise (1794–1862), married to Edgeworth's half-sister Harriett.
22 Ibid.
23 General Jean Humbert (1755–1823), French general, leader of French force into Ireland in 1798.

2. *WARTIME GEOGRAPHY* 1940–1945

1 Wild, odd, singular.
2 I am grateful to the National Archives, London, for assistance in tracing these reports.

3 James Dillon, Irish politician, leader of the opposition Fine Gael party at this time.
4 Lord Craigavon, James Craig, (1871–1940), Prime Minister of Northern Ireland.
5 Frank McDermot, pro-British Irish Senator, against neutrality.
6 Sir John Keane (1873–1956), Anglo-Irish landlord and member of the Irish Senate.
7 Senator Robinson, possibly David Robinson, Fianna Fáil Senator.
8 Oliver St John Gogarty (1878–1957) Irish Writer
9 Lord Halifax, Edward Frederick Lindley Wood, 1st Earl of Halifax (1881–1959) British Tory politician, British ambassador to the US.
10 *Heimkunst* – folk art.
11 Erskine Hamilton Childers (1905–1974), President of Ireland from 1973 until his death in 1974.
12 William T. Cosgrave (1880–1965), president of the executive council of the Irish Free State, leader of Fine Gael.
13 It wasn't.
14 Eoin O'Duffy (1892–1944), Commissioner of the Garda Ṣíochána, leader of Fine Gael (1933–34).
15 *The Great Dictator* is a comedy film released in October 1940. It was written, directed, produced by, and starred Charlie Chaplin.
16 Esmé Stuart Lennox Robinson (1886–1958), Irish dramatist, poet and theatre producer and director.
17 'Boule de Suif' is a short story of the Franco-Prussion war by the late-19th century French writer Guy de Maupassant
18 Ethel Mary Dell, (1881–1939), author
19 O'Connor Sligo – possibly . Sir Domnhnall Ó Conchobhair Sligo, c.(1556–1588).
20 The Earl of Desmond, Gerald Fitzgerald, 16th Earl of Desmond (1558–1583), leader of the Munster Rebellion.
21 Sir George Carew, Lord President of Munster (1555–1629).
22 William Cecil, 1st Baron Burghley (1520–1598), chief advisor of Queen Elizabeth.
23 Robert Dudley, 1st Earl of Leicester (1532–1588), English nobleman, close friend of Elizabeth.
24 Robert Cole Bowen, Bowen's grandfather.
25 Neville Chamberlain (18 March 1869–9 November 1940), Prime Minister of Great Britain.
26 Elizabeth Yeats (Lolly) (1869–1940), designer and print maker, printer.
27 Dorothy Richardson (1873–1957), novelist.
28 William Orpen, 1878–1931), Irish painter.
29 Walter Sickert (1860–1942), painter
30 Theodor Leschetitzky (1830–1915), Polish, London-based pianist and teacher.
31 Evie Hone (1894–1955), Irish artist.
32 Andre Lhote (1885–1962), French painter and sculptor.
33 Albert Gleizes (1881–1953), painter.

3. *PRINTS ON THE LANDSCAPE* 1940–1945

1 Strongbow – Anglo-Norman invaders of Ireland named after Strongbow, Richard de Clare, Earl of Pembroke (1130–1176).
2 Delusions of grandeur, megalomania.
3 Constantia Maxwell (1886–1962), writer and Professor of Economics at Trinity College, Dublin.
4 Dorothea Herbert (1770–1829), Anglo-Irish writer and memorialist.

5 Edith Somerville (1858–1949) and Violet Florence Martin (1862–1915), cousins, partners and Anglo-Irish writers.
6 Built for Catherine de Medici, Queen of France (13 April 1519–5 January 1589).
7 Ernst Lubitsch (January 28, 1892–November 30, 1947) was a German-born film director.
8 Andrey Januaryevich Vyshinskiy (10 December 1883–22 November 1954) was a Russian and Soviet jurist and diplomat and served as the Soviet Foreign Minister from 1949 to 1953.
9 E. Bowen has put 'Knowl'. It looks obvious that it should be 'Bartram-Haugh'.

4. *A New Ireland* 1950s

1 Stephen Lucius Gwynn (1864–1950).
2 Richard Boyle, 1st Earl of Cork (1566–1643).
3 James Butler, 1st Duke of Ormonde (1610–88).
4 John Redmond (1856–1918), Irish nationalist politician.
5 Edward Carson, Baron Carson (9 February 1854–22 October 1935), an Irish and British barrister, judge and politician. He was leader of the Irish Unionist Alliance and Ulster Unionist Party between 1910 and 1921.
6 John Aloysius Costello (1891–1976), Taoiseach from 1948–51 and 1954–57.

5. *A Clean End* 1960s

1 Bowen wrote this narration script for 'Kinsale, Son et Lumiere', a light and sound show performed at Charlesfort Castle in Kinsale on 22 May 1966. Thanks to the Harry Ransom Center for permission to use this unpublished manuscript.
2 Strongbow – Anglo-Norman invaders of Ireland named after Strongbow, Richard de Clare, Earl of Pembroke (1130–1176).
3 Charles Blount, 8th Baron Mountjoy and 1st Earl of Devonshire (1563–1606), Lord Deputy of Ireland under Queen Elizabeth I, then Lord Lieutenant.
4 Aodh Ruadh Ó Domhnaill, anglicized Hugh Roe Ó Donnell (1572–1602) was King of Tír Chonaill (or Tyrconnell), who led a rebellion against English government in Ireland.
5 Juan del Águila y Arellano (1545–1602). Spanish commander of the invasion of Ireland.
6 Richard Boyle, 1st Earl of Cork (1566–1643).
7 Roger Boyle, 1st Earl of Orrery (1621–79), soldier, statesman and dramatist.
8 James Butler, 1st Duke of Ormonde (1610–88).
9 The Ladies of Llangollen were Lady Eleanor Butler (1739–1829) and the Honourable Sarah Ponsonby (1755–1832).

Bowen's Irish Writings: a bibliography

The Last September (London: Constable, 1929)

Dublin Under the Georges, by Constantia Maxwell, 25 July 1936, *New Statesman and Nation*

A Biography of Dublin, by Christine Longford, 7 November 1936, *New Statesman and Nation*

Letter from Ireland, 28 October 1937, *Night and Day*

My Ireland, by Lord Dunsany, 26 June 1937, *New Statesman and Nation*

Agreeable Reading: Review of *The Farm by Lough Gur* by Lady Carbery, 9 October 1937, *New Statesman and Nation*

Island Life: Review of *Land's End* and *No More Music,* 15 March 1938, *New Statesman and Nation*

Dublin Old and New, by Stephen Gwynn, 17 May 1938, *New Statesman and Nation*

Then and Now: Review of Three Homes by Lennox Robinson, T. Robinson, and Nora Dorman, and *Irish Holiday* by Dorothy Hartley, 17 September 1938, *New Statesman and Nation*

Irish Life in the Seventeenth Century: After Cromwell by Edward MacLysaght, 6 May 1939, *New Statesman and Nation*

The Sword of Light by Desmond Ryan, 6 May 1939, *New Statesman and Nation*

The Moores of Moore Hall, by Joseph Hone, 25 November 1939, *New Statesman and Nation*

Finnegans Wake, 1939, *Purpose* 11.3.

The Big House, October 1940, *The Bell.*

Report from Ireland Ministry of Information, 9 November 1940

James Joyce by Herbert Gorman, 14 March 1941, *The Spectator.*

Eire, 12 April 1941, *New Statesman and Nation*

James Joyce, *The Bell,* 1 6 1941

Truth about Ireland – Atlantic Gateway, by Jim Phelan (Bodley Head), September 5 1941, *The Spectator*

Reports for the Ministry of Information, by Elizabeth Cameron, 9 and 20 February, and 12, 19, 25–31 July 1942

Bowen's Court (London: Longman, 1942)

Dubliner: Review of *Pictures in the Hallway* by Sean O'Casey, 1 May 1942, *The Spectator* 168

Weeping Earl, *The Great O'Neill* by Sean O'Faolain, 6 March 1943, *New Statesman and Nation*

Seven Winters: Memories of a Dublin Childhood (London: Longmans, 1943)

The Desire to Please: A Story of Hamilton Rowan and the United Irishmen by Harold Nicolson, 22 May 1943, *New Statesman and Nation*

The Most Unforgettable Character I've Met, 1944, *Windmill*

Mainie Jellett, 3 December 1944, *The Bell* 9

Post script to the US edition of *The Demon Lover and other Stories*, 1945

Ireland Makes Irish, 15 August 1946, *Vogue*

How They Live in Ireland, 1946 *Contact*

Writings from Paris Peace Conference, 1946, *Cork Examiner*

Introduction to the Cresset Press edition of *Uncle Silas*, by Sheridan Le Fanu, 1947

The Heat of the Day (London: Jonathan Cape, 1949)

Christmas at Bowen's Court, December 1950, *Flair* 1.11

Review of *Come Back to Erin* by Sean O'Faolain, December 1950, *The Bell*

Life in the Irish Counties: Review of *The Fire in the Dust* by Francis MacManus, 11 February 1951, *New York Herald Tribune*

The Shelbourne (London: Harrap, 1951)

Exploring Ireland: Review of *Wait Now!* by Rachel Knappett, 4 May 1952, *Observer*

Come to Ireland, *Ireland and the Irish*, by Charles Duff, 1952, unpublished, Harry Ransom Center

A City Growing: Review of *Dublin 1660–1860* by Maurice Craig, *Observer*, 18 May 1952

The Anglo-Irish by Brian Fitzgerald, 16 November 1952, *Observer*

Preface to second US edition of *The Last September* 1952

The Stranger in Ireland by Constantia Maxwell, *The Deserters* by Honor Tracey, June 1954, *Tatler*

Ireland 1950, 1950s, unpublished essay, Harry Ransom Center

Ireland, 1954, *House and Garden*

A World of Love (London: Cape, 1955)

A Kite's Dinner: Poems, 1938–1954 by Sheila Wingfield, 1955, *Tatler* 215, 19 January 1955

Essence of Ireland: Review of *The Patriot Son* by Mary Lavin, 11 April 1956, *Tatler* 220

James Joyce's Dublin, Patricia Hutchins, *8 May* 1957, *Tatler*

Lifelong Attachment: Review of *George Moore: Letters 1895–1933 to Lady Cunard*, edited by Rupert Hart-Davis, 16 October 1957, *Tatler* 226

Bowen's Court, 1958, *Holiday*

Kinsale, Son et Lumiere, 22 May 1966, Harry Ransom Center

Introduction to *The House by the Church-yard*, by Sheridan Le Fanu, 1968

The Irish Cousins by Violet Powell, 31 January 1970, *The Spectator*

General Bowen Bibliography

Works by Elizabeth Bowen

Encounters (London: Sidgwick and Jackson, 1923).
Ann Lee and Other Stories (London: Sidgwick and Jackson, 1926).
The Hotel (London: Constable, 1927).
Joining Charles (London: Constable, 1929).
The Last September (London: Constable, 1929).
Friends and Relations (London: Constable, 1931).
To the North (London: Gollancz, 1932).
The Cat Jumps and Other Stories (London: Gollancz, 1934).
The House in Paris (London: Gollancz, 1935).
The Death of the Heart (London: Gollancz, 1938).
Look at All Those Roses (London: Gollancz, 1941).
Bowen's Court (London: Longman, 1942).
Seven Winters: Memories of a Dublin Childhood (London: Longmans, 1943).
English Novelists (London: Collins, 1945).
The Demon Lover and Other Stories. (London: Cape, 1945).
The Heat of the Day (London: Jonathan Cape, 1949).
Collected Impressions (London: Longmans, 1950).
The Shelbourne (London: Harrap, 1951).
A World of Love (London: Cape, 1955).
A Time in Rome (London: Longmans, 1960).
Afterthought (London: Longman, 1962).
The Little Girls (London: Cape, 1964).
A Day in the Dark and Other Stories (London: Cape, 1965).
The Good Tiger (London: Cape, 1965).
Eva Trout, or Changing Scenes (London: Jonathan Cape, 1969).
Pictures and Conversations, ed. Spencer Curtis Brown (London: Allan Lane, 1975).

Selected works on Elizabeth Bowen

Backus, Margot. *The Gothic Family Romance: Heterosexuality, Child Sacrifice, and the Anglo-Irish Colonial Order* (Durham, NC: Duke University Press, 1999)

Bennett, Andrew and Nicholas Royle. *Elizabeth Bowen and the Dissolution of the Novel* (Hampshire: Macmillan, 1995)

Christensen, Liz, *Elizabeth Bowen, The Later Fiction* (Museum Tusculanum Press, University of Copenhagen, 2001).

Coughlan, P. 'Women and Desire in the Work of Elizabeth Bowen' in E. Walshe, ed., *Sex, Nation and Dissent in Irish Writing* (Cork: Cork University Press, 1997).

Corcoran, Neil. *Elizabeth Bowen: The Enforced Return* (Oxford: Oxford University Press, 2004).

Craig, Patricia. *Elizabeth Bowen* (London: Penguin, 1986).

Ellmann, Maud. *Elizabeth Bowen: The Shadow Across the Page* (Edinburgh: Edinburgh University Press, 2003).

Farrell, Marcia. Elizabeth Bowen: A Selected Bibliography, *MFS Modern Fiction Studies,* Volume 53, No. 2, Summer 2007.

Foster, R.F. *Paddy and Mr Punch: Connections in Irish and English History* (London: Penguin, 1993).

—. *The Irish Story*. (London: Penguin, 2001).

Glendinning, Victoria. *Elizabeth Bowen: Portrait of a Writer* (London: Weidenfeld and Nicolson, 1977).

Hepburn, Allan. Ed. *People, Places, Things: Essays by Elizabeth Bowen* (Edinburgh: Edinburgh University Press, 2008).

—. Ed. *Listening In: Broadcasts, Speeches and Interviews by Elizabeth Bowen* (Edinburgh: Edinburgh University Press, 2010).

Hoogland, Rene. *Elizabeth Bowen: A Reputation in Writing* (New York: New York University Press, 1994).

Jordan, Heather Bryant. *How Will the Heart Endure? Elizabeth Bowen and the Landscape of War* (Ann Arbor: University of Michigan Press, 1992).

Kreilkamp, Vera. *The Anglo-Irish Novel and the Big House* (Syracuse, NY: Syracuse University Press, 1998).

Lassner, Phyllis. *Elizabeth Bowen* (Basingstoke: MacMillan, 1990).

Lee, Hermione. *Elizabeth Bowen: An Estimation* (Totowa, NJ: Barnes and Noble, 1981).

—. Ed. *The Mulberry Tree: Writings of Elizabeth Bowen* (London: Virago, 1986)

O'Faolain, Sean. 'A Reading and Remembrance of Elizabeth Bowen', *London Review of Books* (4–17 March, 1982), 15–16.

Osborn, Susan. Ed. *Elizabeth Bowen: New Critical Perspectives* (Cork: Cork University Press, 2009).

Walshe Éibhear. Ed. *Elizabeth Bowen: Visions and Revisions* (Dublin: Irish Academic Press, 2009).

Wills, Clair. *That Neutral Island* (London: Faber and Faber, 2007).

Index